I Can't Draw a Straight Line

I Can't Draw
a Straight Line

Bringing Art
into the Lives
of Older Adults

Shirley K. Hubalek, B.F.A.

HEALTH
PROFESSIONS
PRESS

Baltimore • London • Toronto • Sydney

Health Professions Press, Inc.
Post Office Box 10624
Baltimore, Maryland 21285-0624

Typeset by Signature Typesetting & Design, Baltimore, Maryland.
Manufactured in the United States of America by
The Maple Press Company, York, Pennsylvania.

The inclusion of resources in the Appendixes should not be construed as an endorsement of any particular product, but are the resources of which the author is aware and are accurate to the best of her knowledge at the time of publication.

Cover painting by Katherine Frey, Baltimore, Maryland. Used with permission.

Library of Congress Cataloging-in-Publication Data

Hubalek, Shirley K.
   I can't draw a straight line : bringing art into the lives of older adults / Shirley K. Hubalek.
     p. cm.
   Includes bibliographical references and index.
   ISBN 1-878812-34-3
   1. Art and the aged.   2. Aged—Education—Art.   3. Art therapy.   I. Title.
N72.A33H83   1996
618.97'065156—dc20
                                                 96-28549
                                                      CIP

British Library Cataloguing in Publication Data are available from the British Library.

Contents

v

Preface

This book, which outlines my method of assessing the interests and needs of an art group, building a group, developing lesson plans, and helping group members learn to create and evaluate art, was born out of my search for materials to guide me as I planned lessons and facilitated art groups for older adults and adults with disabilities in nursing facilities, adult day centers, and other settings.

I began my career working with older adults in an outreach program sponsored by several community colleges in the Baltimore area. In the mid-1980s art education materials for group facilitators working with older adults were almost nonexistent. My colleagues and I searched constantly for materials to guide us. Most of us adapted art education materials geared toward children. I felt that older adult participants, who were creative, interested in art, and hungry for knowledge, deserved more than this haphazard approach. I believed that there was a way to organize a curriculum for older adults that was based on sound artistic principles and used lesson plans that they could comprehend and accomplish. I scoured public and university libraries, wrote to professional organizations, and attended seminars and workshops, gathering information about forming groups, teaching adults and people with disabilities, and organizing curricula.

Slowly, a structure for my curriculum emerged, and I began to experiment with lesson plans and group activities. As I tried these new ideas, art group participants began to grasp my instruction more quickly and their ability to draw and paint and understand art improved dramatically. Their level of satisfaction with their artwork grew, and they no longer called their work "childish." I was doing something right!

After a year of using my curriculum in various settings, I decided that the principles and lessons worked and that other group facilitators might find my ideas helpful. I wanted to share these ideas with others.

I Can't Draw a Straight Line is not intended to be an art therapy manual, although developing the curriculum and writing the book have been therapeutic for me. Soon after I began work on the book, my fiancé was killed in a tragic accident. Writing became a lifeline to the future for me. Every word that I put on paper affirmed a belief in myself, that there was life beyond loss. I understood on a deeper level than before that creative work is a therapeutic, healing activity.

The members of my art groups, especially the older adults, and I grew closer as we shared thoughts and feelings about the pain of loss. As the participants worked on their drawings and paintings, I observed that they experienced the same self-affirmation, healing, and respark of belief in a future that I experienced as I wrote. I found that art has great value in all of our lives. It does have the power to heal if we open our hearts to that power.

I would like to thank Marie Santora for sharing her wisdom, knowledge, and faith and perseverance. Without her, this book would never have been written. I would also like to acknowledge the residents of Ridgeway Manor Nursing Center, Charlestown Care Center, and St. Martin's Home for the Aged, who lent their creative spirits to the development of this art program. The following people also gave encouragement and assistance: Jacqueline Wurzel, who read the first draft; Tommy Thornton, who typed the first chapters into the computer; and Peter Grimes, who was my computer consultant.

In loving memory of
Lawrence James "Larry" Williams
1959–1991
A kindred spirit and gifted writer

Introduction

"I don't know why I'm in here. I can't draw a straight line."

You have heard this statement from a first-time participant in an art group if you are facilitating an art group for residents of a nursing facility, clients of an adult day services center, or older adults with physical or mental disabilities. Many adults, with and without disabilities, make this statement because they tend to judge their attempts to draw or paint under two misconceptions: An artist must be able to draw a straight line, and art must be realistic or identifiable. Thus, participants come into an art class expecting to fail. The facilitator for the group must convince participants that they can succeed. The facilitator can accomplish this by using the lesson plans contained in this book.

These lesson plans have been used with many older adults. I have found that participants who are initially fearful of creating art receive support and encouragement to begin their exploration of the visual arts, specifically drawing and painting, through the approach outlined in the lesson plans. Creating art provides participants in the group with a sense of achievement and self-esteem. As older adults gain understanding about and confidence in creating art, they become more independent and more willing to explore their thoughts and feelings. They grow increasingly curious about art in general and begin to look forward to the group sessions. Creating art also sharpens participants' ability to observe other people and the environment and provides an outlet for self-expression, which can be lacking in care settings.

An atmosphere of personal success can be fostered by the group facilitator through the technique of building a community (see Part 1 of the curriculum) and by helping participants learn to draw and paint in an individually satisfying, realistic manner. As participants gain confidence, they can be introduced to other styles of art that do not contain realistic-looking

1

images. (Many participants call these styles "modern art.") This learning process may take many weeks and progress may not be steady. However, with persistence, many older people begin to enjoy drawing and painting and develop an appreciation of other styles of artistic expression.

Fostering an atmosphere of personal success is not a simple task, especially with older adults with physical and mental disabilities. These older adults bring special challenges into the classroom, such as hearing and sight impairments, chronic pain, depression, anxiety, grief, and lethargy. Many participants with disabilities report that focusing their minds on creating art often "opens a window from the pain," even if only momentarily, and allows healing and peace to enter the body and the soul. They forget about themselves when they concentrate on creating art.

When working with older adults with disabilities, facilitators should remember that the creative process itself is the goal. During the act of creating art participants are able to use their remaining physical, mental, emotional, and social abilities. Participants organize and reorganize ideas, thoughts, feelings, memories, and materials and become creators, and thus gain control of something, perhaps for the first time since being admitted to the facility. With admission to a facility, participants in the group give up control of so much (e.g., their privacy, their mobility, their independence, many of their possessions). Many residents feel as though much of life has been taken away from them. However, when they create art participants can reach into their minds and use whatever thoughts and feelings they desire. They alone decide what to put on paper.

By realizing that they are in control of their art, participants regain some control over their lives and are able to achieve self-fulfillment, self-esteem, and self-direction. In essence the art group is not just a setting in which to learn about art, but somewhere to explore life and to heal. For example, you may encounter participants who constantly ask you what colors to use in a painting. Tell them to explore. Explain that the art they create is their own; they are in total control. They may use whatever colors they want. Your task as group facilitator is "to re-animate dead nerves, to reopen the doors of perception" (Hoffman, Greenberg, & Fitzner, 1980, p. 81).

Grandma Moses began painting in her late 70s. In her autobiography, *My Life's History*, she wrote about memory and hope: "What a strange thing is memory, and hope, one looks backward, the other forward. The one is of today, the other is the Tomorrow. Memory is history recorded in our brain, memory is a painter, it paints pictures of the past" (Fowler & McCutcheon, 1991, p. 175). Through the techniques of exploration used in drawing and painting, many older adults with disabilities can tap into their memories. Drawing and painting become the methods through which they are able to reflect on their past, reanimate their lives in the present, and envision hope in the future.

Once participants begin putting their private thoughts, ideas, and memories on canvas and paper, the worlds of today and tomorrow begin to look a bit different to them. Today becomes worth living because the day is spent creating something tangible, rather than sitting idle, waiting for time to pass. The art created in the group session can be used to involve participants in group discussions about the past and how the past relates to the present. Tomorrow becomes a time to look forward to because it holds the possibility of meeting with the class again, creating new works of art, joining in discussions with others, and opening more doors into the future. By engaging an older person in an art group you are not only providing him or her with an activity that is enjoyable but, through the use of reminiscence, discussions, and positive feedback, you are also using the class as a valuable therapeutic tool.

Section I

Planning

A critical step in building a successful art program is planning. Planning begins with assessment of the interest, physical skill, and intellectual or cognitive levels of the people with whom you will be working. Once you have made these assessments, you can determine the size of the group and the physical space for the group, set goals, and assemble the basic art materials.

Assessing the Interest Level

The interest level of the group can be assessed by surveying, or asking, each resident or client whether he or she is interested in participating in an art class at the nursing facility/adult day center/senior center. Even if little or no interest is expressed, do not immediately conclude that you should not offer an art class. Instead, try another method. One method I have found effective is to recruit an artist from the community to show his or her work to the group. A visit from an artist can sometimes motivate individuals to participate in an art class. It is important to select an artist whose work you feel, on the basis of your resident/client survey, would be of interest to the people you will be teaching. The artist must be able to communicate effectively and present his or her work in a way that your group will find interesting. During the artist's presentation note the reactions and the level of interest of the audience. Following the presentation, ask the members of the group whether they found the presentation interesting and whether they might be interested in creating their own artwork.

Assessing the Physical Skill Level

Because drawing and painting utilize sensory motor skills, such as hand–eye coordination; vision; hearing; and upper body, hand, and shoulder movements, it is important to assess what each person in your group can physically accomplish. In order to make this assessment, directly observe prospective group members as they perform their activities of daily living (ADLs). Observe whether they are able to use eating utensils, to grasp and move objects on a table in front of them, to brush their teeth, or to comb their hair. If necessary, consult with the facility's occupational or physical therapy departments for their assessment.

The individual's personality and will are also important in assessing the level of physical skill. Some people with disabilities are willing to try almost anything, whereas other people with disabilities are not willing. Older adults with disabilities who are determined to create art but are unable to use standard equipment often can be accommodated by making adaptations to art equipment. *The International Directory of Recreation-Oriented Assistive Device Sources*, edited by John A. Nesbitt, and *The Source Book for the Disabled*, by Glorya Hale (see Select Bibliography [p. 183] for further information), provide comprehensive lists of resources for adaptive equipment.

Assessing the Intellectual or Cognitive Level

The intellectual or cognitive level of the group must be assessed in order to determine how you will lead the group. The members of the group must be addressed on a level the members can readily understand. To begin the assessment, question each participant about his or her level of education, whether high school, college, or technical school. Ask whether he or she has previously taken any art classes or created artwork. (The participants who have studied art should be questioned regarding the satisfaction they derived from their study.) Ask each participant whether he or she has a favorite artist or personally knows any artists. The answers you receive will help you assess the level of knowledge of the group and the sophistication of that knowledge.

When planning an art program, be aware that some participants may have illnesses or conditions that impair their thought processes or attention spans. To lead an art group for individuals who have significant cognitive impairments the facilitator needs much patience, calm, and perseverance. Assess your own abilities and then ask staff members at the facility or center for an honest appraisal of your abilities in these areas before deciding to lead such a group.

DETERMINING THE SIZE OF THE GROUP

In determining the size of the group, assess how many participants you feel you can comfortably lead. This will depend on the results of your assessments of the physical skill level and the cognitive skill level of participants in the group. Groups that are made up of individuals with high levels of physical and cognitive skills can be as large as 12–15 participants because each individual has the ability to work without assistive devices and/or constant supervision. Groups that comprise individuals with physical or cognitive impairments must be limited in size to four or five participants, unless more than one facilitator is present. The reasons for this limitation are that people with these impairments need considerable individual attention. Because older adults with cognitive impairment are easily distracted, a facilitator must be readily available to redirect their attention to the task before them. Individuals with cognitive and physical disabilities may need assistance in manipulating the art materials.

DETERMINING THE PHYSICAL SPACE AND ITS ELEMENTS

Once you have determined the size of the group, you are able to determine the physical space in which the art class will be held. The physical space is crucial to the success of the group because many participants have a physical, visual, or cognitive impairment. The space must be large enough, bright enough, and free of distractions in order to allow group members the comfort they need to enjoy the art activities. The space must comfortably accommodate the number of participants that you feel you can lead. Numerous factors, such as amount of foot traffic, noise levels, lighting, amount of storage and display areas, and type of furniture, must also be considered. The space must be an area through which the facility personnel do not pass as they work. The space must also be as quiet as possible in order for art group participants to concentrate and hear instructions. Individuals with cognitive impairments are especially sensitive to noise and other distractions. Turning off or lowering the volume of televisions, radios, or stereos in the area will also help control the noise in the environment.

Proper lighting of the space is essential for older participants. As people age, the eye changes. The lens thickens and the muscles that control pupil size weaken. As a result, older eyes need more than twice as much light as younger eyes to function properly. Older eyes also do not adapt quickly to changes in light levels, and glare is often a problem. Glaucoma, cataracts, dry eyes, presbyopia (a reduced flexibility in the lens of the eye that makes it difficult to focus on near objects), and retinal disorders are common among older adults and can have an impact on how much or what kind of lighting would be best. Keep in mind that glare from windows or interior lighting may cause discomfort in the participants. Be prepared to make adjustments as necessary (e.g., closing blinds or curtains). Poor or inadequate lighting should be corrected; using high-wattage light bulbs or lamps can be helpful.

Having access to running water is also important. Participants will need water to paint and to clean art tools and their hands after each session. Make sure that you have an adequate supply of paper towels to assist in cleanup. For the convenience of the participants, try to find a space for the group that is located near restrooms, especially for participants with bladder or bowel management difficulties.

Because storage space is at a premium in many facilities investigate your facility to find a suitable, safe storage area for art supplies. A cabinet or sturdy shelves can be placed in the art classroom for storage. A wheeled cart is handy for storing and transporting supplies to the class.

Tables and chairs that will be used by the participants must be selected carefully. Chairs must provide proper support and be sturdy and comfortable. Avoid using metal folding chairs because they do not offer support when sitting for long periods doing artwork. The tables you select must be sturdy, easy to clean, and of a height that allows individuals to sit at them comfortably as they create artwork. It is essential that tables have enough clearance so that wheelchairs can fit under them. Special work boards that fit over the arms of a wheelchair to provide a stable, sturdy, and comfortable work surface for participants with wheelchairs can be made or purchased. Appendix D lists sources for the work boards.

Finally, you will need to find an area in which to display the finished artwork of the group participants. It is important that the artwork be displayed so that the participants are able to receive positive feedback from people in the facility and in the community. Staff and visitors take great interest in the artwork created by the group. The display space can be as simple as a bulletin board or as elaborate as an area designed specifically to be an art gallery.

Once you have assessed the interest level, the physical skill level, and the cognitive level of potential participants and determined the size of the group and the physical space and its elements, tour the facility to locate an appropriate classroom space, a storage area, and a gallery area.

SETTING GOALS

Setting goals is a process through which you will form the framework for your art program. Setting goals proceeds by asking yourself the following questions: What do I realistically expect to accomplish with this art program? Who will facilitate the group? How long should each class run? How many classes should I schedule before I evaluate the program? A good way to help you clarify your thoughts and set realistic goals is to put them in writing.

What Do I Realistically Expect to Accomplish?

The goal you will be most concerned with is what you would like to accomplish with the participants. To do this, honestly assess what you feel able to accomplish. Avoid wishful thinking. Do not overextend yourself. Your goals can be expanded later, after you establish a pattern of successes. Perhaps you wish to develop a comprehensive art program for older adults. By combining the sound artistic principles contained in this book and your own creativity, you can develop a comprehensive art program. Perhaps you do not wish to invest the time needed to develop a comprehensive program. Perhaps you do not feel such a program would benefit or be interesting to your participants. As an alternative to a broad-based program, you may find it effective to use only a few of the lessons contained in Section II or to teach parts of the section, "Exposing Older Adults to Art History."

As an example of setting a realistic initial goal, you may wish to establish interest in an art program over a 10-week period in a core group of four or five participants. This goal is not product oriented (i.e., oriented toward producing a finished piece), but interest oriented (i.e., oriented toward establishing interest in an art program). In this way, the interest level is first established and the product follows. Thus, if you have a small but interested group, other, perhaps larger, groups may follow. Higher goals can then be built upon the one achieved.

When assessing what you wish to accomplish with the art program, you must take into account any disabilities with which the participants are living. For example, participants with cognitive impairments may be able to accomplish a great deal just by remaining alert but completing only a part of the art activity. The product (e.g., a finished piece of art) may not be as important as the process of building a community (see Section II, Part 1) and/or physical and mental stimulation for some participants with significant disabilities. The creation of art involves thinking and doing, not simply making things. The art of creation involves solving problems, and interacting with others encourages this process. Each group will be different, so be aware that the product is not the most important part of the art program.

Who Will Facilitate the Group?

Once the goal of what you wish to accomplish has been set, you need to determine who will facilitate, or lead, the group. If you are not going to act as the group's facilitator, decide who on your staff is best qualified to do so. Training in art is not necessary. The essential qualities of a good group facilitator are enthusiasm, patience, a sincere desire to lead and build a group, the willingness to learn about building a community, and the desire to research books and magazines for use in effective art lessons.

How Long Should Each Class Run?

The next step in the goal-setting process is to decide on the length of each class session. The length of each session will depend on the attention span and the extent of the disabilities or level of functioning of the participants and on how much time the facilitator can devote to the group. The length of a class that comprises people with disabilities who are high functioning (e.g., little cognitive loss, good motor skills) may be 2 hours, but 1–1½ hours is best for these groups. The best length of a class that comprises people with cognitive impairments is 45 minutes to 1 hour. I have determined these class lengths over a 12-year period with hundreds of group participants. These are not hard-and-fast rules, however. You may want to experiment to determine the optimum session length for your groups.

How Many Classes Should I Schedule Before I Evaluate the Program?

Another important aspect of the goal-setting process is deciding how many classes to hold before evaluating your program. Making this decision is dependent on what you set as your goal of what you wish to accomplish. However, 8–10 sessions is usually a sufficient number of classes to hold before you evaluate whether your goals have been accomplished. Complete guidelines for evaluating your program can be found in Section III, "Evaluation."

ASSEMBLING BASIC ART MATERIALS

The final step in planning an art program for older adults is assembling the art supplies that are used in most art classes (Table 1; see Appendix C, "Sources for Art Supplies"). As you gather these materials, keep in mind that some participants may have physical disabilities and will need to have adaptations made to the art materials (e.g., larger brushes may be needed, brush handles may need to be made longer, the work surface may need to be changed in favor of a work board that fits over the arms of a chair or wheelchair). Ideas for adapting art materials for participants with disabilities are scattered throughout the text,

Table 1.   Basic art materials

Paper

White 8½" × 11" paper (typing or photocopy paper is acceptable)

Heavyweight drawing paper (9" × 12" or larger)

Kraft paper (white or brown; by the roll)

Multicolor construction paper

Large newsprint pad

Newspapers (to protect work surfaces from paint or markers)

Painting media and supplies

Watercolor sets (cake-type paint)

Tempera nontoxic poster paints (at minimum, supply must include the primary colors red, blue, and yellow, and black and white)

Paintbrushes (e.g., round, bristle, nylon, camel hair, flat, fan)

Oriental watercolor brushes (inexpensive, with bamboo handles, in a variety of sizes)

Paper plates

Paper or plastic cups and bowls

Egg cartons or muffin tins

Drawing media

Pencils with erasers

Felt-tip colored markers (permanent and nonpermanent)

Oil pastels (Craypas)

Charcoal (vine charcoal and CharKoal)

Facilitator's supplies

Easel

Black thick-line felt-tip marker

Slide projector

Projection screen or white wall

VCR

Record player, tape player, and/or CD player

Other supplies

Aprons (plastic disposable are acceptable; one for each participant)

Cellophane tape

Masking tape

Rulers

Soap

Stapler

Paper towels

Trash cans

and a listing of companies that offer products for people with disabilities can be found in Appendix D.

FACILITATING AN ART GROUP FOR OLDER ADULTS WITH MILD TO MODERATE COGNITIVE IMPAIRMENT

Facilitating an art group for older people with moderate cognitive impairment requires knowledge about cognitive impairment and skill in working with older adults with such impairment. The level of functioning of people with cognitive impairment varies according to their particular impairment. People with moderate cognitive impairment have some remaining motor abilities, may possess verbal skills, and may be able to follow simple directions. As some impairment progresses, however, individuals will exhibit a lack of ability to use or understand language and will lose the ability to comprehend visual and other sensory stimuli.

Lesson plans C1–C5 were designed for facilitators directing art groups for older adults with mild to moderate cognitive impairment. Before you begin facilitating a group of older adults with cognitive impairment, become familiar with the type of cognitive impairment of each individual in the group by meeting with the recreation director, activities director, or head nurse. A great deal of literature exists on cognitive impairment. If you wish to learn more, consult the Select Bibliography, which begins on page 183.

Size of the Group

Because some participants with cognitive impairment require almost constant guidance and assistance, the art group must be limited in size, especially when only one group facilitator is present. Groups with one facilitator should consist of no more than four to five participants. Art group management becomes difficult when an art group participant who is capable of completing tasks when the facilitator provides individual attention becomes passive if the facilitator leaves him or her to assist another member of the group. This may diminish the art experience for some members of the group. As long as the group is small in size and the facilitator is able to return frequently to each participant to provide individual attention and assistance, all members can have a positive art experience.

Space for the Group

The physical space in which the art group is to be held must be located away from noisier areas of the facility and must be free from distractions because individuals with cognitive impairment are easily distracted. You must also take special care when arranging the seating for the group as you will need to have immediate access to members. A round table, a horseshoe-shaped table, or tables placed in a U shape are the best choices for art groups comprising people with cognitive impairment because they allow you to physically reach all of the participants easily and to maintain eye contact with them while you are seated. If you use a horseshoe-shaped table or tables arranged in a U-shaped configuration, seat the participants around the large part of the horseshoe or U shape; you should sit in the narrow space of the horseshoe shape.

Supplies for the Group

Lesson plans C1–C5 require supplies in addition to those listed in Table 1:

- Heavyweight watercolor paper (9" × 12" sheets)
- Sketchbook (8" × 10" pad)
- White tissue paper (several packages)
- Lightweight cardboard or tag board (three or four 8" × 10" sheets)
- Cardboard dividers for boxed fruit or eggs (one for each participant and one for the facilitator)
- Plastic squeeze bottles (similar to the condiment containers used in restaurants; one or two for every color of paint)
- Paintbrushes 1" flat, soft bristles and 2" utility brushes (one for each participant and one for the facilitator)
- Glue (white, nontoxic)
- Adhesive stars (white)
- Scissors

- Hole punch
- Curl-type ribbon
- Small rubber ball

The foundation for Lesson Plans C1–C5 is five of the six basic elements of art: line, color, shape, pattern, value, and form. (Proportion and space are not taught because people with cognitive impairment generally have difficulty with the concepts.)

Section II

Curriculum

The art curriculum I have designed is specific to older adults with disabilities. It incorporates the three areas of art program development outlined by Hoffman, Greenberg, and Fitzner (1980):

Social exchange: building a community
Basic art knowledge: materials and technical skills
Critical thinking: broadening the base of what is art and the creative act

Each area is introduced briefly, and practical ideas and methods are provided in order to accomplish the goals you have set for your participants.

Part 1

Social Exchange:
Building a Community

Build the *support* and *enthusiasm* of the facility staff through friendliness and cooperation.

Create an *atmosphere conducive to creative work* through the *establishment of a stable environment* and the *performance of exercises at the beginning of each class* that are designed to stimulate the mind and body.

The foundation of the art curriculum is building a community. A community is an *interacting* group of diverse people sharing a pursuit (in this case, creating art) in a given location. The word *interacting* is especially important in the community of the art group because in order for individuals to achieve success in the program, they must break down the barriers that exist among members of the group. The community of the art group comprises the older adult participants, the group facilitator, and the facility or center staff. This is a diverse group—various ages, backgrounds, personalities—the members of which need to feel comfortable with one another in order for the participants and the program to succeed. Some participants may be fearful of interacting at first, but this feeling can be overcome by understanding two aspects of fear. The first aspect is that fear is caused by a person's anticipation of danger. Participants may perceive this danger to be others who may judge them or their artwork negatively. The second aspect is that fear is a lack of faith or self-confidence. If participants lack faith or confidence that they will be able to live up to their own expectations or those of the group, they will be fearful. Building a community eases participants' fear and helps them to build faith or confidence in themselves.

ELEMENTS OF COMMUNITY BUILDING

Two elements are necessary to build a community: the support and enthusiasm of the facility activities department and other staff and the creation of an atmosphere within the group that is conducive to sharing thoughts and feelings.

Support and Enthusiasm of the Facility Activities Department and Other Staff

The support and enthusiasm of facility staff for the program go a long way in helping you establish community within the art group. If staff feel free to compliment participants on their artwork, participants will begin to gain confidence and to look forward to being together again at the next session. To encourage support and enthusiasm it is important that you establish a good rapport with facility staff. Do this by introducing yourself, informing staff about what you are doing, and being cooperative and friendly.

An Atmosphere Conducive to Sharing Thoughts and Feelings

Through the process of creating an atmosphere that is conducive to sharing thoughts and feelings, participants are helped to understand that although living in a nursing facility or having a disability may be sterile and isolating, it does not mean that they are isolated from the rest of humanity. They come to understand that they share similarities with people who do not live in nursing facilities and who do not have disabilities. The process itself has two parts: establishing a stable environment for the group and performing exercises at the beginning of each class that are designed to stimulate the mind and body and to promote a feeling of community.

Establishing a Stable Environment for the Group

During the planning phase you determined the space in which the art classes would be held and the elements that made the space appropriate for your group. In order to create a stable environment for the group, the space and those elements should remain the same for each class meeting, as should the members of the group, if possible. These factors help foster trust in the participants that will ease their fears and build their self-confidence.

17

Your behavior as the facilitator plays a crucial role in creating a stable environment. You must be consistent. When you are on time and prepared for each class, participants understand that you are someone on whom they can rely. They understand that you value them and the class. This consistency helps establish trust, which enables participants to feel safe in expressing themselves. Consistency also helps to reduce catastrophic behavior. Maintaining a good sense of humor is an effective way to dispel tension and fear in everyone. A shared laugh helps to create a sense of community. Being "creatively flexible" is another behavior that helps you to create a stable environment for participants because it helps you when circumstances (e.g., room changes, illnesses) are defeating your efforts to demonstrate consistency. Creative flexibility is the ability to assess the situation, assess what you can realistically accomplish, and make on-the-spot adjustments to your lesson plan, such as making minor changes in the lesson or teaching a different lesson. You can develop creative flexibility through experience working with participants. Do not be critical of yourself or your ability to be creatively flexible if you are just beginning work with older adults. You will gain confidence and experience with time.

Performing Exercises to Stimulate Mind and Body and to Promote Community

Begin each session by performing an exercise that indicates to all of the group members that it is time to think about art. Because many participants may be idle or bored during the day, the exercise should also promote alertness among them. The exercise should also foster the feeling of community within the group by encouraging participants to interact. Many forms of expression can be used, such as relaxation techniques, movement, music, and discussion.

Relaxation/Breathing and Movement Exercise

Relaxation/breathing and movement exercises stimulate the body and the mind. When the body and mind are stimulated the ability to do creative work is enhanced. To begin the exercises, explain to the group members what they are about to do. Explain to the group that this is a breathing and movement exercise that requires everyone who can stand to do so and to raise the right arm while inhaling on the count of one and to lower the right arm while exhaling on the count of two. Reassure participants that anyone who is unable to stand may remain seated and anyone who is unable to raise his or her arms need only do the breathing. Demonstrate the exercise. Ask the group members to try it along with you. Repeat the exercise using the left arm. After two repetitions, explain to participants that the next step in the breathing and movement exercise requires everyone to raise both arms while inhaling on the count of one and to lower both arms while exhaling on the count of two. Reassure participants that anyone who is unable to raise his or her arms may do the breathing only. Demonstrate the exercise. Ask the participants to try it along with you.

Music Exercise

Music is another form of expression that stimulates mind and body, promotes community, and can be used to begin a session. Use music that is simple and known to all participants. Sing-along songs, such as "Take Me Out to the Ball Game," are good choices. If you have chosen to conduct a lesson around a theme, you can use a song to introduce the theme. As an example, you choose the theme "summertime." You may wish to begin the session by leading the participants in singing "In the Good Old Summertime," and then moving on to a discussion about summer picnics. You may then instruct participants to paint pictures of items that they might take on a picnic. To conclude the lesson, you may assemble the paintings in the space you have designated as an art gallery as a picnic scene.

Discussion Exercise

Discussion can also be used to begin a session. Topics selected should promote the exchange of ideas and encourage verbal expression. Possible discussion topics include events that have happened since the last session, upcoming events, a review of the previous lesson, or a lively discussion about a famous work of art.

Remember to keep the discussion focused and brief. If participants try to monopolize the conversation or ramble, redirect the discussion to the original point. However, if you sense that the group members wish to discuss the topic further, suggest that they discuss it after class or during the next session. Thank the participants for their enthusiasm and participation before redirecting the focus.

Get Acquainted Game

An excellent way to create an atmosphere that is conducive to sharing thoughts and feelings and to introduce the participants to creating artwork is to conduct the Get Acquainted Game. Conduct this game as an introductory lesson before you begin Lesson A1. The Get Acquainted Game allows you to evaluate the participants' motor skills, cognitive skills, and artistic experience before beginning lessons A1–A10.

Supplies

Chalkboard or easel with an oversize pad of paper
Tables and chairs
Blank white 3" × 5" index cards
Felt-tip markers in various colors; two for each participant and one for yourself
Cellophane tape

Procedure

- Arrange the Room—Arrange tables and chairs for the participants in a U-shape or in a horseshoe formation. Place a pad of oversize paper on the easel. Place the easel and pad at the opening of the horseshoe or U-shape. If you are using a chalkboard, arrange the tables and chairs in a U-shape or in a horseshoe formation in front of the board. Stand next to the easel or in front of the board to facilitate the game.

- Lead the Discussion—The Get Acquainted Game begins with a discussion that is designed to allow all members of the group to interact with you and with each other. In some facilities in which you may conduct art classes you may find that many participants do not know the people sitting beside them. Such isolation is contrary to the concept of building a community. To help participants defeat isolation and feel comfortable and to provide structure to this part of the game, introduce yourself to the group. Tell participants that you would like to get to know all of them by name and that you will need their help to do so. Then ask everyone in the group to introduce him- or herself. After everyone has done so, try to correctly address each person by his or her name. This part of the exercise encourages participants to talk and to speculate whether you can remember who is who. You will not always be right and may need to ask the participants for assistance. By asking for help, you demonstrate to the group that you are human too and that you also need help remembering at times.

- Lead the Name Tag Demonstration—Explain to the group that in this part of the game everyone will create his or her own name tag and that participants should watch as you create a name tag for yourself. Take a 3" × 5" index card and write your first name using a felt-tip marker in your favorite color. Then, draw some circles around the edges of the

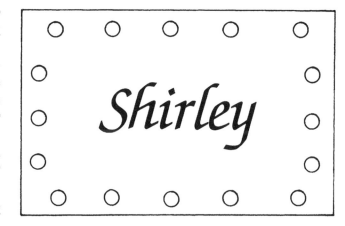

card using a marker in another color. Your name tag should look similar to the example shown. When you have finished, encourage interaction by asking the group how you might make the name tag differently. Write their suggestions on the oversize pad. Take another index card and design your name tag using their suggestions.

- Guide Participants in Creating the Name Tag—Give several 3" × 5" cards to each participant. Use cellophane tape to secure the cards on the table or work board for participants who need this assistance (e.g., people who do not have the use of both hands). Tell each participant to choose two felt-tip markers, each of a different color. Instruct everyone to write his or her first name on the card and to draw a design around the name. They can use their own ideas or one of the ideas that you wrote on the oversize pad.

- Conduct the Game—Explain to participants that they will now use the tags to play the Get Acquainted Game. However, if the group comprises people with more than moderate cognitive impairments, ask each participant to display his or her name tag and introduce him- or herself.

To begin the game, ask each participant to display or hold up his or her name tag and state his or her name. After all participants have "introduced" themselves, ask each participant to exchange his or her name tag with that of the person to the right and introduce him- or herself. This introduction can be as simple as handing the name tag to the person on the right and saying, "Hi. My name is Shirley. What's your name?" The person on the right reciprocates.

After the name tag introductions have been made, gather all the tags, mix them up, and distribute them to the participants. Be sure that no one has his or her own name tag. Ask each participant to display the tag, read the name, and give it to the correct person. If it is not convenient for the participants to move around the room, ask them to point to the person whose tag they possess. You may then give that tag to the correct person.

Part 2

Basic Art Knowledge: Materials and Technical Skills

Foster *self-confidence* and *independence* in participants. Allow more confident participants to make their own choices, and be alert and sensitive to the need of less confident participants for *support and guidance*.

Introduce art group participants to the six elements of art: line, shape, color, pattern, value and form, and space and perspective using the lessons that follow. The lessons are designed to promote a positive, creative art experience for all participants, including the facilitator.

The heart of the curriculum is the lesson plans, which enable you to introduce various art materials and techniques to the participants and to show them how to use the materials to create works of art. As you introduce the art materials to the participants, it is important to foster self-confidence in them. You must help participants realize that they can use the materials and their developing skills to successfully create works of art.

PRINCIPLES THAT BUILD PARTICIPANTS' CONFIDENCE

The "draw-along-with-me " technique helps participants to achieve success by modeling someone else's work. Stand at an easel in front of the group. On an oversize pad draw a small segment and ask the participants to draw what you have drawn. Initially, participants depend on you to make decisions for them and to establish a pace at which they can work comfortably. By the third lesson you should begin to encourage the members of the group to make their own decisions regarding their drawings and to proceed at their own pace.

In addition to the draw-along-with-me technique, incorporate the following principles into your teaching method to build the participants' confidence:

- *Lesson plan.* Introduce elements of art in a logical sequence so that each lesson builds on the preceding lesson.
- *Slow pace.* Try to accomplish only as much as participants with disabilities are able to understand and are capable of physically.
- *Flexibility.* Adapt the lesson to fit the capabilities of participants if you sense they are not grasping the objectives.
- *Encouragement.* Encourage and support the participants' efforts and accomplishments.
- *Patience.* Exercise patience with the participants, but especially with yourself.

HOW TO DEVELOP THE LESSON PLAN

It is important to write and use a lesson plan for each session. Although it can be a painstaking, time-consuming process, writing a lesson plan is the best way for you to clarify what you wish to achieve and the ways you will do so. The plan will also help prevent you from becoming sidetracked from your goals for the participants during the lesson. Use the following headings to write lesson plans:

- *Subject.* A word or phrase that states the concept you will teach in the lesson (e.g., "color")
- *Objective.* Several phrases that list what the participants should achieve in the lesson (e.g., "construct a color wheel, learn primary colors, learn secondary colors")
- *Supplies.* A list of materials needed in order for participants to complete the lesson
- *Procedure.* Step-by-step instructions that detail how you will accomplish your objectives

These headings are incorporated in the 25 lessons that follow.

Writing a lesson plan will help you to focus your ideas and goals, but keep in mind that it is not a rule book. Remember that in working with older people with disabilities you need to be creatively flexible. During a session you may notice that some of the participants are not feeling well or do not seem interested in the lesson. Be sensitive to the needs of participants. Abandon the lesson plan and do something else, such as hold a discussion. Sometimes, a brief discussion about the participants' problems gives everyone permission to "let off steam" and allows you to resume teaching the lesson. In some cases, you may find it necessary to create a new lesson on the spot. As you acquire skills and experience using the techniques and lesson plans, your confidence will grow and you will be able to create a new lesson plan if the need arises.

TOOLS OF THE TRADE

I call the three sets of lessons that follow the "tools of the trade" because they are based on the six basic elements, or tools, of art. Participants must be able to recognize and use these elements in order to create any work of art. The six basic elements of art are as follows:

1. *Line.* Line is the fundamental element of art. Line can also be described as "marks."
2. *Shape.* Shape is flat, two-dimensional areas in a work of art. These areas can be geometric (e.g., square, round, triangular) or organic (irregular in outline).
3. *Pattern.* Pattern is repeated lines, shapes, or colors in a work of art.
4. *Color*
5. *Value and form.* Value is the darkness or lightness (grays) in a work of art. Form is three-dimensional mass (e.g., cube, sphere, pyramid) created by using value.
6. *Space and perspective.* Space is the feeling of depth in a work of art. Perspective is a method of drawing that is used to create space.

Before you introduce participants to the "tools of the trade" (use with Lesson A1 only), assemble a few tools, such as a hammer, a saw, and a screwdriver, and place them in a toolbox. Take the toolbox with you to the first session and ask the participants, "What are these things?" "Who uses these things?" and "What can you do with these things?" Answers to the questions will vary, but the idea you want to communicate is that these tools are used by a carpenter in building. Then explain to the group that they also will be using tools, the tools that build a work of art.

The lessons that follow introduce participants to each element, or tool, of art and provide an art activity that uses each element. Once one element is learned, another element is introduced and builds upon the previous element. Participants gradually acquire the knowledge and use of all the elements, which they can then begin to incorporate into their own artwork. The lessons in Set A are the easiest and are designed to be used as the introductory set. The lessons in Set B are more difficult. They are designed to be used after the lessons in Set A have been completed or as the introductory set for a more advanced group of participants. The lessons in Set C are designed to be used in teaching people with mild to moderate cognitive impairment. The emphasis in these lessons is on providing a positive, creative art experience to participants and on emphasizing hand–eye coordination, mental and motor skills coordination, motion repetition, spatial relationship recognition, and color recognition.

Lesson Plans

Tools of the Trade

Lesson Plan A1

SUBJECT: Elements of art: Line

OBJECTIVES: Ensure that participants are able to recognize the element of art, line, in nature and in works of art.

Help participants to become accustomed to drawing lines on paper.

Instruct participants in creating a completed line drawing.

Help participants to understand that drawing can be a fun, expressive activity.

SUPPLIES: Typing paper (several sheets for each participant)

Easel with pad of oversize paper (large newsprint pad) (for facilitator's use)

Black thick-line felt-tip marker (for facilitator's use with oversize pad)

CharKoal brand charcoal (one stick for each participant)

Felt-tip marker (one marker for each participant)

Cellophane tape

Line drawing, "single tulip" (included in this lesson)

Dot drawing, "single tulip" (included in this lesson)

Line drawing, "two tulips" (included in this lesson)

Visual examples (advertisements and pictures from magazines that show the use of line and reproductions of line drawings from books)

PROCEDURE:

Arranging the Room

Arrange tables and chairs for the participants in a U or horseshoe shape. If a participant in a wheelchair wants to use a work board, attach the board to the wheelchair. Set the pad of oversize paper on the easel and place them in the opening of the U or horseshoe. Stand next to the easel to conduct the lesson.

Leading the Discussion

Begin Lesson A1 by writing "Tools of the Trade: Line" on the oversize pad using the felt-tip marker or on the chalkboard (if available). Initiate a discussion in which you explain that the purpose of this lesson is to help the participants recognize and identify the element of art called line in their surroundings, in nature, and in works of art. First, draw a straight line on the pad and ask the participants what it is. Allow them time to respond. Draw additional lines that are straight, jagged, scalloped, horizontal, and vertical. Ask the participants to describe these lines. Second, ask them where they see line both indoors and outdoors. (Examples of some of the objects with line that they may observe are curtain rods, picture frames, wooden chair legs, telephone poles, and tree branches.) Third, show examples of advertisements, pictures of urban and rural scenes from magazines, and line drawings from books. Ask the participants to point out lines in these examples and describe them.

Leading the Drawing Demonstration

Pass out several sheets of white 8½" × 11" paper, a felt-tip marker, and a stick of CharKoal brand charcoal to each participant. Remove the caps from the markers and use cellophane tape to tack down the corners of the paper for participants who need assistance. Return to the easel.

Explain to the group that you are going to use a marker to make different kinds of lines on your pad of paper. Then draw straight, squiggly, jagged, curly, horizontal, vertical, and curved lines. Use the draw-along-with-me technique, asking participants to use a marker to draw similar lines on the sheets of typing paper. Encourage the group to be creative when they draw their lines. (*Note*: Do not draw too quickly when you use the draw-along-with-me technique. Remember the physical and/or mental disabilities that group members may have and draw at a pace that is comfortable for all participants.)

Next, ask participants to use the stick of charcoal to draw lines. Explain that they can draw any kind of line, that they may use as many sheets of paper as they need, and that this exercise is designed to give everyone an opportunity to experiment and have fun with line. Display a positive attitude and be supportive of the participants' attempts to draw. Remind them that they can start over at any time and that there is no need to worry about errors.

You may encounter negative comments from the group such as, "This isn't art" or "We're not drawing anything." If they make negative comments, remind group members that although what they are drawing may not be considered art, they are learning to use a tool called line with which they will create art later in the lesson.

Creating the Line Drawing

Display the line drawing, "single tulip" (p. 29). As you show the drawing to the group, ask them to explain what kind of drawing it is and what basic element of art was used to draw the tulip. (*The correct responses are a line drawing and line.*) Explain to group members that everyone will draw the tulip; you will draw first and they will draw along with you.

Pass out the dot drawing, "single tulip" (p. 30), to the participants who need it. (Participants who need the dot drawing are people who are confused, frustrated, or cannot decide where or how to begin a drawing. Often, these participants are able to connect dots to create a drawing because the dots help them to focus their thoughts and guide them in the drawing experience.) Ask these participants to follow the directions you provide to the entire group. The participants will be able to create the tulip by following your instructions and connecting the dots. Distribute a sheet of typing paper and one felt-tip marker to the other participants. To avoid confusion, remove the stick of charcoal.

Continue to show the line drawing, "single tulip," and ask the group members to study the drawing carefully. Ask them what they see in it. (*The correct responses are a tulip, leaves, a stem, and the ground.*) Then, ask the participants the following questions (the correct responses follow the questions in italics):

- Do the tulip and leaves take up the entire page? (*Yes*)
- Are all the lines the same? (*No*)
- How do the lines differ? (*Some lines are long, some lines are curved, some lines are jagged*)
- Should the paper be turned vertically or horizontally when you begin drawing? (*Vertically*)
- Where would be a good place to start drawing? (*The ground at the bottom of the paper*) Point to this area on the newsprint pad.

After discussing the single tulip drawing, request that the participants draw along with you as you demonstrate how to draw the tulip. Instruct the participants to take a clean sheet of paper and their marker and to turn the paper so that it is vertical. When the group has done so, ask the participants to draw along with you as you draw a straight line across the bottom of your paper (Figure 1).

Line drawing, "single tulip."

Dot drawing, "single tulip."

Ask the participants what they should draw next. (*The correct response is the stem.*) Then ask them whether the lines of the stem are curved or straight and where the lines should be drawn on the paper. After the group has responded correctly, ask the members to draw along with you as you draw two curved lines side by side (Figure 2).

Then, ask the participants progressively more difficult questions, such as what should be drawn next? (*The correct response is the flower.*), Where does the flower go on the page? (*The correct response is on top of the stem.*) and What shape is it? (*The correct response is a U shape.*) After the questions have been answered by the participants, tell everyone to draw along with you as you draw a U shape (Figure 3). (You may wish to pause to allow the participants to admire the work they have completed thus far. Encourage the participants by complimenting their drawings. Resume drawing the tulip by first asking the group what type of line is used to draw the top of the flower shape. (*The correct response is a jagged line.*) Then instruct the group to draw this jagged line along with you (Figure 4).

The final part of the tulip to be drawn is the leaves. Ask the group where the leaves are located. (*The correct response is on both sides of the stem.*) Ask the participants what type of lines are used to draw the stem. (*The correct response is curved lines.*) Ask the participants to draw along with you as you draw one curved line. Then draw the other curved line to form the leaf, and ask the group to draw along with you (Figures 5 and 6).

Once participants have drawn the leaf along with you, ask the following questions: What should you draw next? (*The correct response is other leaf.*) and How many and what types of lines are used to draw this leaf? (*The correct response is two curved lines.*) Instruct participants to draw the two curved lines along with you (Figure 7).

As the members of the group put the final touches on their drawings, ask them to admire their line drawings of the single tulip. If some participants are not happy with their drawing, repeat the steps used to create the drawing until everyone is satisfied with his or her drawing. Remember to encourage the participants as they complete each step of the drawing.

After you have ensured that everyone is happy with his or her drawing, ask if anyone would like to add other objects, such as grass or sunshine, to his or her drawing. Encourage participants to do so, but do not push them. If group members drew the single tulip with ease, ask them to attempt the line drawing, "two tulips," included in this lesson (p. 34). Use the same step-by-step procedure for creating this drawing as you did with the line drawing, "single tulip," which you have just completed.

Ending the Lesson

Signing artwork, showing it to the group, and displaying it in a special area function as a closing exercise and signify that the lesson is concluding. The closing exercise allows participants to see the tulips everyone has drawn and to provide positive feedback and encouragement to one another. This interaction reinforces the concept of building a community among the members of the group. To encourage constructive (positive) criticism, you should always make positive statements about the participants' artwork. You may find that participants sometimes negatively appraise their own artwork. Always try to counter these negative comments with positive criticism. Ask participants why they do not like their drawings. Ask them to be specific about what they think is wrong. Their responses will help you to assist them in making the drawing more to their liking.

Begin the closing exercise by asking the participants to choose their own favorite of their drawings, to sign it, and to show it to the group. Some participants may be reluctant or too shy to sign their drawing or to show it to the group. **Do not push them**. Often, other members of the group will ask to see their drawings. This request may prompt participants who are shy to show their work. Ask the participants if they would like to display their drawings after the conclusion of the session. If they agree to your request, hang the drawings in the gallery area you selected during the planning stage of the program.

After all participants have contributed to the closing exercise, explain to them that the first lesson has concluded. Thank everyone for participating and tell the members of the group that you are pleased with their progress. Remind the group that you will return for the second lesson on (day, date, and time).

The participants' artwork should be removed periodically and saved in individual portfolios for a review and evaluation session (see Part 3 of this section) that is held after the completion of each set of lessons. The portfolios can be created by stapling two large sheets of heavyweight drawing paper together to form a large envelope. Participants may decorate their portfolios, which then become works of art as well. You may wish to devote a part of Lesson A1 or A2 to this endeavor.

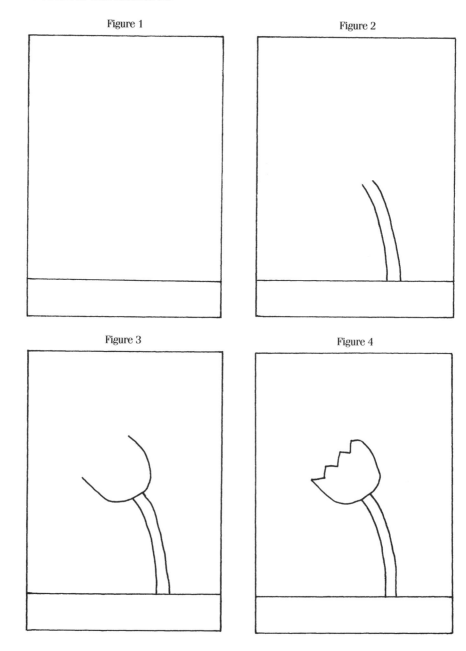

Figure 1   Figure 2

Figure 3   Figure 4

Figure 5

Figure 6

Figure 7

Line drawing, "two tulips."

Lesson Plan A2

SUBJECT: Elements of art: Color (Wear clothing or accessories to the class that are colorful; enlist the help of an assistant if your class consists of more than five participants; an assistant can help you to distribute supplies and to ensure that participants do not drink the paint or water)

OBJECTIVES: Ensure that participants are able to recognize the element of art, color, in nature and in works of art.

Ensure that participants learn the three primary colors red, yellow, and blue.

Ensure that participants learn the three secondary colors orange, purple, and green.

Ensure that participants learn the art of mixing color.

Instruct participants in constructing a color wheel.

SUPPLIES: Heavyweight drawing paper (one sheet for each participant)

Tempera nontoxic poster paints (red, yellow, blue)

Paintbrushes (¼" flat bristle; two brushes for each participant)

Black permanent ink felt-tip markers (one marker for each participant)

Pencils

Aprons (one for each participant)

Paper towels

Cellophane tape

Paper plates (two plates for each participant)

Plastic or paper cups (to fill with water)

Easel with pad of oversize paper (large newsprint pad) (for facilitator's use)

Black thick-line felt-tip marker (for facilitator's use with oversize pad)

Trash can

Small tables

Newspaper or other protective covering for tables

Color wheel (included in this lesson, which can be filled in by participants who are unable to construct their own)

Large circle pattern (included in this lesson)

PROCEDURE:

Arranging the Room

Arrange the tables and chairs for the participants in a U or horseshoe shape. If a participant in a wheelchair wants to use a work board, attach the board to the wheelchair. Cover the tables and work boards with newspaper or another protective covering. Set the pad of oversize paper on the easel and place them in the opening of the U or horseshoe. Stand next to the easel to conduct the lesson. Place the following supplies on a table near you: tempera paints (red, yellow, blue), paper plates, paper towels, two paintbrushes (¼" flat bristle), two plastic or paper cups (to hold water), and permanent ink felt-tip markers.

Leading the Color Mixing Demonstration

Begin the demonstration by writing "Tools of the Trade: Color" on the oversize pad using various colors of felt-tip markers or on the chalkboard (if available). Pour the red, yellow, and blue paints around the edge of a paper plate. Leave space in the center for mixing col-

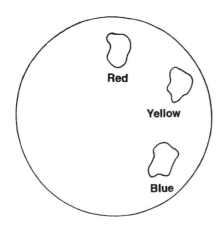
ors. This paper plate is your palette. Explain to group members that a palette is a surface on which various colors of paint are arranged and mixed (see figure at left).

Inform the participants that in this lesson they will learn about color theory and color mixing. Ask everyone in the group to watch carefully as you use a paintbrush to take some paint from your palette and apply it to the oversize pad in a circle pattern. Ask the participants to name the color you painted on the pad. After they have named the color red, rinse and wipe the brush thoroughly. Follow the same steps with yellow paint and blue paint. Explain to the participants that red, yellow, and blue are called *primary colors*, which means that all other colors are made from these three colors.

Next, explain to the participants that you will mix the colors orange, purple, and green, which together are called *secondary colors* because they are made from the primary colors. Begin the demonstration by mixing orange. Ask everyone to watch carefully as you use a paintbrush to take a dab of red paint and place it in the center of your palette. Then, rinse the brush in the cup of water and wipe it thoroughly using a paper towel. Take the brush again and place a dab of yellow paint into the dab of red paint. Use your brush to mix the colors together to create orange. Then, rinse the brush in the cup of water and wipe it thoroughly using a paper towel. Repeat the procedure using blue and red to create purple and blue and yellow to create green. Set the palette aside and take a clean paper plate to continue the demonstration. Rinse the brush in the cup of water and wipe it thoroughly using a paper towel. Ask the participants if they have any questions. Answer their questions. Repeat the mixing of colors to help participants understand anything that is unclear to them.

Creating the Color Wheel

Explain to the group members that the next part of the lesson consists of creating their own color wheel. Begin the color wheel demonstration by drawing a large circle on your oversize pad (Figure 8). Ask the participants to tell you what you have just drawn. If they correctly answer that it is a circle, explain that this circle will be used to make the color wheel. Explain to participants that a color wheel is a circle divided into six equal parts. An artist uses the wheel to organize colors in order to understand how colors relate to one another and to use them harmoniously.

Divide the circle into six equal parts. First, draw a horizontal line across the circle. Second, draw a large "X" across the circle as if you were cutting a pie. You have now divided the circle into six equal parts (Figures 9 and 10).

Take a clean paper plate palette and arrange the colors red, yellow, and blue around the edge of the palette as you did when you demonstrated the primary colors. Paint the circle as shown in Figure 11. Rinse the brush in a cup of water and wipe it thoroughly using a paper towel.

After you have arranged the primary colors, point to the blank space between yellow and red. Ask the participants to name the color that is located in the blank space. (*The correct response is orange.*) Explain that orange lies between yellow and red because orange is a mixture of yellow and red. Mix the orange paint on your palette. Take the paintbrush and paint orange in the correct space (Figure 12). Rinse the brush in a cup of water and wipe it thoroughly using a paper towel.

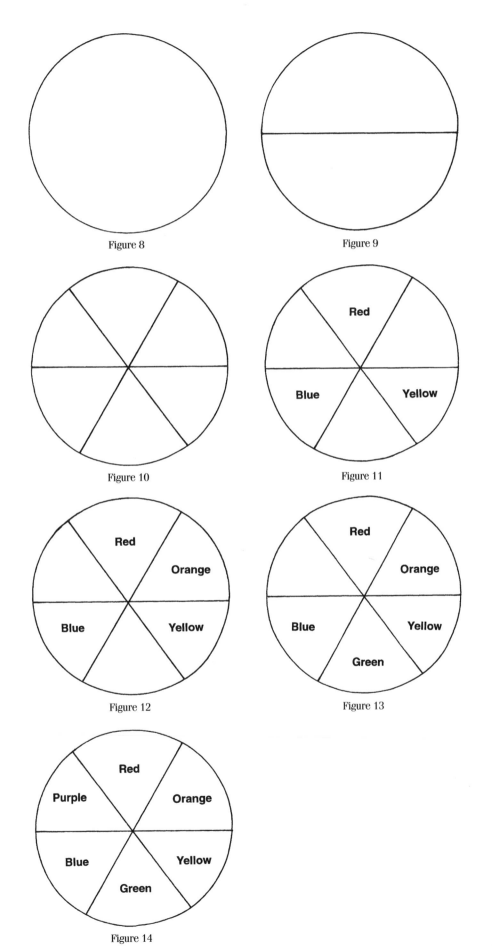

Figure 8

Figure 9

Figure 10

Figure 11

Figure 12

Figure 13

Figure 14

37

Next, point to the blank space between yellow and blue. Ask the participants to name the color that is located in the blank space. (*The correct response is green.*) Explain that green lies between yellow and blue because green is a mixture of yellow and blue. Mix the green paint on your palette. Take the paintbrush and paint green in the correct space (Figure 13). Rinse the brush in a cup of water and wipe it thoroughly using a paper towel.

To complete the color wheel, point to the blank space between blue and red. Ask the participants to name the color that is located in the blank space. (*The correct response is purple.*) Explain that purple lies between blue and red because purple is a mixture of blue and red. Mix the purple paint on your pallette (Figure 14). Take the paintbrush and paint purple in the correct space.

After you have completed the color wheel demonstration, ask the participants if they have any questions. Answer their questions. Repeat the mixing of any colors to help participants understand steps that are unclear.

Explain to the participants that you will create another color wheel and that they will create one along with you. Provide each participant with the following:[1]

- Heavyweight drawing paper
- Two paper plates, each with a dab of red, yellow, and blue paint placed around the edge of the plate
- Two paintbrushes
- Felt-tip permanent ink marker or pencil
- Paper towels
- Paper or plastic cup filled with water
- Large circle pattern included in this lesson (for participants who need assistance [e.g., those who are unable to draw a large circle or are too determined to draw a perfectly round circle]; also, tack down the edges of their papers with cellophane tape)

After you have distributed the materials and everyone is ready to begin, ask the participants to draw and paint along with you as you repeat the process of creating the color wheel.

Ending the Lesson

After everyone has completed his or her color wheel, ask the participants to sign their project and show it to the group as part of the closing exercise. Ask whether anyone would like to display his or her color wheel in the gallery area. Hang the artwork of the participants who wish to display it, and remember to provide positive feedback to all participants.

Explain to the group that the second lesson has concluded. Thank everyone for participating and tell the members of the group that you are pleased with their progress. Remind the group that you will return for the third lesson on (day, date, and time).

---

[1]You may be tempted to distribute these supplies at the beginning of class with the other art supplies. Do not do so. Many participants tend to "play" with supplies and do not attend to the introduction to the lesson. Also, participants with dementia tend to become confused by and preoccupied with the supplies in front of them.

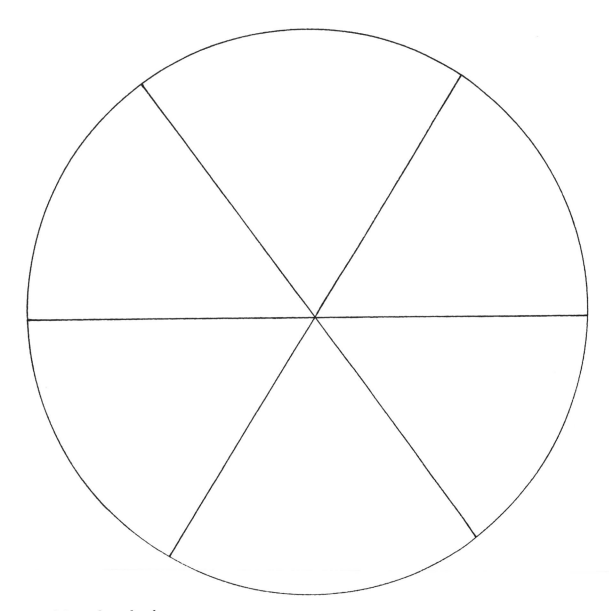

Outline of the color wheel.

Large circle pattern.

Lesson Plan A3

SUBJECT:	Elements of art: Shape
OBJECTIVES:	Ensure that participants can identify the three basic shapes square, triangle, and circle.
	Ensure that participants are able to recognize the element of art, shape, in nature and in works of art.
	Introduce the participants to painter Josef Albers. A brief biographical sketch is included in this lesson.
	Ensure understanding of the categories of color outlined in Lesson A2.
	Instruct participants in creating a design using squares and color.
SUPPLIES:	Drawing paper (several sheets for each participant)
	Easel with pad of oversize paper (large newsprint pad) (for facilitator's use)
	Oil pastels (one box for each participant and one box for the facilitator)
	Black thick-line felt-tip marker (for the facilitator's use)
	Cellophane tape
	Reproductions of Josef Albers's paintings (obtain from books or other sources)
	Color wheel (included in this lesson; already filled in)
	Squares drawing (included in this lesson)
PROCEDURE:	

Arranging the Room

Arrange the tables and chairs for the participants in a U or horseshoe shape. If a participant in a wheelchair wants to use a work board, attach the board to the wheelchair. Set the pad of oversize paper on the easel and place them in the opening of the U or horseshoe. Stand next to the easel to conduct the lesson.

Leading the Discussion

Begin the lesson by writing "Tools of the Trade: Shape" on the oversize pad or on the chalkboard (if available). Using the black marker, draw a circle, a square, and a triangle on the pad (see below). Ask the participants to name the shapes you have drawn. After they have answered correctly, explain to the group that they will be using these basic shapes during the lesson.

In order to ascertain the level of the participants' ability to recognize shape in the environment, ask whether anyone sees the three basic shapes in the classroom. Ask participants to point out the shapes to the rest of the group. (*Participants may point out a circular doorknob, a square picture frame, or a curtain with a triangle print.*)

After you have helped participants to become acquainted with the element of shape, introduce Josef Albers and his series of paintings *Homage to the Square*. Read the bio-

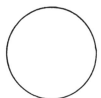 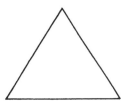

41

graphical sketch of Albers below and show reproductions of *Homage to the Square* to the group. Ask participants to explain why they like or dislike Albers' paintings and what colors the artist used in his paintings.

As the group views Albers' paintings, explain that in these paintings one color interacts with the color next to it and that this interaction affects how the viewer interprets the colors. Point out this phenomenon in the paintings.

After the group has studied Albers' paintings, review what the participants learned about color in Lesson A2. Display the color wheel (see figure at right). Ask the participants to name the primary and secondary colors. (*The correct responses are the primary colors are red, yellow, and blue, and the secondary colors are orange, purple, and green.*)

After the participants have named the secondary colors, ask them to explain how they would create the secondary colors using the primary colors. (*The correct response is to mix red and yellow to get orange, to mix blue and red to get purple, and to mix blue and yellow to get green.*

Leading the Drawing Demonstration

To begin leading the drawing process, explain to the participants that in this lesson they will create a design using squares of different colors, much like Josef Albers did in *Homage to the Square*. Inform them that they will use oil pastels to create their artwork. Explain that colored pigment and oil are mixed together and rolled into sticks that are called oil pastels, and that many artists use these pastels in their work. (*Note:* It is important that you avoid referring to oil pastels as "crayons" because this word connotes a medium used primarily by children and this tends to stigmatize older adults. Some may even dismiss the art group as childish and inappropriate for them and leave.)

Distribute several sheets of heavyweight drawing paper and a box of oil pastels to each participant. Also, distribute "squares drawing" included in this lesson to participants who are unable to draw the squares or who are preoccupied with drawing "perfect" squares. These participants may need assistance in holding the drawing paper steady as they draw. You should turn their papers to the vertical position and tack the corners of the paper to the table or work board using cellophane tape. Instruct the entire group (even the participants who received the "squares drawing" to draw along with you as you create a design using squares of different colors. Ask participants to find a red, a blue, and a green pastel in their box of pastels. (The oil pastels are labeled so that participants with some color blindness can use the pastels.) Inform them that these are the colors they will use for their drawings today. Reassure participants that because this drawing is a freehand drawing, they should not worry about making straight lines. Ask the participants to become

Josef Albers

Josef Albers, an important painter and teacher of the 20th century, was born in 1888 in Westphalia, Germany. He studied art at the Royal Art School in Berlin from 1913 to 1915 and at the Bauhaus in Weimar, Germany, where he later taught. The Bauhaus (literally translated, architecture house*) was the most important school of architecture and design of the 20th century. Founded in 1919 by Walter Gropius, the Bauhaus undertook the synthesis of 20th century technology, craftsmanship, and design aesthetics. In 1926 the school was moved into a new building, designed by Gropius, located in Dessau, Germany. Although the Bauhaus was closed by the Nazis in 1933, the Gropius building still stands in Dessau.*

While at the Bauhaus, Albers became interested in how colors interact and how colors influence human emotions. He began his study by using colored glass fragments to create works of art. As his study progressed, he found that using painted squares in his work was more effective than using the colored glass fragments. Albers created the paintings in his series Homage to the Square *by using various sizes and colors of painted squares.*

In addition to Homage to the Square, *Albers wrote a book entitled* Interaction of Color. *In this book the painter describes his theory of color, which is based on what he discovered about color through the creation of his paintings.*

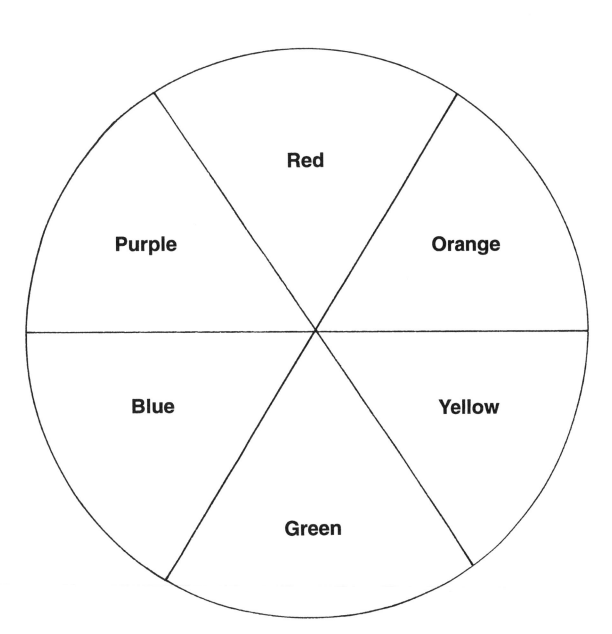

The color wheel.

familiar with the pastel sticks by selecting one of the three oil pastels. Explain to the participants that colored pigments and oil are mixed together to create these pastels. Demonstrate this media on the oversize pad by choosing a pastel and drawing lines all over a page of the pad. Ask the participants to do the same on a sheet of drawing paper in order to get the feel of this medium. Allow 1–3 minutes for the participants to work with the pastel. Then begin the drawing process.

To begin the drawing process, turn the paper on the easel pad to the vertical position and ask that participants do the same. Draw three squares, one inside the other, on your paper using the blue oil pastel and ask that participants do the same (Figure 15). After everyone has drawn the three squares, tell the group members that you will use a red oil pastel in the next step of the drawing process, coloring in the smallest square in the drawing. As you color in the square on your oversize pad, ask group members to select the red oil pastel and color in the smallest square on their drawings (Figure 16).

Next, you will lead the group in coloring in the next-smallest square. Select the green oil pastel to color in this square and inform participants about what you are doing. Ask the participants to work with you as you color in the next-smallest square (Figure 17). Then, select the blue oil pastel and use it to color in the largest square. As you color in the largest square, ask the participants to join you by coloring in the largest square (Figure 18).

As group members complete their designs, ask them whether they like the colors they used in their designs and how this color scheme makes them feel. Ask participants to explain why they like or dislike their designs or the colors. As the members of the group discuss their artwork, remind them that a particular color does not always look the same in all circumstances. The colors surrounding a color affect this color. Because of the laws of physics (including the transmission of light) and optical principles and the physiology involved in visual perception, colors interact with one another. This interaction allows us to perceive a color differently depending on the color that surrounds it. This is Josef Albers's theory of color. Show his *Homage to the Square* again as an example of this principle.

If there is enough time and the participants are able or willing to do so, create another design using the same colors in a different configuration (Figures 18 and 19). To begin, ask the participants to use a fresh sheet of paper. Distribute another copy of "squares drawing" to participants who need it.

If you would like to continue doing this type of design work with the participants at this point or in the future, use shapes, such as the square and circle, and any three colors in your designs (Figures 20 and 21).

Ending the Lesson

At the conclusion of the lesson, reinforce the participants' self-esteem by telling them that they are making great progress and that their work is good. Ask the participants to sign their designs and show them to the rest of the group. Ask whether anyone would like to display his or her designs in the gallery area. Explain to the group that you will hang all the designs after they participate in a closing breathing/relaxation exercise. Tell participants that this exercise helps to release the tension that built up while they created their designs. Explain what you are going to do and then ask group members to follow your instructions. The following exercise can be used with almost any group, and should be done two or three times.

Ask participants to close their eyes. *On the count of one, slowly take a deep breath through the nose. On the count of two, slowly exhale through the mouth.*

After everyone has completed the closing breathing/relaxation exercise, explain that Lesson 3 has concluded. Thank everyone for participating and tell the members of the group that you are pleased with their progress. Remind the group that you will return for the fourth lesson on (day, date, and time). Hang the designs in the gallery area.

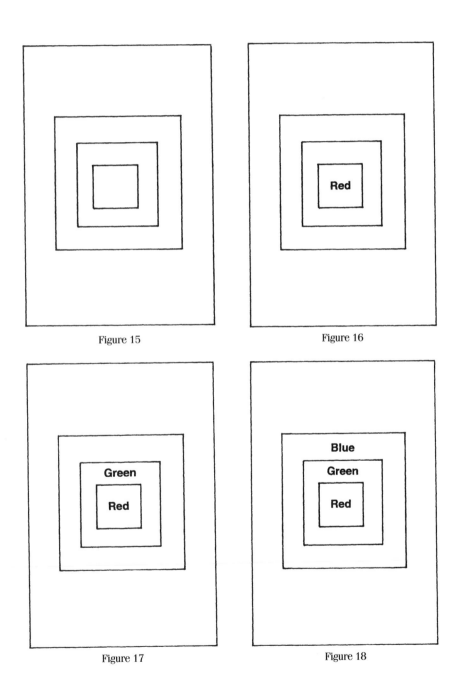

Figure 15

Figure 16

Figure 17

Figure 18

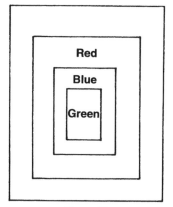

Figure 19

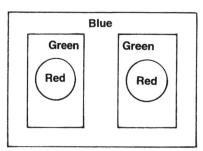

Figure 20

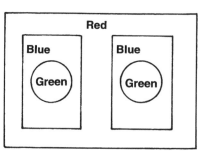

Figure 21

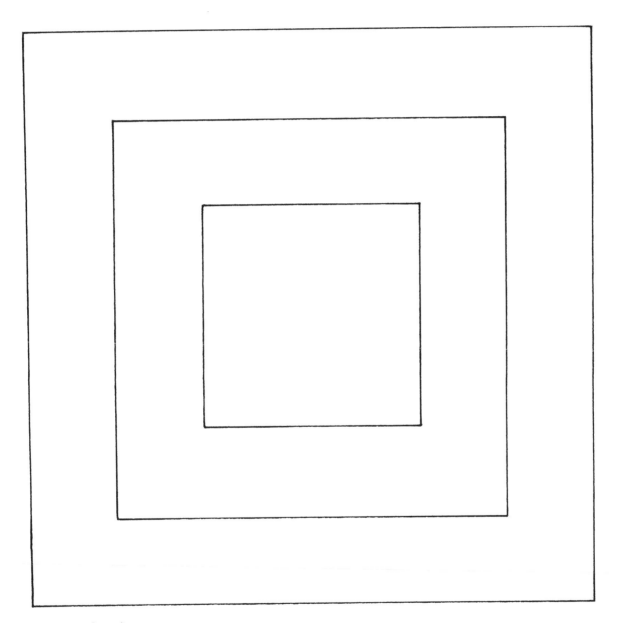

Squares drawing.

Lesson Plan A4

SUBJECT:	Elements of art: Pattern
OBJECTIVES:	Ensure that participants are able to recognize and identify the element of art, pattern, in nature and in works of art.
	Help participants to complete the art project incorporating pattern.
SUPPLIES:	White 8½" × 11" paper (several sheets for each participant)
	Felt-tip markers (several colors for each participant and several colors for the facilitator)
	Cellophane tape
	Easel with pad of oversize paper (large newsprint pad) (for the facilitator's use)
	Black thick-line felt-tip marker (for the facilitator's use)
	"Circles 1" (included in this lesson)
	"Circles 2" (included in this lesson)
PROCEDURE:	

Arranging the Room

Arrange the tables and chairs for the participants in a U or horseshoe shape. If a participant in a wheelchair wants to use a work board, attach the board to the wheelchair. Set the pad of oversize paper on the easel and place them in the opening of the U or horseshoe. Stand next to the easel to conduct the lesson.

Leading the Discussion

Begin the lesson by writing "Tools of the Trade: Pattern" on the oversize pad using the thick-line marker or on the chalkboard (if available). Inform the participants that this lesson is concerned with the element of art, pattern. Explain to the group that a pattern is a repetition of a shape and/or a color. Ask participants to point out examples of pattern they see in the classroom. (Examples of patterns that they may observe are designs in the curtains, table-cloths, other participants' clothing, or other fabrics.) Then discuss the various examples of pattern found in the room.

Leading the Drawing Demonstration

Once you feel sure that everyone can recognize and identify pattern, explain to group members that in this lesson they will create a design using pattern. Distribute several sheets of white 8½" × 11" paper and several felt-tip markers of various colors to each participant. Distribute "circles 1" to participants who need this outline. (Participants who need "circles 1" will follow the same directions you provide to others in the class.) Some participants may need assistance in removing the caps from the felt-tip markers and in stabilizing the paper. Tack the corners of the paper (horizontal orientation) using cellophane tape to the table or work board. Ask the rest of the group to turn their papers to the horizontal position.

Ask the group to draw along with you as you draw two large circles on the oversize pad (Figure 22). Tell participants that they may use any color. Reassure group members that because this drawing is a freehand drawing, they should not worry about making perfectly round circles. Some participants may ask to make several attempts at drawing circles. Encourage participants to do so.

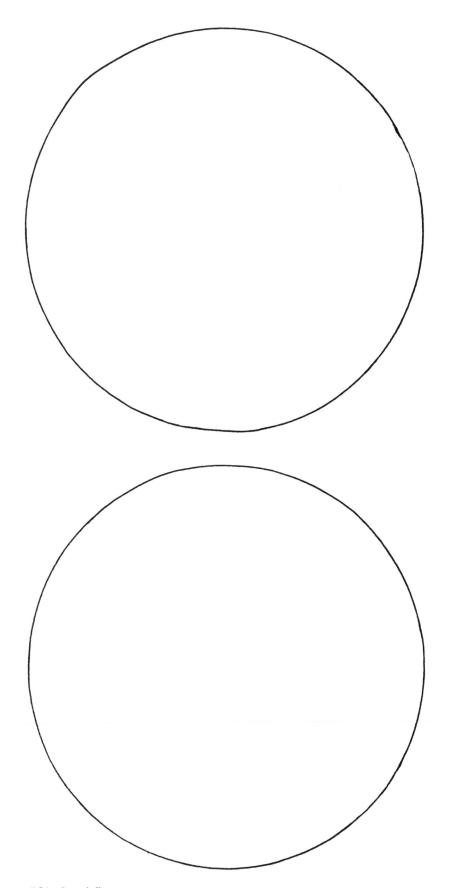

"Circles 1."

After everyone draws the two large circles to his or her satisfaction, explain to participants that they will now use skills that they learned in earlier lessons to create a design. Tell them that they will use line and color to create a repeated pattern. Explain that zigzag lines and dots can be used as a repeated pattern in their design. As you select three colors to use in creating the repeated pattern design, inform the group members that they should select any three colors to use in creating their design. Then demonstrate drawing the repeated pattern design (Figure 23).

Once you complete the demonstration, ask the participants to use your examples as guides and draw a design on the paper. Allow everyone ample time to complete his or her design. You will need to use judgment to gauge the time needed to complete the design. Do not push participants to finish quickly, and provide assistance to participants who are having difficulty thinking of design patterns.

When everyone is satisfied with his or her design tell the participants that you have an idea for another design that you want them to try to draw. Ask the participants to take a clean sheet of paper and turn it to the horizontal position. Distribute "circles 2" to the participants who need it. Draw several circles on your oversize pad and ask all of the participants to do the same on their paper. Explain to the group that these circles may intertwine and that they can use zigzags, dots, lines, or any line or shape as a repeated pattern (Figure 24).

Encourage the participants to work independently and to create as many pieces as they want. If the group needs to be fed ideas, draw some on the oversize pad (Figure 25).

Ending the Lesson

To conclude Lesson A4, ask the participants to sign their designs and show them to the rest of the group. Ask whether anyone would like to display his or her designs in the gallery area. Explain to the group that you will hang all the designs after they participate in a closing breathing/relaxation exercise. Tell participants that this exercise releases the tension that built up while they created their designs and encourages members of the group to form bonds with one another. Explain what you are going to do and then lead the group in the following exercise. Repeat this exercise two or three times.

Join hands, if you can, close your eyes. On the count of one, slowly take a deep breath. On the count of two, slowly exhale with a sigh.

When everyone has completed the breathing/relaxation exercise, explain that Lesson 4 has concluded. Thank everyone for participating and tell the members of the group that you are pleased with their progress. Remind the group that you will return for the fifth lesson on (day, date, and time). After the group leaves the room, hang the artwork in the gallery area.

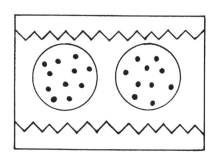

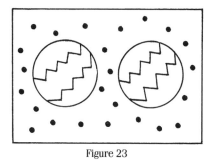

Figure 23

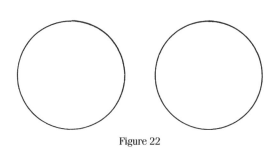

Figure 22

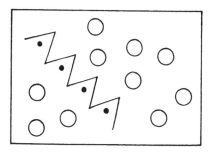

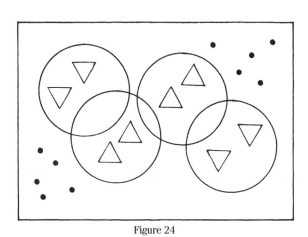

Figure 24

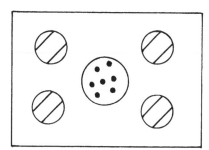

Figure 25

"Circles 2."

Lesson Plan A5

SUBJECT:	Still life: The use of line
OBJECTIVES:	Ensure that participants are able to recognize and understand still life as an art form.
	Help participants to successfully draw a simple still life using the element of art, line.
SUPPLIES:	Heavyweight drawing paper (several sheets for each participant)
	Large sheet of white paper (for use in creating the still life)
	Brown or black felt-tip markers (one for each participant)
	Red apples (several)
	Green grapes (one large bunch or several small bunches)
	Small table (on which to set the apples and grapes)
	Easel with pad of oversize paper (large newsprint pad) (for the facilitator's use)
	Black thick-line felt-tip marker (for the facilitator's use)
	Cellophane tape
	Reproductions of still lifes (check the library for books about still life painting and drawing [books about learning to draw or paint usually contain a section about still life]; art magazines [see Appendix F] and postcards are other good sources)
	Still life drawing (included in this lesson)

PROCEDURE:

Arranging the Room

Arrange the tables and chairs for the participants in a U or horseshoe shape. If a participant in a wheelchair wants to use a work board, attach the board to the wheelchair. Set the pad of oversize paper on the easel and place them in the opening of the U or horseshoe. Place the small table to be used for the still life in the center of the U-shape or horseshoe area. Stand next to the easel to conduct the lesson.

Leading the Discussion

Begin the session by writing "Tools of the Trade: Still Life" on the oversize pad using the thick-line marker or on the chalkboard (if available). Using the books, magazines, postcards, or other media you have gathered, ask participants to name the type of art. Wait for a response. If no one answers correctly, explain that this type of art is called still life and that still life is a composition of inanimate objects. Discuss the objects that are depicted in the examples by directing the participants' attention to the shapes, sizes, and textures. Ask them to tell you the colors they see in the still life examples.

After a thorough discussion of the reproduction examples, ask the participants what objects they would like to use in a still life. The objects can be any inanimate objects, but fruit, vegetables, and simple vases are probably the best objects to use because the objects have simple shapes and the participants are familiar with the forms.

Inform the group that you have brought some objects to class that will be used in creating a still life. Show participants a red apple, the green grapes, and the sheet of white paper.

Leading the Drawing Demonstration

Distribute several sheets of heavyweight drawing paper and a brown or black felt-tip marker to each participant. Also, distribute "dot drawing, still life" to the participants who need it. (Remind these participants that they should follow the directions you will provide to the entire group. These participants will be able to create a still life drawing by following the directions and connecting the dots.) Tack down the corners of the heavyweight drawing paper with cellophane tape for the participants who need their paper stabilized, and remove the caps from the markers as well.

Move to the small table in the middle of the U or horseshoe. Place the large sheet of white paper on the table, the apple on top of the paper, and the green grapes next to the apple (Figure 26). As you place the objects, ask the group to describe the color, shape, and texture of the objects.

After you have arranged the objects, explain to the participants that in this lesson they will draw a still life along with you. (*Note*: The still lifes included as examples in this lesson use a horizontal arrangement, for uniformity. However, you may try vertical arrangements if you wish.) Ask the group if they have any questions before they begin drawing.

Begin the drawing demonstration by turning your oversize pad to the horizontal position and asking the participants to do the same with the heavyweight paper. Inform participants that when they begin a still life, they should always start with the largest shape. Instruct the participants to draw along with you as you draw the largest shape, the round apple shape. Then draw the smaller shapes, the round shape of the grapes and the horizontal lines for the table. To complete the still life, draw the diagonal lines that represent the large sheet of paper on which the objects rest (Figure 26). Draw the shapes as slowly as the group needs you to draw them.

Remember to provide encouragement to group members and permission to start over if participants become confused or if they are not satisfied with their attempts at drawing the objects. If some participants become too confused or frustrated to draw, ask them to stop, take a deep breath, and begin again. Allow participants to start over two or three times. Reassure group members that you are there to help. Sometimes, touching a participant on the shoulder encourages him or her to try again. Should you sense that a group member does not want to participate at that moment, give him or her permission to stop and watch while the rest of the group works. If the participant voices a desire to leave the group or begins making negative comments about the group, its members, or art in general, remind the individual that it is all right to leave. Explain that he or she is welcome to return to class on another day. Do not allow a problem behavior to take up a large amount of class time, however. Give the disruptive participant the options previously stated and redirect your attention to others in the group. If a group member insists on making negative comments and continues to exhibit disruptive problem behavior, seek assistance from the activity or recreation coordinator or a member of the facility staff.

After you dismiss the class, discuss the problem behavior with the activity or recreation coordinator or the director of nursing if you are the coordinator. Ask whether the person exhibiting the behavior would be happier in another type of group.

After everyone has completed the drawings to his or her satisfaction and if time permits, ask the participants to verbally assist you in arranging the objects in other configurations. As you can see in Figure 27, some possible changes are adding another apple or separating the grapes into several groups. If you sense that the participants seem comfortable about drawing independently, ask them to draw the new arrangement, but do not draw along with them. Before the participants begin drawing ask them whether the drawing paper should be placed horizontally or vertically (their response will depend on the orientation of the still life). Ask them what object should they draw first. (*The correct response is to begin with the apple or the largest shape.*) These questions will help to guide the participants who are less sure of themselves, but who wish to draw independently.

Ending the Lesson

To conclude Lesson 5, ask the participants to sign their work and show it to the rest of the group. Ask whether anyone would like to display his or her still life in the gallery area. Explain to the group that you will hang all the still lifes after they participate in a closing breathing/relaxation exercise. Tell participants that this exercise releases the tension that built up while they created their artwork and encourages members of the group to form bonds with one another. Explain what you are going to do and then lead the group in the following exercise:

Join hands, if you can. Close your eyes. On the count of one, take a deep breath through your nose. On the count of two, exhale through the mouth.

When everyone has completed the breathing/relaxation exercise, explain that Lesson 5 has concluded. Thank everyone for participating and tell the members of the group that you are excited about their progress. Tell participants that you have noticed that their confidence is growing and has grown so much since the first session. Explain that you believe more of them will soon be able to draw and paint with little help from you. Remind the group that you will return for the sixth lesson on (day, date, and time). After the group leaves the room, hang the artwork in the gallery area.

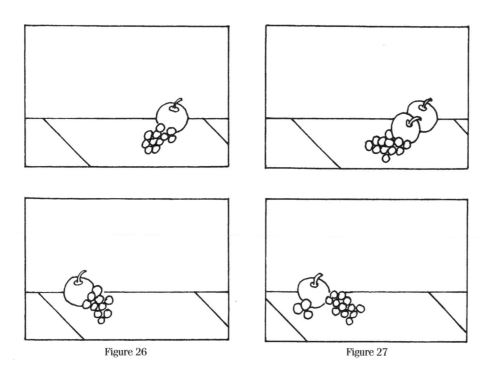

Figure 26   Figure 27

Lesson Plan A6

Subject:	Still life: Line and color
Objectives:	Help participants to successfully draw a simple still life using line.
	Ensure that participants learn the basic techniques of watercolor.
	Help participants to successfully paint a still life using watercolor.
Supplies:	Heavyweight drawing paper (several sheets for each participant)
	Black or brown permanent ink felt-tip markers (one for each participant and one for the facilitator; permanent ink is needed so that the drawing will not run when the watercolor is applied)
	Basic watercolor sets with brushes (one for each participant and one for the facilitator)
	Cups or bowls of water (one for each participant and one for the facilitator)
	Red apple and green grapes
	Paper towels
	Dot drawing, still life (included in this lesson)
	Cellophane tape
	Small table (for the objects included in the still life)
	Easel with pad of oversize paper (large newsprint pad) (for the facilitator's use)

Procedure:

Arranging the Room

Arrange the tables and chairs for the participants in a U or horseshoe shape. If a participant in a wheelchair wants to use a work board, attach the board to the wheelchair. Set the pad of oversize paper on the easel and place them in the opening of the U or horseshoe. Place the small table that will be used in creating the still life in the center of the U or horseshoe. If you are able to recruit an assistant to help you during the session, ask him or her to set up the table for the still life.

Leading the Discussion

Begin the session by writing "Tools of the Trade: Still Life" on the oversize pad or on the chalkboard (if available). Distribute several sheets of paper, a permanent ink marker, a basic watercolor set with brush, a bowl of water, and some paper towels to all participants. The "dot drawing, still life" is distributed to participants who need it. (Remember that the participants who need the dot drawing are people who are confused, frustrated easily, or cannot decide where or how to begin a drawing. The dots help them to focus on and guide their drawing. Remind these participants to follow the directions you provide to the entire group. These participants will be able to create a still life drawing by following the directions and connecting the dots.) Tack down the corners of the paper with cellophane tape for participants who have difficulty keeping their papers stable. Also, remove the caps from the markers of the group members who require this assistance. Return to the easel and ask if anyone can define the word *still life* and can tell the group anything about this type of painting. After the correct response is given, inform the participants that in addition to drawing a still life, they will be using watercolors to paint their still life drawing.

Facilitators should note that this lesson may be too long for some groups, but that it can easily be broken into two sessions: Session 1) draw the still life and introduce the watercolor techniques and Session 2) review the watercolor techniques and paint the still life drawn in the first session. A breaking point for the sessions is indicated in the text with three asterisks.

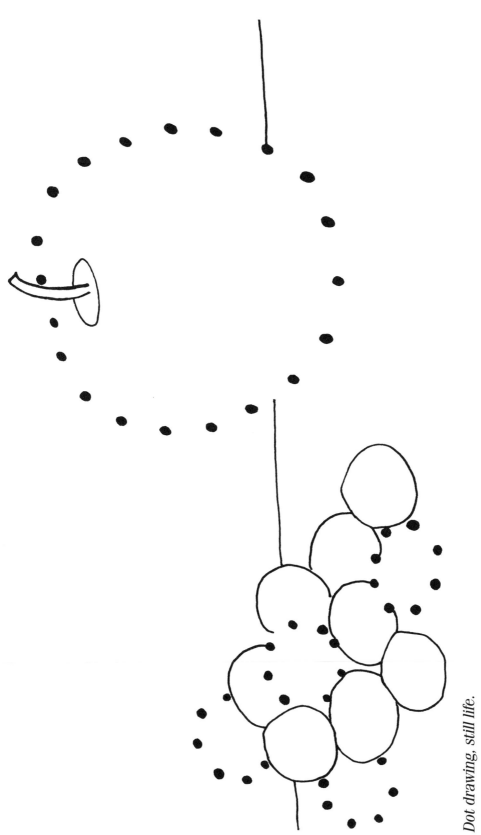

Dot drawing, still life.

Leading the Drawing Demonstration

Explain to the group that you will draw a still life using a vertical format. Arrange the still life (red apple and green grapes) on the small table. Then turn your oversize pad to the vertical position. Ask the participants to watch as you draw the example on the oversize pad. Beginning with the largest shape, draw the apple shape, then the shape of the grapes, and finally the horizontal lines for the table (Figure 28). As you complete your still life, ask whether anyone has any questions. Answer the questions and instruct the participants to begin drawing their own still lifes. Remind them to turn their papers to the vertical position and to draw the shape of the apple, the shape of the grapes, and then the horizontal lines that represent the table. Encourage participants to complete their drawings without your help. However, if some participants ask for assistance, offer your guidance.

After everyone has completed a drawing, ask the group members to set their drawings aside while you demonstrate some watercolor techniques that they will use in painting their still lifes.

Demonstrating the Watercolor Techniques

Begin the demonstration by using a permanent ink marker to draw and label five squares on the oversize pad (Figure 29). Inform the group that you will demonstrate five watercolor painting techniques. Explain that these techniques will be used in the still life that they will paint later in the lesson. As you begin the demonstration, tell the group that for watercolor painting, it is important to keep their paper on a flat, horizontal surface, and that the brush must be wet before dipping it into the paint.

The first technique you will demonstrate is the **wash technique**. Load a brush first with water and then any color. Apply the brush to the square labeled "Wash." Explain to the participants that the wash technique is used to create large areas of color, such as skies.

The second technique you will demonstrate is the **wet-in-wet technique**. Load a brush with water and apply it to the first square labeled "Wet-in-wet." Ask the group to watch carefully as you load the wet brush with any color and apply directly to the wet square. The color will run rapidly. Then apply red paint to the second square labeled "wet-in-wet." Clean the brush thoroughly and then apply blue paint directly to the wet, red square. Ask the partici-

Figure 28

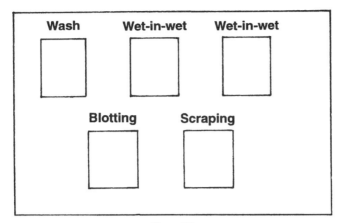

Figure 29

pants to watch carefully as the colors run together to form purple. Demonstrate other color mixtures by using blank areas on the pad to mix red and yellow to make orange and to mix blue and yellow to create green.

Demonstrate the technique called **blotting** next. Load a brush first with water and then any color. Apply the brush to the square labeled "Blotting." While the area is still wet, instruct the group to watch as you use a wadded-up paper towel to blot the wet area. Explain to participants that this technique may be used for textures such as grass. Texture is created by the paper towel drawing away some of the liquid and leaving a pattern in its place.

The fourth technique you will demonstrate is called **scraping**. Begin by loading a brush first with water and then with any color. Apply the brush to the square labeled "Scraping." While the square is wet, take the end of your brush and scrape the wet color. Explain to participants that this technique may be used for textures such as grass or rough surfaces.

Demonstrate the final technique, **lines and strokes**, by loading a brush first with water and then with any color. Move the brush around the paper, making lines and short strokes. Tell participants that this technique may be used to create lines and flower petals.

After allowing time for the participants to ask and receive answers to their questions about the demonstration, ask the group to try some of the techniques you demonstrated. Instruct everyone to take a clean sheet of paper and his or her brush. Inform the participants that they do not need to make squares on their papers as you did in order to demonstrate the techniques. Guide the participants through the five watercolor techniques by demonstrating a technique on the oversize pad of paper and directing them to try it on their own paper.

***

Leading the Watercolor Painting Demonstration

Inform the participants that now that they have tried all the watercolor techniques, they will learn to add color to the still life drawing they completed earlier. Ask them to watch carefully while you paint.

Begin the demonstration by explaining to the group that because it is the largest area, you will start with the background of the still life. Using the wet-in-wet technique and two colors, paint the background. The two background colors should blend. You may also want to try the blotting or scraping techniques as you paint the background. Allow the colors to dry before continuing to paint.

Once the background is dry, explain that you will paint the next largest area, the apple, using the wash technique. Paint the apple and allow the paint to dry before you move on to the grapes. Instruct everyone to watch as you use the wash technique to paint the grapes. After the paint dries, use the wash technique to paint the foreground. The foreground is the area on which the apple and grapes sit. Try the blotting and scraping techniques in the foreground to add interest to this area of the painting. Use two small strokes to add stems to the apple and grapes (Figure 30). When you complete the still life painting, ask the participants whether they have any questions. Reserve some time to thoroughly answer the questions.

After you have answered all the questions, tell the participants that they can paint their still life drawings by using your demonstration as a guide. Reassure them that you will be glad to help them if they need help, but that they now possess the ability to paint the drawing completely on their own.

Ending the Lesson

To conclude Lesson 6, ask the participants to sign their work and show it to the rest of the group. Ask whether anyone would like to display his or her work in the gallery area. Explain to the group that you will hang all the paintings after they participate in a closing breathing/relaxation exercise. Tell participants that this exercise releases the tension that built up while they created their artwork and encourages the members of the group to form bonds with one another. Explain what you are going to do and then lead the group in the following exercise:

Join hands, if you can. Close your eyes. On the count of one, slowly take a deep breath through your nose. On the count of two, slowly exhale through the mouth.

When everyone has completed the breathing/relaxation exercise, explain that Lesson 6 has concluded. Thank everyone for participating and tell the members of the group that you are pleased with their progress. Remind the group that you will return for the seventh lesson on (day, date, and time). After the group leaves the room, hang the artwork in the gallery area.

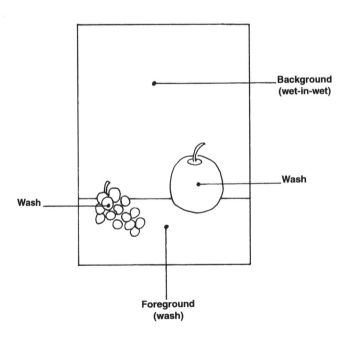

Figure 30

Lesson Plan A7

SUBJECT: Still life: Line, color, and pattern

OBJECTIVES: Help participants to become aware of the element of art, pattern, in still life painting and drawing.

Instruct participants in successfully drawing a simple still life using the elements of art, line and color.

Instruct participants in incorporating pattern into a still life painting.

SUPPLIES: Heavyweight drawing paper (several sheets for each participant)

Black or brown permanent ink felt-tip markers (one for each participant)

Basic watercolor sets with brushes (one for each participant and one for the facilitator)

Cup or bowl of water (one for each participant, one for the facilitator)

Paper towels

Cellophane tape

Reproductions of still lifes that incorporate pattern

Dot drawing, still life (included in this lesson)

Easel with pad of oversize paper (large newsprint pad) (for the facilitator's use)

Black thick-line felt-tip marker (permanent ink) (for the facilitator's use)

Several red apples and oranges and a bunch of green grapes

Small table (for the objects included in the still life)

PROCEDURE:

Arranging the Room

Arrange tables and chairs for the participants in a U or horseshoe shape. If a participant in a wheelchair wants to use a work board, attach the board to the wheelchair. Set the pad of oversize paper on the easel and place them in the opening of the U or horseshoe. Place the small table that will be used in creating the still life in the center of the U or horseshoe.

Leading the Discussion

Write "Tools of the Trade: Still Life: Line, Color, and Pattern" on the oversize pad or on the chalkboard (if available). As you begin the lesson, remind the group that a pattern is a repetitive series of shapes and/or colors. Explain that artists use pattern to lend more interest to their artwork and to give the piece a textural quality. Ask participants to point out patterns in the room. (The patterns they observe may be found in draperies, tablecloths, or clothing.) To reinforce the concept of pattern and to incorporate the type of art the group has been studying, show the class reproductions of still lifes that use pattern.

Leading the Drawing Demonstration[1]

Explain to the participants that in this lesson everyone will draw and paint a still life that incorporates the element of art, pattern. Distribute several sheets of heavyweight drawing paper, a felt-tip marker, watercolor sets with brushes, and cups or bowls of water to each participant. Also, pass out "dot drawing, still life" to the participants who need it. (Remind these participants to follow the directions you provide to the entire group. These partici-

---

[1]If you feel that participants are confident enough to draw independently, you may skip the drawing demonstration.

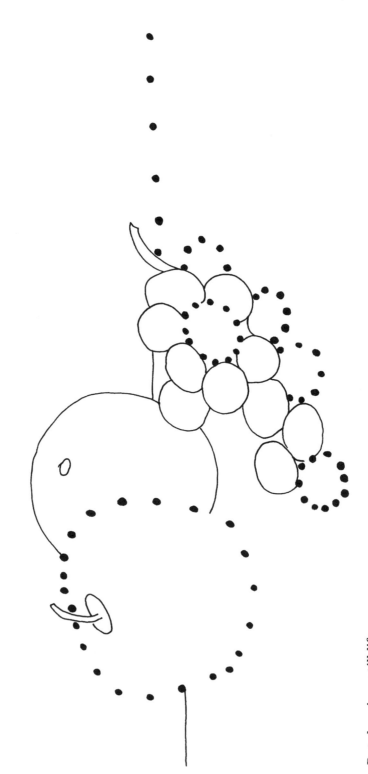

Dot drawing, still life.

pants will be able to create a still life drawing by following the directions and connecting the dots. Ask the participants to add their own patterns, such as stripes or circles, to the wall behind the still life objects. Tack down the corners of the drawing paper using cellophane tape for participants who have difficulty stabilizing the paper. In addition, remove the caps from the markers of the participants who require this assistance.

In setting up the still life on the small table in the center of the U or horseshoe, you should ask the participants if they would like to offer suggestions about arranging the still life. Incorporate their suggestions (if any are offered) into the setup. For example, they may want you to include more fruit, or if you or anyone in your group has experience in drawing, to use a vertical arrangement (Figure 31).

Once the still life setup is agreed upon, ask the group to draw along with you as you draw this still life.

Begin the drawing demonstration by asking the participants to decide whether the drawing paper should be oriented horizontally or vertically and with what part of the still life should you start drawing. (*The correct responses are horizontally and with the basic shapes of the fruit, beginning with the largest fruit.*)

Start by drawing the basic shapes of the fruit and complete the piece by drawing the lines to indicate the small table. Draw slowly enough so that all participants can draw along with you. Remember also to encourage the learners and make positive comments about their work in order to boost their self-esteem and preserve their interest in the art class. Ask everyone to continue drawing along with you until each person has created a drawing with which he or she is satisfied.

Once the drawings are complete, ask group members to name some patterns that could be added to the still life drawings. Examples of patterns that could be added are stripes (for a tablecloth) or a floral pattern (for wallpaper) (Figure 32). While you and the participants add various patterns to the drawings, ask the participants to explain why an artist would want to add pattern to his or her artwork. (*The correct response is that pattern makes the piece more interesting and gives it a textural quality.*)

Leading the Watercolor Painting Demonstration

When everyone has added pattern to his or her drawings, review the five watercolor techniques (wash, wet-in-wet, blotting, scraping, and lines and strokes) that you taught in Lesson A6. A good way to review is by quickly demonstrating each technique on the oversize pad. As you demonstrate each technique, ask the participants to identify it.

After reviewing the watercolor techniques with the participants ask them what colors could be added to their drawings to make them come alive. Allow a few minutes for replies and then invite everyone to use his or her watercolors and the various techniques to add color to the still life drawings. Remind the participants to dip their brushes into the cup or bowl of water before they dip into the paint. Advise group members to keep their still life either horizontal or flat while they paint.

Using various watercolor techniques and colors, paint your still life drawing as the participants paint theirs. Remain alert to participants who may need encouragement and guidance throughout the painting process.

Ending the Lesson

To conclude Lesson 7, ask the participants to sign their work and show it to the rest of the group. Ask whether anyone would like to display his or her designs in the gallery area. Explain to the group that you will hang all the designs after they participate in a closing breathing/relaxation exercise. Tell participants that this exercise releases the tension that built up while they created their artwork and encourages the members of the group to form bonds with one another. Explain what you are going to do and then lead the group in the following exercise:

Join hands, if you can. Close your eyes. On the count of one, slowly take a deep breath through the nose. On the count of two, slowly exhale through the mouth.

When everyone has completed the breathing/relaxation exercise, explain that Lesson 7 has concluded. Thank everyone for participating and tell the members of the group that you are pleased with their progress. Remind the group that you will return for the eighth lesson on (day, date, and time). After the group leaves the room, hang the artwork in the gallery area.

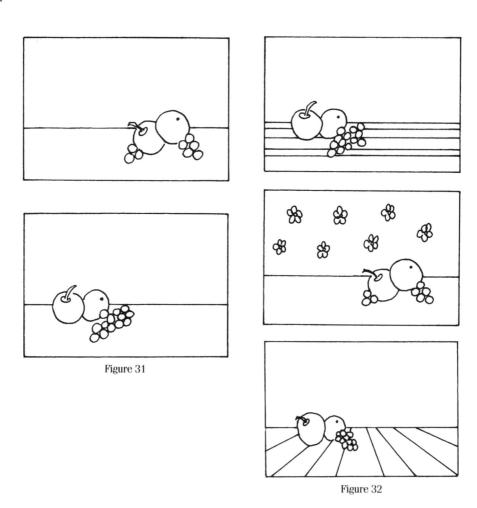

Figure 31

Figure 32

Lesson Plan A8

SUBJECT: Value and form

OBJECTIVES: Ensure that participants are able to define the terms *value* and *form* and to recognize value and form in works of art.

Help participants to draw a cylinder using value to create form.

Instruct participants in creating a still life drawing that incorporates several cylinders.

SUPPLIES: Heavyweight drawing paper (several sheets for each participant)

Vine charcoal (several sticks for each participant and for the facilitator)

Black felt-tip markers (one for each participant)

Cellophane tape

Easel with pad of oversize paper (large newsprint pad) (for the facilitator's use)

Black thick-line felt-tip marker (for the facilitator's use)

Charcoal drawings of a cube, a sphere, and a cylinder (included in this lesson)

"Line drawing, cylinder" (included in this lesson)

"Line drawing, two cylinders" (included in this lesson)

Reproductions of drawings that contain value and form (drawings by Rembrandt, Michelangelo, or van Gogh are good examples)

PROCEDURE:

Arranging the Room

Arrange tables and chairs for the participants in a U or horseshoe shape. If a participant in a wheelchair wants to use a work board, attach the board to the wheelchair. Set the pad of oversize paper on the easel and place them in the opening of the U or horseshoe. Stand next to the easel to conduct the lesson.

Leading the Discussion

Begin the lesson by writing "Tools of the Trade: Value and Form" on the oversize pad or on the chalkboard (if available). Then write the word *Value* below the title of the lesson. Explain to the participants that value is the darkness and lightness in a drawing and that value also can be described as the shadows or shading in a drawing. To illustrate value, show the group reproductions of works of art that contain value. Display works (drawings are best) that primarily use black, white, and gray tones. Books that feature the drawings of the masters, such as Rembrandt, Michelangelo, and van Gogh, can be obtained from the library. Allow approximately 5 minutes for group members to study the drawings.

After everyone has had time to study the reproductions, select one example and ask participants where the darkest and the lightest values are in the drawing and whether the work is a landscape, a still life, a seascape, or a portrait. Ask the group members to describe the objects depicted in the drawing and to determine whether the objects appear realistic and three-dimensional. If they respond that the objects appear realistic to them, ask what they think the artist did to make them appear three-dimensional. (*The correct response is the objects appear realistic because the artist used many values [grays or shadows] in the artwork.*)

Charcoal drawing of a cube.

Charcoal drawing of a sphere.

Charcoal drawing of a cylinder.

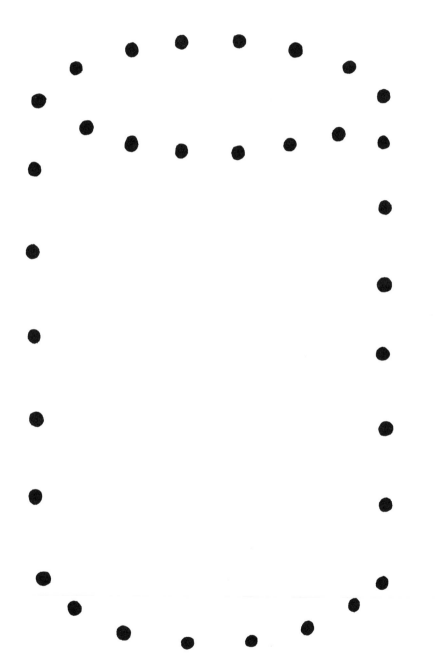

Dot drawing, cylinder.

After the participants have responded, continue the lesson by writing the word *Form* on the oversize pad. Explain to the participants that form is three-dimensional mass created by using value. Some examples of form that will help you to explain this concept are a cube, a sphere, and a cylinder. Illustrate these examples by displaying the samples of the cube, the sphere, and the cylinder, found on pages 66–69. Ask the group to look at the drawings for a few moments and then point out the darkest and lightest areas on each drawing. Explain that because the artist used the technique of value, the drawings appear realistic and three-dimensional.

Inform the group that there are at least two other three-dimensional forms with which they will work. Ask the participants to identify the forms. (*The correct response is a pyramid and a cone.*) Conclude the discussion about form by asking the participants to point out some three-dimensional forms that they observe in the room. Some forms they may observe are a piece of chalk, a cardboard box, and a chair. After the participants have identified several three-dimensional forms located in the room, tell them that everyone will use a felt-tip marker and a stick of charcoal to draw a three-dimensional form. Distribute several sheets of heavyweight drawing paper, a black felt-tip marker, and a stick of vine charcoal to each participant. Also, distribute the "dot drawing, cylinder" to participants who need it. Remember to remove the caps from the markers and tape the corners of the heavyweight drawing paper (placed in a vertical orientation) for participants who require this assistance. Instruct these participants to follow the directions you provide to the entire group. These participants will be able to create a line drawing of a cylinder by following the directions and connecting the dots.

Leading the Drawing Demonstration

Begin the drawing demonstration by asking the group to draw along with you as you draw the cylinder. (*Note:* Do not draw too quickly when you use the draw-along-with-me technique. Remember the physical or mental disabilities that group members may have and draw at a pace that is comfortable for all participants.) Instruct everyone to turn his or her drawing paper to the vertical position and to take the felt-tip marker and draw an upward curving line at the bottom of the paper (Figure 33). Ask participants to draw two vertical lines upward from the curved line at the bottom of the paper. The lines must be the same length (Figure 34). Instruct participants to draw a downward-curving line at the top that joins the two vertical lines. Then direct the group to draw an upward-curving line just below the downward-curving line (Figures 35 and 36). When all of the participants have completed this step, tell them that they have just drawn a cylinder. To complete the drawing, ask the participants to draw two horizontal lines to indicate that the cylinder is placed on another object (Figure 37).

After participants have completed the drawings, ask them to evaluate what they have drawn. If some participants are not satisfied with their drawings, or even if they are, ask them to take another sheet of heavyweight drawing paper and draw another cylinder. When all drawings are complete, ask the participants to choose the drawing they think is the best. This drawing will be used in the next portion of the lesson, adding the element of value to a drawing.

Explain to the members of the group that they will add value, or shading and shadows, to their drawings of the cylinder and that they will use a drawing media that is new to them, vine charcoal. Ask everyone to pick up their stick of vine charcoal and examine it. Inform the group that vine charcoal is made from actual vines that have been processed into the charcoal they are holding. Explain that the stick of charcoal is very light and fragile. Reassure the participants that it is all right to break the charcoal into smaller, easier-to-handle pieces. To illustrate your point, break a stick of charcoal into smaller pieces.

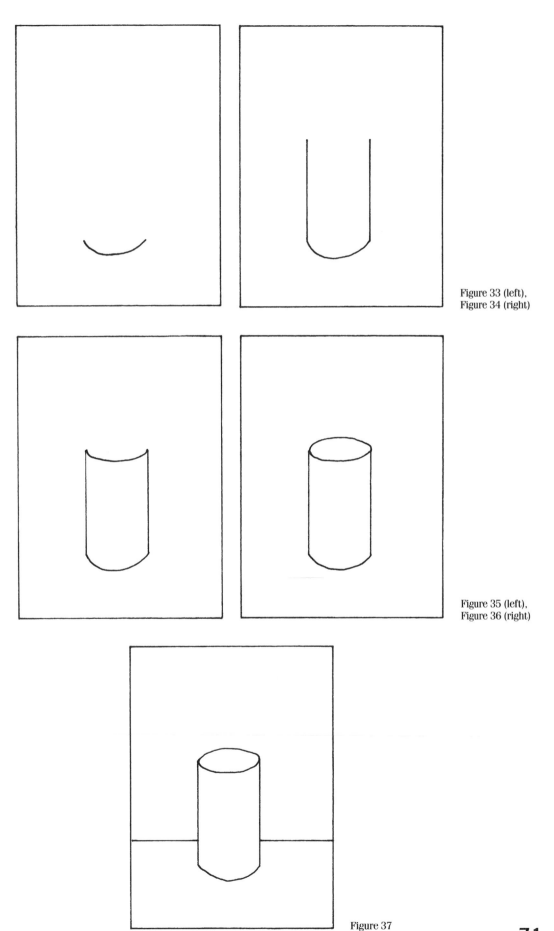

Figure 33 (left),
Figure 34 (right)

Figure 35 (left),
Figure 36 (right)

Figure 37

71

Begin adding value to the drawing of the cylinder by asking participants to place the drawing they have chosen on the table or work board in front of them and to draw along with you. Set the scene by telling them that the light is hitting the cylinder on the left side, making a shadow on the right side. As you shade the right side of your cylinder drawing, ask the group to take the charcoal and draw along with you (Figure 38). Advise participants that the inside of the cylinder is also dark because no light is falling into it. Ask everyone to incorporate that value by shading the inside of the cylinder (Figure 39). Because there also would be a shadow lying on the surface on which the cylinder is sitting, ask the participants to use the charcoal to fill in the shadow. Instruct them to make the shadow gradually smaller as they move away from the cylinder (Figure 40).

After the group has finished shading the cylinder, ask the group members to review their drawings and to ask questions regarding the shading process. Allow sufficient time for participants' questions before proceeding with the lesson.

The next part of the lesson involves drawing a still life of two cylinders of different sizes. Begin by distributing the "dot drawing, two cylinders," to participants who need it. (Remind these participants to follow the directions you provide to the entire group. These participants will be able to create the line drawing of two cylinders by following the directions and connecting the dots.) Tape the corners of the drawing paper and remove the caps from the markers for the participants who require assistance. Ensure that everyone has several sheets of clean heavyweight drawing paper. Direct participants to use their felt-tip markers as they draw along with you. Lead the group through the steps seen in Figures 38–40 depicting the assembly of the cylinder (Figure 41).

Tell the group to draw along with you as you draw a smaller cylinder next to the one already drawn. Ask the participants to draw a curved line below and to the right of the first cylinder (Figure 42). Then ask them to draw two short vertical lines up from the curved line. (Often, participants will draw the lines too long if you do not emphasize that the vertical lines should be short [Figure 43].) Ask the participants to draw a downward-curving line that joins the two vertical lines. To complete the cylinder, ask everyone to draw an upward-curving line just below the downward-curving line (Figures 44 and 45). Inform the participants that they have now drawn two cylinders. Ask the participants to complete the drawing by drawing three lines to indicate that the cylinders are placed atop another object (Figure 46).

Direct the members of the group to incorporate value, or shading, in their drawings. Remind them that the light is hitting the cylinders on the left side, making a shadow on the right side. Ask everyone to use his or her stick of vine charcoal to incorporate value in the cylinders. Instruct everyone to draw along with you as you shade the right sides of the cylinders. Remind the participants that they must also shade the inside of the cylinder (Figure 47). To complete the drawings, ask everyone to incorporate the shadows on the surface on which the cylinders are placed. Remind the participants to make the shadows gradually smaller as they move away from the cylinders (Figure 48).

Ending the Lesson

To conclude Lesson 8, ask the participants to sign their work and show it to the rest of the group. Ask whether anyone would like to display his or her designs in the gallery area. Explain to the group that you will hang all the designs after they participate in a closing breathing/relaxation exercise. Tell participants that this exercise releases the tension that built up while they created their artwork and encourages the members of the group to form bonds with one another. Explain what you are going to do and then lead the group in the following exercise:

Join hands, if you can. Close your eyes. On the count of one, slowly take a deep breath through the nose. On the count of two, slowly exhale through the mouth.

When everyone has completed the breathing/relaxation exercise, explain that Lesson 8 has concluded. Thank everyone for participating and tell the members of the group that you are pleased with their progress. Remind the group that you will return for the ninth lesson on (day, date, and time). After the group leaves the room, hang the artwork in the gallery area.

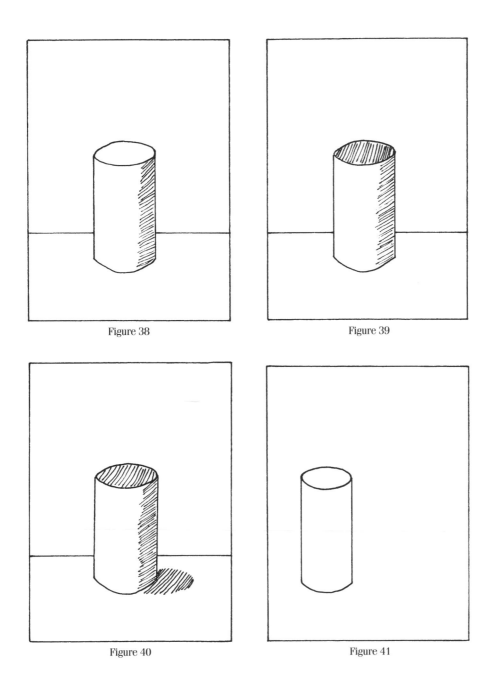

Figure 38   Figure 39

Figure 40   Figure 41

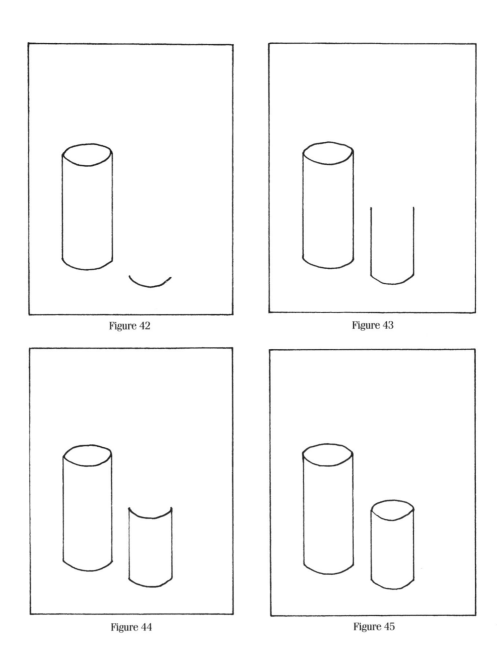

Figure 42

Figure 43

Figure 44

Figure 45

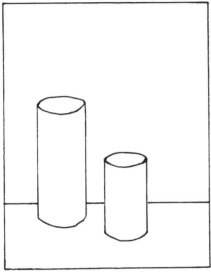

Figure 46

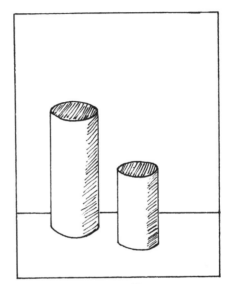

Figure 47

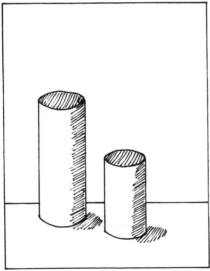

Figure 48

Dot drawing, two cylinders.

Lesson Plan A9

SUBJECT: Perspective and space

OBJECTIVES: Ensure that participants are able to recognize the elements of art, perspective and space, in works of nature and in art.

Help participants draw a simple landscape that exhibits a knowledge of perspective and space.

SUPPLIES: Heavyweight drawing paper (several sheets for each participant)

Felt-tip marker (assorted colors; one for each participant)

Cellophane tape

Easel with pad of oversize paper (large newsprint pad) (for the facilitator's use)

Thick-line felt-tip marker (for the facilitator's use)

"Drawing example, perspective and space" (included in this lesson)

"Dot drawing, landscape" (included in this lesson)

Reproductions of drawings, paintings, or photographs that illustrate the use of perspective and space (gather several landscapes)

PROCEDURE:

Arranging the Room

Arrange tables and chairs for the participants in a U or horseshoe shape. If a participant in a wheelchair wants to use a work board, attach the board to the wheelchair. Set the pad of oversize paper on the easel and place them in the opening of the U or horseshoe. Stand next to the easel to conduct the lesson.

Leading the Discussion

Begin the lesson by writing "Tools of the Trade: Perspective and Space" on the oversize pad or chalkboard (if available). Explain to the participants that perspective is a method of drawing that is used to create three-dimensional space, or depth, in works of art, and that space is the sense of depth that comes from a painting or drawing. Make the group aware that artists use perspective to create the illusion of three-dimensional space in the mind of the viewer. To illustrate your points, show the group the drawing example (p. 78) and examples of drawings, paintings, and photographs from various media that incorporate perspective and space. After everyone has examined the examples of perspective and space, ask whether anyone has questions regarding the examples. Answer any of the participants' questions.

Explain that landscapes make great use of perspective and that they will draw a landscape that incorporates perspective during this session. Ask the participants if anyone can define the word *landscape*. (*The correct response is a picture representing a view of natural scenery*.) After group members have responded to this question, explain to them that a good way to generate ideas for their landscape drawings is by visualizing an actual landscape. Tell participants that to visualize a beautiful landscape they should close their eyes and think of a beautiful outdoor scene. The landscape can be from a childhood memory, a vacation spot, or even somewhere they lived before they came to the nursing facility, or whatever the circumstances. Ask the participants to identify objects found in their visualized landscape. List their responses on the oversize pad. Before proceeding to the drawing demonstration, ask the group members to open their eyes.

77

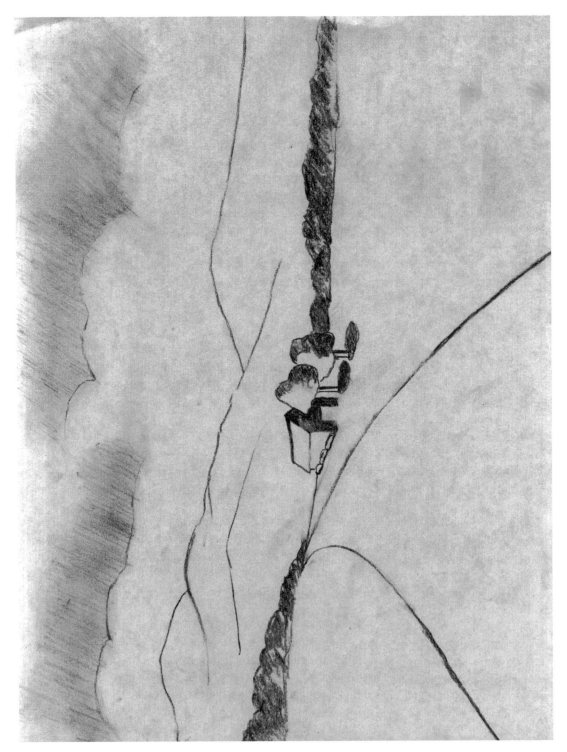

Drawing example, perspective and space.

Leading the Drawing Demonstration

The landscape drawing demonstration begins as you inform participants that they will draw a landscape using the ideas they offered during the visualization. Distribute several sheets of heavyweight drawing paper and a felt-tip marker to each participant. Also distribute "dot drawing, landscape" to participants who need it. (Remind these participants to follow the directions you provide to the entire group. These participants will be able to create a landscape drawing by following the directions and connecting the dots.) Remove the caps from the markers and tack down (with cellophane tape) the corners of the papers of the participants who need this assistance. Ensure that their drawing paper is in a horizontal orientation.

The text that follows is only an example of the procedure for drawing any simple landscape. Your group's landscape may differ because your participants may identify other objects during their landscape visualization. Remember to draw slowly enough for the participants to comprehend and to ask questions.

Your landscape may contain mountains beyond the horizon, a stream, some clouds, and a tree. Ask the participants to watch as you turn your oversize pad to the horizontal position and then as you draw a line across the paper (Figure 49). Explain to the group that this is the horizon line. The horizon line divides the page and helps the artist compare shapes and sizes seen in the landscape. Then draw several lines to indicate mountains in the background. To do so, start slightly above the horizon line and draw inverted V-shaped lines to represent mountain peaks. You may wish to slightly round off the tops of the peaks and make the mountains various sizes and heights (Figure 50).

Next, move to the foreground and begin to draw lines to represent a stream. Start slightly off center from the horizon line and draw one squiggly line from the horizon line down to the bottom of the page. Add another squiggly line starting slightly to the left of the first squiggly line (Figures 51 and 52).

To form clouds, draw several curved lines. A triangle can represent a tree. Complete the tree by adding a small rectangle at the bottom of the triangle (for the tree trunk; Figure 53). Ask group members whether they have any questions about drawing a landscape. Allow time for them to think and for you to answer any of their questions.

Inform participants that they will now draw their own landscapes using the ideas they offered during the visualization. You may wish to review their ideas briefly, especially if some participants have short-term memory impairments. Encourage them to begin drawing their landscapes without your help. Keep in mind that some of the participants may have a great deal of difficulty conceptualizing a picture without a visual aid. If some of your participants are not able to start without drawing along with you, hand out one of the reproductions for them to use as a guide or draw a few ideas on the oversize pad. Use simple shapes, such as triangles and rectangles, to design a landscape that is easy for participants to understand and draw. If you use the examples of the sailboat and the road leading to the mountains (Figure 54), remember to begin by first drawing the horizon line and then the mountains, the trees, or the boat. Complete the examples by drawing the diagonal lines to indicate the road. Remind group members that they may start over if they are not satisfied with their drawings.

Ending the Lesson

To conclude Lesson 9, ask the participants to sign their work and show it to the rest of the group. You may want to ask each participant to tell the group about his or her landscape drawing. Initiate the "show and tell" discussion by asking if the drawing is of a place he or

Dot drawing, landscape.

she has seen, visited, or lived. Also ask the participant if this is a place he or she would like to be and why the participant feels this way. Ask whether anyone would like to display his or her landscape in the gallery area. Explain to the group that you will hang all the landscapes after they participate in a closing breathing/relaxation exercise. Tell participants that this exercise releases the tension that built up while they created their artwork and encourages the members of the group to form bonds with one another. Explain what you are going to do and then lead the group in the following exercise:

Join hands, if you can. Close your eyes. Visualize the landscape you drew. On the count of one, slowly take a deep breath through the nose. On the count of two, slowly exhale through the mouth.

Allow some quiet time as the group members visualize their landscapes.

When everyone has completed the visualization/relaxation exercise, explain that Lesson 9 has concluded. Thank everyone for participating and tell the members of the group that you are pleased with their progress. Remind the group that you will return for the tenth and final lesson on (day, date, and time). After the group leaves the room, hang the artwork in the gallery area.

Figure 49

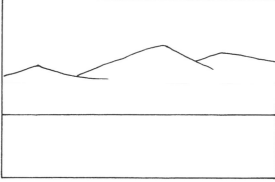

Figure 50

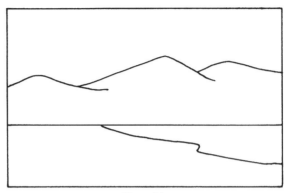

Figure 51

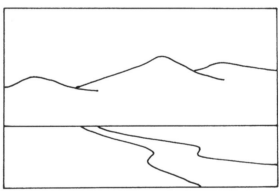

Figure 52

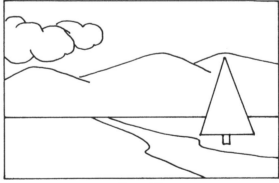

Figure 53

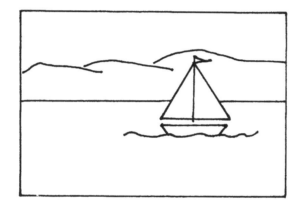

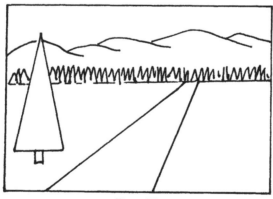

Figure 54

Lesson Plan A10

SUBJECT: Perspective and space

OBJECTIVES: Ensure that participants are able to recognize perspective and space in nature and in works of art.

Introduce participants to the oil pastel blending techniques.

Help participants draw and paint a simple landscape.

SUPPLIES: Heavyweight drawing paper (several sheets for each participant)

Craypas oil pastels (one set for each participant and one set for the facilitator)

Cellophane tape

Easel with pad of oversize paper (large newsprint pad) (for the facilitator's use)

"Drawing example, perspective and space" (see p. 78)

"Dot drawing, landscape" (see p. 80)

Participants' landscape drawings from Lesson Plan A9

Reproductions of works of art that illustrate perspective and space

PROCEDURE:

Arranging the Room

Arrange tables and chairs for the participants in a U or horseshoe shape. If a participant in a wheelchair wants to use a work board, attach the board to the wheelchair. Set the pad of oversize paper on the easel and place them in the opening of the U or horseshoe. For this lesson, you will want to display the participants' landscape drawings from the previous lesson where they can be seen easily by the participants. Stand next to the easel to conduct the lesson.

Leading the Discussion

Begin the lesson by writing "Tools of the Trade: Perspective and Space" on the oversize pad or chalkboard (if available). Distribute several sheets of heavyweight drawing paper and a set of oil pastels to each participant. Some participants may need help in stabilizing the paper while they draw. Tack down the corners of the drawing paper using cellophane tape.

Begin the discussion by reviewing the art terms *perspective* and *space* with the participants. Ask the group to define perspective. Wait for responses. (Keep in mind that depending on the type of disabilities or impairments of your participants, not all will remember the definition from the previous session. Be patient and do not push group members.) If no one responds with the correct answer, explain to the group that perspective is a method of drawing that is used to create space, or depth, in works of art. Ask the participants to describe the concept of space when seen in drawing or painting. Wait for responses. If no one responds with a correct answer, explain to the group that space is the sense of depth that comes from a painting or drawing.

Continue the discussion by showing reproductions of paintings and photographs that illustrate perspective and space to the group. "Drawing example, perspective and space" (see p. 78) may be used for this purpose, as well as works by the photographer Ansel Adams and the painter John Constable.

Inform participants that they will be using oil pastels in this lesson (*Note:* Remember to use the term "oil pastel" and not the word "crayon" when discussing this medium. "Crayon" connotes a medium used primarily by children and this tends to stigmatize older adults.) Explain that colored pigment and oil are mixed together and rolled into the sticks that are called oil pastels, and that many artists use these pastels in their work. Remind the participants that they used oil pastels to create the design using squares in Lesson A3.

Demonstrating the Oil Pastel Blending Techniques

Select the yellow pastel from your box of pastels. Apply a layer of yellow pastel to a small but easily visible area of your oversize pad. Ask participants to do the same on their papers. Then apply a layer of red pastel directly atop the layer of yellow and ask the group to do the same. The colors will blend together. Explain that any colors can be blended in this way. Demonstrate layering blue pastel over yellow and red pastel over blue. Ask the group to also try blending these colors.

Explain to group members that they can create a transition area from one color to another. Demonstrate how to create this transition area by applying a layer of pastel to a small area of the paper and then placing another color next to and overlapping the first color slightly. The colors will blend in the area where the two colors overlap.

Leading the Drawing Demonstration

Begin the drawing process by showing the participants' landscape drawings from Lesson A9. As you show these drawings to the group, explain that in this lesson they will have the opportunity to use these drawings and the oil pastels to create a new landscape.

Ask the participants to choose one of their landscapes from Lesson A9 to use as a guide. Allow ample time for less agile people to make their selection. Instruct group members to use a clean sheet of heavyweight drawing paper and copy their previous drawing onto this sheet. A good way to help them copy the landscape from Lesson A9 is to ask the participants to place their old landscape above or to one side of the clean sheet of drawing paper. Doing so will make it easier for group members to see their drawings.

After everyone has arranged his or her drawing area, ask whether anyone has any questions. The participants may ask a variety of questions, such as the following:

Q: *How do I start?*
A: Turn your paper to the horizontal position, draw a horizon line, and add whatever was in the Lesson A9 landscape (e.g., trees, mountains, a stream). (You may want to sketch on the oversize pad to help them get started.)

Q: *I don't remember this. Is this mine?*
A: Yes. You drew that in the last class.

Q: *What color should I use to draw the landscape?*
A: You can use any color to create the drawing.

Then instruct participants to begin drawing on a clean sheet of paper. Remind participants that you have plenty of paper, that they may draw as many landscapes as they like, and that they may begin again if they are not satisfied with their drawing.

Some participants may be unable to draw a landscape without the guidance of a drawing aid. These participants should be given "dot drawing, landscape" (see p. 80). Help these learners to connect the dots and to apply color to the drawing using the oil pastels.

When everyone has finished drawing, instruct the participants to apply color to the objects in the drawing by using the oil pastels and the blending techniques they practiced earlier in the lesson.

Ending the Lesson

To conclude Lesson 10, ask the participants to sign their work and show it to the rest of the group. You may want to ask each participant to tell the group about his or her landscape. Initiate the "show and tell" discussion by asking if the drawing is of a place he or she has seen, visited, or lived. Also ask the participant if this is a place he or she would like to be and why the participant feels this way.

Ask whether anyone would like to display his or her landscape in the gallery area. Explain to the group that you will hang all the landscapes after they participate in a closing breathing/relaxation exercise. Tell participants that this exercise releases the tension that built up while they created their artwork and encourages the members of the group to form bonds with one another. Explain what you are going to do and then lead the group in the following exercise:

Join hands, if you can. Close your eyes. Visualize the landscape you just finished. On the count of one, slowly take a deep breath through the nose. On the count of two, slowly exhale through the mouth.

Allow a few minutes for the group to complete the relaxation exercise. Then explain to the group members that they have finished the beginning set of drawing and painting lessons, and that the class sessions will continue with lessons designed to teach critical thinking about art. (However, if the group is ready to move on to the more advanced B lessons, save the critical thinking and art history sections until after these lessons are completed.) Tell the participants that they will review and evaluate their own artwork using the six basic elements of art they learned in the 10 previous lessons. Explain that after they review and evaluate their own artwork, they will view and learn about works of art created by master artists throughout history. Tell the participants that they will also have the opportunity to create their own works of art using ideas found in masterworks. Be sure to mention that an art exhibition of the participants' artwork or the work of a guest artist can be organized at the end of the section on art history.

Before dismissing the class, thank the group members for participating, praise their work generously, and give yourself a big pat on the back for a job well done. You may want to give each group member a certificate of completion (blank forms are available in most office supply outlet stores or you can make them yourself). After the group leaves the room, hang all the oil pastel landscapes in the gallery area for residents, staff, and visitors to admire.

Lesson Plan B1

SUBJECT:	Elements of art: Line
OBJECTIVES:	Ensure that participants are able to understand and recognize the element of art, line, in nature and in works of art.
	Help participants to create a line drawing.
SUPPLIES:	White 8½" × 11" paper (several sheets for each participant)
	Felt-tip marker (one marker for each participant)
	Cellophane tape
	Easel with pad of oversize paper (large newsprint pad) (for facilitator's use)
	Bold color thick-line felt-tip marker (for the facilitator's use)
	"Line drawing, flowers" (included in this lesson)
	Visual examples (advertisements and pictures from magazines that show the use of line and reproductions of line drawings from books)

PROCEDURE:

Arranging the Room

Arrange tables and chairs for the participants in a U or horseshoe shape. If a participant in a wheelchair wants to use a work board, attach the board to the wheelchair. Set the pad of oversize paper on the easel and place them in the opening of the U or horseshoe. Stand next to the easel to conduct the lesson.

Leading the Discussion

Begin Lesson B1 by writing "Tools of the Trade: Line" on the oversize pad using the felt-tip marker or on the chalkboard (if available). Initiate a discussion in which you explain that the purpose of this lesson is to help the participants recognize, identify, and understand the element of art called line in their surroundings, in nature, and in works of art. First, draw a straight line on the oversize pad and ask the participants to describe what you have drawn. Allow them time to respond. Draw additional lines that are straight, jagged, scalloped, horizontal, and vertical. Ask the participants to describe these lines. Second, ask them where they see line both indoors and outdoors. (Examples of some objects with line that they may observe are curtain rods, picture frames, wooden chair legs, telephone poles, and tree branches.) Third, show examples of advertisements, pictures of urban and rural scenes from magazines, and line drawings from books. Ask the participants to point out lines in these examples and describe them.

Leading the Drawing Demonstration

Pass out several sheets of white 8½" × 11" paper and a felt-tip marker to each participant. Display "line drawing, flowers" and ask the group to identify the type of drawing. (*The correct response is a line drawing.*) Allow participants enough time to answer. Once the correct response has been provided, explain that "line drawing, flowers" will be their guide for the drawing lesson.

Ask participants what it is they see in the drawing, using the following questions as a guide:

- What kinds of lines are used in the drawing?
- How much of the page is used for the drawing?
- Is the page orientation vertical or horizontal?
- Where on the page is a good place to start drawing?

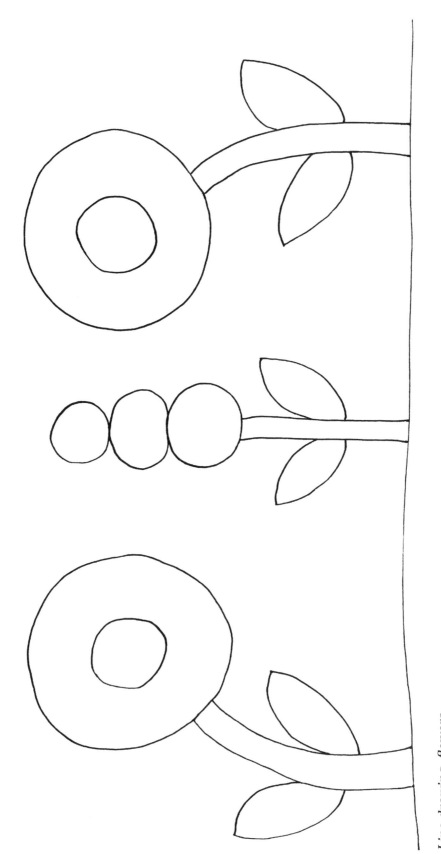

Line drawing, flowers.

88

After the group has answered these questions and you are satisfied that everyone understands how the line drawing is constructed, tell the participants that it is time to begin drawing. Remain aware of the physical disabilities that participants may have, and assure group members that you will draw slowly enough for them to be able to draw along with you. Tell them that you feel positive that everyone will be able to successfully complete a line drawing.

Ask the participants to take a sheet of paper and turn it to the horizontal position and to pick up their felt-tip marker. Use cellophane tape to tack down the corners of the paper onto the table or work board for participants who find it difficult to stabilize their paper. Remove the caps from the markers of the people who may need this assistance. Ensure that all participants are ready to draw along with you. Remind participants that they can start over at any time and that there is no need to worry about errors. Ask group members to place one hand at the bottom of the paper because this is where they will begin drawing.

Using "line drawing, flowers," which you have displayed for the group to see as a point of reference, begin the demonstration by drawing a straight line across the bottom of the paper (Figure 55). Ask everyone to draw along with you.

After the participants complete the horizontal line, ask them to tell you what to draw next. (*The correct response is the flower on the left, beginning with the stem.*) Then ask them whether the lines are straight or curved. When they respond correctly, draw the lines for the stem of the flower, and ask the group to draw along with you (Figure 56). Once they have drawn the stem, ask the group members to tell you what to draw next. (*The correct response is the leaves on the stem.*) Explain that each leaf is drawn using two curved lines. Demonstrate how the leaves are drawn by drawing one curved line that is attached to the stem. Explain that you are starting on the lower right side of the stem and are drawing a line that curves upward. Add another curved line to complete the leaf. Inform the group that you are starting from the tip of the leaf and are drawing a curved line over to the stem (Figures 57 and 58).

When group members complete the leaf, ask them to complete the leaf on the left side of the stem. Tell the group that this leaf is drawn using two curved lines, as was the previous leaf. Ask participants to draw along with you as you add these lines to your drawing (Figure 59).

Explain that the next part of the drawing is the flower blossom, which is drawn on top of the stem. Tell the group that the general shape of the blossom is a circle. Draw the flower blossom and ask everyone to draw along with you (Figure 60). After you have drawn the blossom, inform the group that a smaller circle is drawn in the center of the blossom. You and the participants should draw this circle (Figure 61).

At this point in the demonstration everyone will have drawn one flower on his or her paper. Ask the participants to admire their work. Inquire of the participants what they should draw next. (*The correct response is the flower in the center.*) Ask someone to explain to the rest of the group how to begin drawing this flower. (*The correct response is to start with the stem, add the leaves, and draw the flower blossom.*)

As with the first flower, begin your drawing of the flower in the center with the two lines that form the stem (Figure 62). Inform the group that the lines for this stem are vertical. Ask everyone to draw the stem along with you. Then, drawing together, you and the participants should add the curved lines for the leaves (Figure 63). Ask the participants how the flower blossom should be drawn. (*The correct response is to draw circles one on top of the other.*) Ask the group to draw along with you as you add these circles to your drawing (Figure 64). Step away from the easel and admire your drawing. Encourage group members to admire their drawings.

Ask the group to look at "line drawing, flowers," and remind the participants that the drawing is almost complete. Ask them what they need to draw to finish it. (*The correct response is the flower on the right.*) Explain that this flower is the same variety as the first flower that they drew but that it curves to the left rather than to the right. Ask whether everyone can see this difference. (Continue to explain if some participants do not understand or have difficulty seeing.) Ask the group members if they would like to draw this flower on their own. After allowing enough time for the participants to draw the flower on the right, draw the flower on your oversize pad (Figure 65). Inform the learners that the drawing is now completed, and that if they would like to add anything (e.g., clouds, grass) to their drawing they may do so.

If most of the group members express that they are not happy with their drawings, ask them if they would like to create another drawing. If so, repeat the drawing demonstration.

Ending the Lesson

Signing artwork, showing it to the group, and displaying it in a special area function as a closing exercise and signify that the lesson is concluding. The closing exercise allows participants to see the flowers everyone has drawn and to provide positive feedback and encouragement to one another. This interaction reinforces the concept of building a community among the members of the group. To encourage positive, constructive criticism among the group members, you should always make positive statements about the participants' artwork. You may find that some participants may be overly negatively critical of their own work. In such cases, be sure to counter negative statements with positive, encouraging criticism. When participants comment negatively on their own work, ask them why they feel this way and to describe that feeling specifically. As you come to understand the source of their feelings, you can help the participants to make the work more to their liking.

Begin the closing exercise by asking the participants to choose their own favorite of their drawings, to sign it, and to show it to the group. Some participants may be reluctant or too shy to sign their drawing or to show it to the group. **Do not push them**. Often, other members of the group will ask to see their drawings. This request may prompt participants who are shy to show their work. Ask the participants if they would like to display their drawings at the conclusion of the class in the gallery area you selected during the planning stage of the program. If they agree to your request, hang the drawings.

After all participants have contributed to the closing exercise, explain to the participants that the first lesson has concluded. Thank everyone for participating and tell the members of the group that you are pleased with their progress. Remind the group that you will return for the second lesson on (day, date, and time).

The participants' artwork should be periodically removed and saved in individual portfolios for a review and evaluation session (see Part 3 of this section) that is held after the completion of each section of lessons. The portfolios can be created by stapling two large sheets of heavyweight drawing paper together to form a large envelope. Participants may decorate their portfolios, which then also become works of art. You may wish to devote a part of Lesson B1 or B2 to this endeavor.

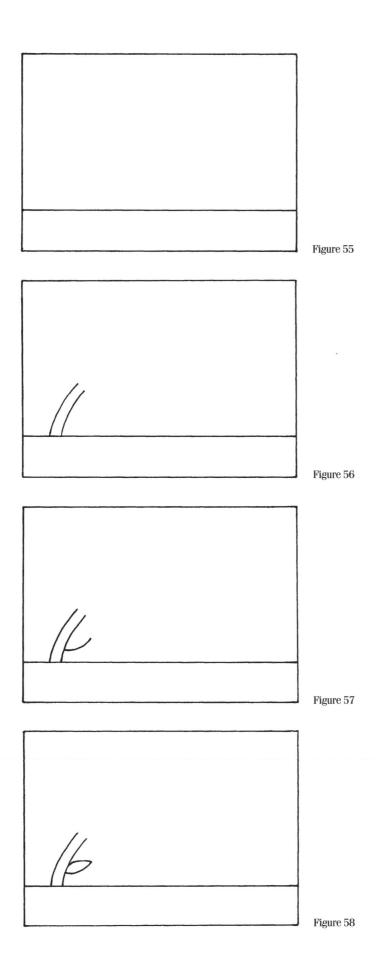

Figure 55

Figure 56

Figure 57

Figure 58

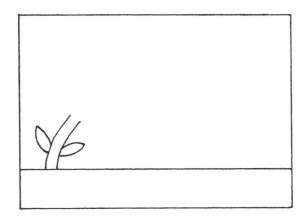

Figure 59

Figure 60

Figure 61

Figure 62

92

Figure 63

Figure 64

Figure 65

Lesson Plan B2

SUBJECT: Elements of art: Color (Wear colorful clothing or accessories to the class; enlist the help of an assistant if your class consists of more than five participants; because this lesson involves the use of liquids and many steps, an assistant can help distribute supplies and ensure that participants do not drink the water or paint.)

OBJECTIVES: Ensure that participants recognize the element of art, color, in nature and in works of art.

Ensure that participants learn the three primary colors: red, yellow, and blue.

Ensure that participants learn the three secondary colors: orange, purple, and green.

Ensure that participants learn the art of mixing color.

Instruct participants in making an art project using a rainbow.

SUPPLIES: Heavyweight drawing paper (two sheets for each participant)

Tempera nontoxic poster paints (red, yellow, blue)

Paintbrushes (¼" flat bristle; one brush for each participant and one for the facilitator)

Black permanent ink felt-tip markers (one marker for each participant and one for the facilitator)

Plastic or paper cups filled with water (one for each participant and one for the facilitator)

Paper towels

Cellophane tape

Paper plates (one plate for each participant and one for the facilitator)

Aprons (one for each participant and one for the facilitator)

Easel with pad of oversize paper (large newsprint pad) (for facilitator's use)

Black thick-line felt-tip marker (for facilitator's use with oversize pad)

Trash can

Newspaper or other protective covering for tables

PROCEDURE:

Arranging the Room

Arrange the tables and chairs for the participants in a U or horseshoe shape. If a participant in a wheelchair wants to use a work board, attach the board to the wheelchair. Cover the tables with newspaper or another protective covering. Set the pad of oversize paper on the easel and place them in the opening of the U or horseshoe. Stand next to the easel to conduct the lesson. Place the following supplies on a table near you: tempera nontoxic paints (red, yellow, blue), paper plates, paper towels, two paintbrushes (¼" flat bristle), two plastic or paper cups (to hold water), and permanent ink felt-tip markers.

Leading the Color Mixing Demonstration

Begin the demonstration by writing "Tools of the Trade: Color" on the oversize pad using various colors of felt-tip markers or on the chalkboard (if available). Pour the paint colors red, yellow, and blue around the edge of a paper plate. Leave space in the center for mixing colors. This paper plate is your palette (Figure 66). Explain that a palette is a surface on which various colors of paint are arranged and mixed. Explain to the participants that in this lesson they will learn about color theory and color mixing.

Ask everyone in the group to watch carefully as you use a paintbrush to take some paint from your palette and apply it to the oversize pad in a circle pattern. Ask the participants to name the color you painted on the pad. After they have named the color red, rinse and wipe the brush thoroughly. Follow the same steps with yellow paint and blue paint. Explain to the participants that red, yellow, and blue are called *primary colors*, which means that all other colors are made from these three colors.

Next, explain to the participants that you will mix the colors orange, purple, and green, which together are called the *secondary colors* because they are made from the primary colors. Begin the demonstration by mixing orange. Ask everyone to watch carefully as you use a paintbrush to take a dab of red paint and place it in the center of your palette. Then, rinse the brush in the cup of water and wipe it thoroughly using a paper towel. Take the brush again and place a dab of yellow paint into the dab of red paint. Mix the colors together to create orange. Then, rinse the brush in the cup of water and wipe it thoroughly using a paper towel. Repeat the procedure using blue and red to create purple and blue and yellow to create green. Set the palette aside and take a clean paper plate to continue the demonstration. Rinse the brush in the cup of water and wipe it thoroughly using a paper towel. Ask the participants if they have any questions and then answer them. Repeat any mixing of colors to help participants understand anything that is unclear to them.

Creating the Art Project

Distribute the following supplies to each participant:

- One paper plate palette with a dab each of yellow, blue, and red paint around the edge of the plate
- One paintbrush
- One permanent ink felt-tip marker
- One sheet of heavyweight drawing paper
- Paper towels
- One cup of water
- One apron

Ensure that all participants are comfortable while they work. Place the palette, cup of water, paintbrush, and paper towels within easy reach of each participant. For example, place the supplies on the person's right side for right-handed participants and on the person's left side for left-handed participants. Remove the caps from the markers for partici-

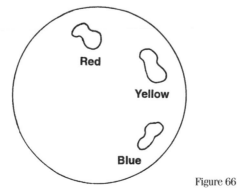

Figure 66

pants who need assistance. Tape down the corners of the sheet of drawing paper for participants who are unable to hold their paper steady. Help participants put on their aprons.

Inform group members that they will create a rainbow design using the primary and secondary colors. Explain that the rainbow can be designed in many ways and that you will draw some examples on the oversize pad using a felt-tip marker and the colors left over from the color mixing demonstration (Figure 67).

Encourage the group to suggest other rainbow designs, but remind participants that the three primary colors and the three secondary colors must be used in the design. Draw and then paint a few of the group's suggestions. Then ask the participants to create their own rainbow designs. Remind the group to draw the designs before painting them. Provide a great deal of encouragement and assist anyone who needs help.

Ending the Lesson

To conclude Lesson 2, ask the participants to sign their work and show it to the rest of the group. Ask whether anyone would like to display his or her designs in the gallery area. Explain to the group members that you will hang all the designs after they participate in a closing breathing/relaxation exercise. Tell participants that this exercise releases the tension that built up while they created their artwork and encourages the members of the group to form bonds with one another. Explain what you are going to do and then lead the group in the following exercise:

Join hands, if you can. Close your eyes. On the count of one, slowly take a deep breath through the nose. On the count of two, slowly exhale through the mouth.

When everyone has completed the breathing/relaxation exercise, explain that Lesson 2 has concluded. Thank everyone for participating and tell the members of the group that you are pleased with their progress. Remind the group that you will return for the third lesson on (day, date, and time). After the group leaves the room, hang the artwork in the gallery area.

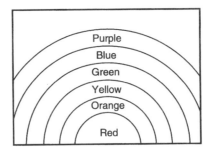

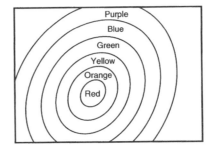

Figure 67

Lesson Plan B3

SUBJECT:	Elements of art: Shape
OBJECTIVES:	Ensure that participants are able to identify the three basic shapes: square, triangle, and circle.
	Ensure that participants are able to identify and discuss shapes as symbols in society (e.g., traffic signs, flags).
	Help participants work together to create a flag for the group or facility.
SUPPLIES:	Roll of brown or white kraft paper
	Tempera nontoxic poster paints (red, yellow, and blue)
	Black felt-tip markers (one for each participant)
	Paper plates (one for each participant)
	Paintbrushes, ¼" (one for each participant)
	Plastic or paper cups filled with water (one for each participant)
	Paper towels
	Easel with pad of oversize paper (large newsprint pad) (for the facilitator's use)
	Black thick-line felt-tip marker (for the facilitator's use)
	Color chart of nautical flags (can be obtained from the public or university library)
	Color chart of U.S. state flags and the U.S. national flag (can be obtained from the public or university library)
	Color chart of U.S. traffic signs (can be obtained from the public or university library)

PROCEDURE:

Arranging the Room

Arrange the tables and chairs for the participants in a U or horseshoe shape. If a participant in a wheelchair wants to use a work board, attach the board to the wheelchair. Set the pad of oversize paper on the easel and place them in the opening of the U or horseshoe. Stand next to the easel to conduct the lesson.

Leading the Discussion

Begin the lesson by writing "Tools of the Trade: Shape" on the oversize pad or on the chalkboard (if available). Initiate a discussion about the shapes that are found in American traffic signs and flags by drawing the shapes of some common traffic signs on the oversize pad (Figure 68). Ask the participants to identify the shapes. Explain that these shapes function as symbols that have a specific meaning in American society. For example, the combination of the octagonal shape and the red color of the stop sign is so recognizable that even without the word STOP written in the center of the octagon, people tend to stop when they see the sign. The color of the sign in combination with a particular shape signifies additional information (e.g., a yellow inverted triangle indicates danger or a warning, a green rectangle indicates direction or location).

Display the color charts of nautical flags, U.S. state flags, and the U.S. national flag. Instruct participants to study the flags for a few minutes. Then use the following questions as a guide for a discussion about the shapes, colors, and meanings of the flags:

- Why are the colors red, white, and blue used in the U.S. flag?
- What is the meaning behind the use of the stars and stripes in the U.S. flag?
- Why is our state flag (whatever color or colors it is)?
- Why are nautical flags used on boats or ships?

At the end of the discussion, explain to the group members that they will create a flag that represents the art group.

Creating the Art Project

Begin the art project by brainstorming design ideas for the flag with the group. (Remember to keep the design simple and use the three basic shapes—circles, triangles, squares—in the design.) Ask group members what colors and shapes they would like to use in the flag. Write or draw their suggestions on the oversize pad. Ask the group what shape the flag should be and how the colors and shapes should be arranged within this outline. Survey the participants as to whether they want to use the name of the facility, a slogan, or a catchy name for the group on the flag. For example, in Figure 69 the name of the facility is Evergreen Acres. The "participants" decided to use blue as a background color and several shades of green in the trees. Triangle shapes were used to create the trees.

Once the design decisions about the flag have been made, roll out a sheet of kraft paper at each table in front of the participants. If your group has several tables of participants, make several flags of the same design.

Ensure everyone receives an opportunity to draw and paint. You may need to move the kraft paper around for participants or ask them to exchange seats in order to give everyone a chance to be creative. Encourage cooperation among the people at each table because the drawing procedure is a group effort. One or several group members may draw the flag design on the kraft paper. The flag must be very large, so assist participants as they draw the flag on the kraft paper using a felt-tip marker.

When the flag has been drawn, inform participants that they will paint it. Distribute a paper paint pallette to each table. Participants at each table should share the palette. Distribute a paintbrush to each participant. Place cups of water and paper towels on the tables within easy reach of group members. Tell the group to paint the background and large areas first and to paint the small details last.

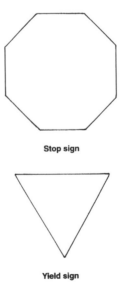

Stop sign

Yield sign   Figure 68

Ending the Lesson

When the flag or flags have been painted, hold it or them up for all to see. Congratulate the group members on their cooperation and fine work. Explain to the group members that to conclude the lesson, they should participate in a closing breathing/relaxation exercise. Tell participants that this exercise releases the tension that built up while they created their artwork and encourages the members of the group to form bonds with one another. Explain what you are going to do and then lead the group in the following exercise:

Join hands, if you can. Close your eyes. On the count of one, slowly take a deep breath through the nose. On the count of two, slowly exhale through the mouth.

When everyone has completed the breathing/relaxation exercise, explain that Lesson 3 has concluded. Thank everyone for participating and tell the members of the group that you are pleased with their progress. Remind the group that you will return for the fourth lesson on (day, date, and time). After the group leaves the room, hang the artwork in the gallery area.

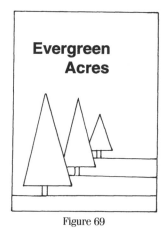

Figure 69

Lesson Plan B4

SUBJECT:	Elements of art: Pattern
OBJECTIVES:	Ensure that participants are able to recognize and identify the element of art, pattern, in nature and in works of art.
	Help participants to successfully draw a repeating pattern that could be used as a wallpaper or fabric design.
SUPPLIES:	Multicolored construction paper (two sheets for each participant)
	White 8½" × 11" paper (several sheets for each participant)
	Felt-tip markers (several colors for each participant and several colors for the facilitator)
	Cellophane tape
	Stapler
	Easel with pad of oversize paper (large newsprint pad) (for the facilitator's use)
	Black thick-line felt-tip marker (for the facilitator's use)
	Wallpaper books (often, paint and wallpaper stores keep old books that store personnel are willing to donate to you)
	"Wallpaper/fabric design project" (included in this lesson)

PROCEDURE:

Arranging the Room

Arrange the tables and chairs for the participants in a U or horseshoe shape. If a participant in a wheelchair wants to use a work board, attach the board to the wheelchair. Set the pad of oversize paper on the easel and place them in the opening of the U or horseshoe. Stand next to the easel to conduct the lesson.

Leading the Discussion

Begin the lesson by writing "Tools of the Trade: Pattern" on the oversize pad using the thick-line marker or on the chalkboard (if available). Design the discussion you lead to ensure that the art group participants are able to recognize and identify the element of art called pattern in nature and in works of art.

Explain to the group that pattern is a repetition of a shape or a color or both. Exhibit examples of repeated patterns in swatches of fabrics (e.g., curtains, tablecloths, clothing) and in wallpaper from wallpaper books. Wallpaper books contain numerous samples of repeated patterns. Then ask group members to identify and describe the patterns that they observe in the classroom. (Examples of patterns that they may observe are stripes, dots, plaids, flowers, and colors that repeat.)

Ask the participants to look outside, if the room has windows, and identify any patterns they observe. (Examples of patterns that they may observe are a pile of leaves, bricks, stairs, or anything that repeats shapes or colors.) Instruct the group to describe other patterns that might be found outdoors. (Examples of other patterns they may observe are zebra patterns, numerous telephone poles in a row, a flock of birds, the patterns on butterfly wings, and snowflakes.) Ensure that participants have a good understanding of patterns by asking whether they have any questions and by reviewing anything that is confusing to them.

Creating the Wallpaper/Fabric Design

Introduce the practical part of the lesson by explaining to group members that they will now create a wallpaper or fabric design. Distribute a copy of the palette for "wallpaper/fabric design project" to each participant. Inform the group that each box will contain a design that each member creates. Using cellophane tape, tack down the corners of the papers of participants who have difficulty stabilizing them. Pass out several sheets of white 8½" × 11" paper to all participants. Then distribute the felt-tip markers and remove the caps from the markers of the participants who need this assistance.

Then ask the participants to watch as you draw the six boxes contained in the palette for the "wallpaper/fabric design project" on your oversize pad. Draw lines to represent stripes in the first box (Figure 70). Point to your stripe pattern and identify it, and ask participants what other patterns may be added. (*One correct response is color.*) Select two colors of felt-tip markers and shade the stripes using these colors. Using various colors of felt-tip markers, draw multicolored dots in the second box and explain that the dots also form a pattern design (Figure 71).

Instruct participants to begin designing by selecting a box on the palette in which to incorporate a pattern. Encourage group members to use one of your examples or to create one of their own, perhaps using one of the pattern designs that were discussed earlier in the lesson (see p. 100). Remind participants that the patterns can be simple or complex. After the learners complete the first pattern, ask them to continue creating patterns in the remaining boxes on their palettes.

When everyone has completed his or her designs, ask group members to select a coordinating color of construction paper to use as a display backing for their design. Staple each palette onto a piece of construction paper. If time is left in the session, ask the participants to select their favorite design pattern from their "wallpaper/fabric design project" palette. Explain to the group that they may enlarge this favorite design onto a sheet of white 8½" × 11" paper. When everyone has completed the enlargement, staple each of the designs onto a coordinating sheet of construction paper.

Ending the Lesson

To conclude Lesson 4, ask the participants to sign their names to their designs and show them to the rest of the group. Ask whether anyone would like to display his or her designs in the gallery area. Explain to the group members that you will hang all the designs after they participate in a closing breathing/relaxation exercise. Tell participants that this exercise releases the tension that built up while they created their designs and encourages members of the group to form bonds with one another. Do the exercise two or three times.

Join hands, if you can. Close your eyes. On the count of one, take a deep breath through the nose. On the count of two, exhale through the mouth.

When everyone has completed the breathing/relaxation exercise, explain that Lesson 4 has concluded. Thank everyone for participating and tell the members of the group that you are pleased with their progress. Remind the group that you will return for the fifth lesson on (day, date, and time). After the group leaves the room, hang the artwork in the gallery area.

Palette for "wallpaper/fabric design project."

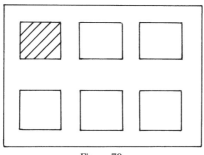

Figure 70

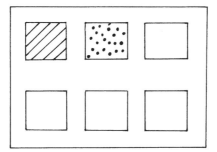

Figure 71

Lesson Plan B5

Subject:	Floral still life: The use of line and color
Objectives:	Ensure that participants are able to recognize and understand still life as an art form.
	Ensure that participants become familiar with floral still life artists. (A brief introduction to floral still life painting is included in this lesson.)
	Help participants to successfully draw a floral still life using line and color.
Supplies:	Heavyweight drawing paper (several sheets for each participant)
	Felt-tip markers (a full spectrum of color for each participant and for the facilitator)
	Cellophane tape
	Easel with pad of oversize paper (large newsprint pad) (for the facilitator's use)
	Black or brown permanent ink felt-tip marker (for the facilitator's use)
	Reproductions of floral still life drawings and paintings from books, magazines, postcards, and other media (impressionists such as van Gogh, Monet, or Manet are good choices; refer to Appendix A for the names of other still life artists)
	Real or artificial flower bouquet with simply-shaped flowers such as carnations or daisies (*Note:* Roses are usually too complicated for beginning participants. Try to avoid them.)
	Small table (on which to set the floral bouquet)

Procedure:

Arranging the Room

Arrange the tables and chairs for the participants in a U or horseshoe shape. If a participant in a wheelchair wants to use a work board, attach the board to the wheelchair. Set the pad of oversize paper on the easel and place them in the opening of the U or horseshoe. Place the small table with the floral bouquet to be used for the still life in the center of the U- or horseshoe-shaped area. Stand next to the easel to conduct the lesson.

Leading the Discussion

Begin the lesson by writing "Tools of the Trade: Floral Still Life—The Use of Line and Color" on the oversize pad using the thick-line marker or on the chalkboard (if available). Using the books, magazines, postcards, or other media you have gathered, show examples of floral still life. Ask participants to name the type of art. Wait for a response. If no one answers correctly, explain that this type of art is called still life, and that still life is a composition of inanimate objects. As you show each example of a still life identify the artist and offer a brief biography of him or her. Explain to the group that many artists paint and draw floral still lifes. Ask the group members to describe the flowers they see in the reproductions, the colors the artist used, the type of lines that were used, and what they see in the background. Encourage the participants to tell you the reasons that they like or dislike the still lifes.

Leading the Drawing Demonstration

Begin the drawing demonstration by asking the group members to tell you what shapes and colors they see in the bouquet. Their answers will vary depending on the flowers you have chosen for the bouquet. Carnations and daisies have a basic, circular shape. Daisies also have circular centers. The stems are linear and can be either straight or curved. Point out to the group that the bouquet as a whole has a basic shape.

Step to the easel and oversize pad and ask the participants to watch as you draw the basic shape of the bouquet using a brown or black felt-tip marker (Figure 72). Explain that because this is a rough sketch the lines need not be exact. The next shape to draw is the basic shape of the vase (Figure 73). Then draw the basic shapes of the individual flowers, stems, and leaves (Figure 74). (If you are drawing daisies, remind the participants that these flowers possess a circular center, with petals radiating out from that center [Figure 75].)

Complete the piece by drawing two horizontal lines to represent a table top (Figure 76). Inform the participants that your line drawing is complete and that it is time for them to create their own drawings of the bouquet.

Distribute several sheets of heavyweight drawing paper and a brown or black permanent felt-tip marker to each participant. Tack down the edges of the paper with cellophane tape for the participants who cannot steady their paper. Remove the caps from the markers for participants who have trouble doing so.

Before the participants begin drawing, ask them whether they should turn their papers to the horizontal or vertical position. (*The correct response is vertical because the bouquet has a vertical shape.*) Instruct the participants to begin their drawing with the basic shapes of the vase, individual flowers, stems, and leaves. Ask them to fill an entire page with their drawing. If members of the group need guidance, repeat the drawing steps that you outlined earlier in the lesson. Strongly encourage everyone as he or she completes each step. If the participants are not happy with their drawings, suggest that they try again on a fresh sheet of drawing paper.

When everyone has finished his or her line drawing of the floral still life, ask the group members to describe the colors they see in the flowers, the stems, the leaves, the vase, the table, and the background. Ask the participants to watch as you add color to your drawing on the oversize pad using felt-tip markers of various colors. It is permissible to color over the lines used in the original drawing. (In fact, doing so lends an expressive quality to the piece.) Add patterns to the table or background if you wish. As you complete your demonstration, ask the participants to add color and patterns to their floral still life drawings.

Ending the Lesson

To conclude Lesson 5, ask the participants to sign their work and show it to the rest of the group. Ask whether anyone would like to display his or her still life in the gallery area. Explain to the group members that you will hang all the still lifes after they participate in a closing breathing/relaxation exercise. Tell participants that this exercise releases the tension that built up while they created their artwork and encourages the members of the group to form bonds with one another. Explain what you are going to do and then lead the group in the following exercise:

Join hands, if you can. Close your eyes. On the count of one, slowly take a deep breath through the nose. On the count of two, slowly exhale through the mouth.

When everyone has completed the breathing/relaxation exercise, explain that Lesson 5 has concluded. Thank everyone for participating and tell the members of the group that you are excited about their progress. Remind the group that you will return for the sixth lesson on (day, date, and time). After the group leaves the room, hang the artwork in the gallery area.

Floral Still Life Painting

Floral still life painting became popular in Europe during the first part of the 19th century, but was largely ignored by American artists until the middle of that century. Floral paintings of the period reflected a familiarity with romantic poetry, the emerging scientific information about flowers, and the symbolic meaning of flowers, especially paintings that included the human figure (e.g., the carnation denoted pride, the daisy suggested innocence, the iris indicated a message, the violet symbolized faithfulness, the water lily revealed eloquence).

The most well-known 19th century floral still life painters were John LaFarge, Childe Hassam, Charles Demuth, and Edouard Manet. Manet (1832–1883) painted a series of floral still lifes during the last years of his life. After several years of illness, his spirits were renewed by the sight of flowers and Manet felt he was inspired to paint them.

These small floral still lifes retained the directness and vitality that characterized his work before he became ill. Because Manet's illness allowed him to work for only short periods, the paintings were probably painted quickly.

The United States produced several still life painters in the mid-19th century, such as George Harvey and Martin Johnson Heade. Heade was best known for his orchid and hummingbird paintings, which were inspired by his trips to Brazil in the mid-1860s. Georgia O'Keeffe, an artist of the 20th century, is known for her bold paintings of very large flowers.

(*Note to facilitators:* Manet's floral still life paintings can be seen in Gordon and Forge's *The Last Flowers of Manet.*)

Figure 72

Figure 73

Figure 74

Figure 75

Figure 76

Lesson Plan B6

SUBJECT: Chinese watercolor painting: The use of line and color

OBJECTIVES: Ensure that participants recognize and understand Chinese watercolor painting.

Ensure that participants learn the basic Chinese watercolor painting techniques.

Help participants to successfully paint a watercolor using the Chinese watercolor painting techniques.

SUPPLIES: Heavyweight drawing paper (several sheets for each participant and for the facilitator)

Cellophane tape

Paper towels

Cup or bowl filled with water (one for each participant and one for the facilitator)

Basic watercolor sets (cake-type paint) (one for each participant and one for the facilitator)

Oriental watercolor brushes (inexpensive, with bamboo handles; one for each participant and one for the facilitator)

Table and chair (for the facilitator's use)

Easel with oversize pad paper (large newsprint pad) (for the facilitator's use)

Black thick-line felt-tip marker (for the facilitator's use)

Reproductions of Chinese watercolor paintings (examples can be found in books from the public or university library)

"Chinese watercolor painting example" (included in this lesson)

Cassette or CD player and cassettes or CDs of traditional Chinese music

PROCEDURE:

Note to the facilitator: Chinese watercolor painting is a very disciplined painting technique, which takes many hours of practice to master. This introductory lesson exposes the participants to art from another culture and gives them an appreciation of it. Before conducting this lesson, practice the techniques outlined—holding the brush, making the strokes, and painting a simple picture.

Arranging the Room

Arrange the tables and chairs for the participants in a U or horseshoe shape. If a participant in a wheelchair wants to use a work board, attach the board to the wheelchair. Place the small table and chair at which you will work in the opening of the U or horseshoe. Set the easel and oversize pad behind your table and chair. Place the supplies you will use within easy reach. As the participants enter the room, begin playing the tape or CD of Chinese music.

Leading the Discussion

Begin the lesson by writing "Tools of the Trade: Chinese Watercolor Painting—The Use of Line and Color" on the oversize pad or on the chalkboard (if available). Turn off the music. Initiate a discussion about Chinese watercolor painting by displaying the reproductions you have gathered. Indicate the linear quality (i.e., lines can be thick or thin, but always highly expressive; Chinese watercolorists use the lines to convey movement and emotion) of this style of art, the delicate colors used, and the long, vertical compositional format. Explain that much of the artwork is created using a brush and ink and is executed using quick, firm strokes of the brush, much like calligraphy. Ask the participants their opinions of the reproductions of Chinese watercolor art you are showing to them and how Chinese art differs from Western art.

Distribute a sheet of heavyweight drawing paper, a cup or bowl of water, a watercolor set, paper towels, and an Oriental watercolor brush to each participant. Tack down (using cellophane tape) the papers of participants who have difficulty stabilizing the papers.

Ask the group members to examine the brushes they will use for their paintings. Explain that the handles are made from bamboo and that the brush hairs are rabbit, sable, or goat. Inform the group that Chinese watercolorists may use many sizes of brushes in painting.

Tell the participants that they will not become proficient in the Chinese watercolor technique during this lesson because it takes many hours of practice to master. The object of the lesson is to provide them with an understanding of this type of art and an appreciation for the art of another culture.

Leading the Stroking Demonstration

Seat yourself at the table in the opening of the U shape to begin the demonstration. First, demonstrate the proper way to hold the watercolor brush. Remember to go slowly enough for all participants to see and understand what you are doing. Explain that your forearm and the base of your wrist rest on the table and that the brush handle points slightly away from you. Instruct participants to grip the brush by placing their thumb above the index and middle fingers (Figure 77). Ask the participants to try holding their brush. (Some participants have difficulty grasping objects and need to use assistive devices [e.g., a padded spork is used in eating]. Foam can be wrapped around the brush handle and secured with rubber bands or tape (Figure 78). [Foam hair curlers can also be used.] Assist participants who need additional help and guidance in holding the brush. Ask group members whether this method of holding the brush feels odd to them and what their reasons are for feeling this way.

Once everyone has practiced holding the brush, tell the group that you will demonstrate four basic strokes used in Chinese watercolor—the hook stroke, the teardrop stroke, the dot stroke, and the stem stroke—and that they will practice the four strokes along with you. Remember to provide encouragement and assist participants who need help. Reassure them that they may use more than one sheet of drawing paper to practice the four basic Chinese watercolor strokes. Explain that in Chinese painting, the artist moves the entire arm and shoulder as he or she creates the strokes. A Chinese painter thinks about and meditates and concentrates on making the stroke before touching the brush to the paper. After this period of concentration, he or she quickly creates the stroke without hesitation.

First, demonstrate the *hook stroke* (Figure 79). Dip your brush into the cup or bowl of water and then into a cake of watercolor paint. You may use any color. Using the lid of the paint box, make a pool of paint and water. The paint should be fairly deep in color. Begin by loading your brush with color from the pool, grasping the brush as seen in Figure 77, placing the tip of the brush on the paper, exerting a slight downward pressure on the brush, and quickly pulling the brush to the right. Create several strokes in close proximity to one another. Ask the group to try to make the hook stroke along with you. Reassure the participants that this is only a practice session before they create an actual painting.

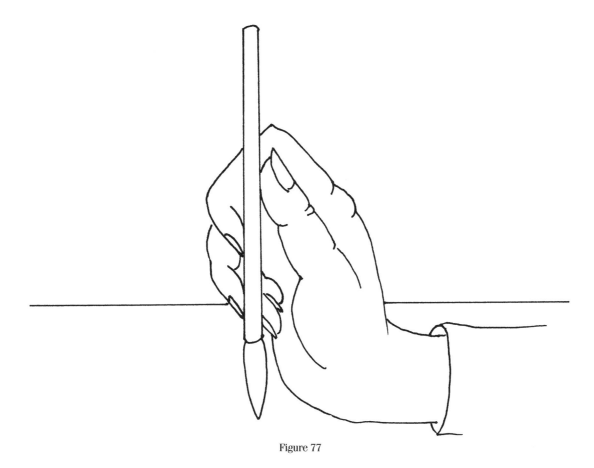

Figure 77

Figure 78

Hook strokes

Figure 79

Teardrop strokes

Figure 80

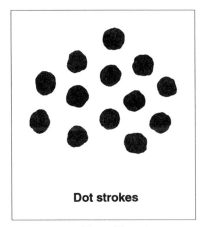

Dot strokes

Figure 81

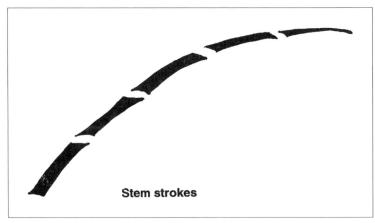

Stem strokes

Figure 82

Second, demonstrate the *teardrop stroke* (Figure 80). Begin by loading your brush from the pool of color in the lid of the paint box. (*Note:* Cleaning and drying the brush is not necessary, but replenishing the pool of color is necessary if you run out of color.) Grasp the brush as seen in Figure 77, with the tip slightly touching the paper. Exert a slight downward pressure on the brush and quickly make a curving movement with the brush in the direction of the lower right-hand corner of the paper. Invite the group to try this stroke.

Third, demonstrate the *dot stroke* (Figure 81) for the group by loading your brush from the pool of color and touching the paper with the brush, lightly twisting it to form a small dot. Explain that Chinese watercolorists make sure that the dots are uniform in size and equidistant from one another, and that they paint the dots in specific groups or patterns. Ask the group to make some dot strokes along with you.

The fourth stroke you will demonstrate is the *stem stroke* (Figure 82). This stroke is always made from left to right. Before you make the stem stroke, load your brush with color from the pool in the lid of the paint box. Then lightly press the brush on the paper and pull it quickly to the right. The stem stroke can be used to create plant stems.

Leading the Painting Demonstration

Explain to the group members that they will now paint a picture using two of the Chinese watercolor painting strokes, the stem stroke and the dot stroke. Display "Chinese watercolor painting example" and inform the participants that this is the painting they will paint. Ensure that all participants have a cup or bowl of clean water and several sheets of fresh heavyweight drawing paper. Reassure everyone that this lesson is an experiment in using Chinese watercolor painting techniques, and that everyone, including you, is learning. Ask that everyone be gentle with him- or herself and not judge his or her attempts too harshly.

Instruct the participants to turn their papers to the vertical position and to mix a pool of water and any color in the lid of their paint boxes. Ask the group members to load their brushes with the chosen color and to paint along with you. Point out that you will begin the painting with the largest area to be painted, the bamboo stems. Create several stems by using the stem stroke and ask the group to paint along with you (Figure 83). As you paint, gently remind the group how the stroke is executed. (Remember that you may need to do so because some participants may have short-term memory losses.) After everyone has completed the stems, explain that you will paint the leaves next using the dot stroke. Ask everyone to paint along with you (Figure 84). As you paint, gently remind the group how the stroke is executed. (Remember that you may need to do so because some participants may

Chinese watercolor painting example

have short-term memory losses.) Paint as many examples as you think are necessary. Remind the participants that they can throw away any painting attempts with which they are not satisfied.

Ending the Lesson

After the participants have practiced the watercolor painting techniques and have painted one or two pictures with which they are satisfied, ask them to sign their paintings and to show their Chinese watercolor paintings to the rest of the group. As the participants view all the paintings, ask the group members to talk about their experience with Chinese water-color painting. Ask them what they liked and disliked about the experience. Ask them whether they would like to create more Chinese watercolor paintings.

Before you dismiss the group, explain that some Chinese watercolorists meditate, and that to close the session, everyone will try a simple meditation/relaxation exercise, which you will lead. (You may wish to play the Chinese music you used at the opening of the session.) You may use the following script:

Relax your shoulders and close your eyes. Take a deep breath and now release it slowly. I want you now to visualize tall grasses swaying in a gentle wind.

Allow a few minutes of quiet time while they visualize the scene. Conclude the meditation by asking everyone to open his or her eyes. Inform the group that Lesson 6 has concluded. Thank everyone for participating and tell the members of the group that you are pleased with their progress. Remind the group that you will return for the seventh lesson on (day, date, and time). After the group leaves the room, hang the artwork in the gallery area.

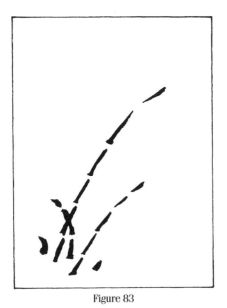

Figure 83

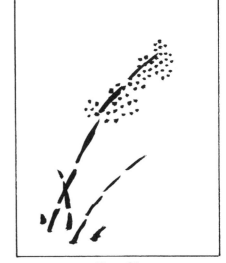

Figure 84

Lesson Plan B7

SUBJECT: Mixed media: The use of line, color, and pattern

OBJECTIVES: Ensure that participants become aware of and understand the use of line, color, and pattern in works of art.

Help participants to successfully draw a simple still life using the elements of line, color, and pattern.

Help participants to successfully create a painting by incorporating two art media, oil pastels and watercolor, in one painting.

SUPPLIES: Heavyweight drawing paper (several sheets for each participant)

Construction paper (various colors; several sheets for each participant)

Oil pastels (one set for each participant and one set for the facilitator)

Watercolor sets (cake-type paint) (one set for each participant and one set for the facilitator)

Paintbrushes, ½" (one for each participant and one for the facilitator)

Cups or bowls of water (one for each participant and one for the facilitator)

Paper towels

Stapler

Real or artificial bouquet of flowers (daisies or carnations)

Small table (on which to display the floral bouquet)

Easel with pad of oversize paper (large newsprint pad) (for the facilitator's use)

Black thick-line felt-tip marker (for the facilitator's use)

Reproductions of works of mixed media art (can be obtained from books, magazines, postcards, and other sources; Rauschenberg, Degas, and Kurt Schwitters are artists who have worked in mixed media)

PROCEDURE:

Arranging the Room

Arrange tables and chairs for the participants in a U or horseshoe shape. If a participant in a wheelchair wants to use a work board, attach the board to the wheelchair. Set the pad of oversize paper on the easel and place them in the opening of the U or horseshoe. Place the small table and floral bouquet in front of the easel. Stand next to the easel to conduct the lesson.

Leading the Discussion

Begin the lesson by writing "Tools of the Trade: Mixed Media—The Use of Line, Color, and Pattern" on the oversize pad using the thick-line marker or on the chalkboard (if available). Initiate a discussion about mixed media art. Explain that mixed media artworks contain more than one art medium. For example, an artist may combine oil pastel and watercolor; ink and watercolor; or fabric, pastel, and charcoal to create a mixed media artwork. Explain that there is no limit to the number of media that can be combined to create a work of art. Then display the reproductions of mixed media art that you have gathered. Ask participants to identify the use of line, color, and pattern in the reproductions. Inform the group about the types of art media that were used to create each piece.

Leading the Demonstration

The demonstration gets underway with you explaining to group members that in this lesson they will create a mixed media artwork. Tell them that they will be using oil pastels and watercolor to create a still life. Then distribute a sheet of heavyweight drawing paper, a box of oil pastels, a watercolor set, a paintbrush, a cup or bowl of water, and paper towels to each participant. Instruct the participants to study the floral bouquet. Ask them to tell you the shapes and colors they see in the bouquet. (*The correct response depends on the flowers used; if you are using carnations or daisies, the correct response is circular; the stems are linear and can be either straight or curved; the colors are whatever you have selected.*) Indicate the basic shape of the bouquet to the group.

Once they have correctly identified the shapes and colors, tell the participants that you will begin to draw the bouquet and that they should draw along with you. Use any color oil pastel to draw the basic shape, or outline, of the bouquet on the oversize pad (Figure 85). Next, draw the basic shape of the vase (Figure 86). Then draw the basic shapes of the individual flowers, stems, and leaves (Figure 87). (If you are drawing daisies, remind the participants that the flowers have a circular center, with petals radiating out from that center [Figure 88].) To complete the drawing, draw two horizontal lines to represent a surface on which the bouquet sits (Figure 89).

When you complete the line drawing, ask the participants to describe the colors they see in the floral still life. Instruct them to use their oil pastels to add those colors to their drawing. Remind group members that they can blend the oil pastels by layering the colors. Use the technique outlined in Lesson A3 to demonstrate blending. Be creative and expressive with color. Assure the participants that when adding color to their drawings, they may go outside the lines they have drawn.

When all the participants are satisfied with their completed drawings, inform them that the next step in creating the mixed media artwork is to add the watercolor paints. Explain to group members that when they apply watercolor paint to their drawings, the areas that are covered by oil pastels will resist the watercolor (because oil and water do not mix). However, the areas on the drawing that do not contain oil pastels will take the watercolor.

Instruct the participants to review the colors in their watercolor sets and to select a color that coordinates with their drawing. Assist participants who cannot make a decision or who have become confused momentarily. Direct the group to use a paintbrush to mix a puddle of water and one color in the lid of the watercolor set. This mix is the watercolor wash. Using the paintbrush, apply the watercolor wash by painting it over the entire drawing. Ask the group to do the same. Advise participants that more than one color can be washed over their drawing if they wish. After the watercolor wash is applied to the oil pastel drawings, allow the paintings to dry. As the paintings dry, ask each participant to select a coordinating sheet of construction paper to use as a mat for his or her completed piece. Staple the construction paper to each participant's work.

Ending the Lesson

To conclude Lesson 7, ask the participants to sign their work and show it to the rest of the group. Ask whether anyone would like to display his or her still lifes in the gallery area. Explain to the group members that you will hang all the still lifes after they participate in a closing breathing/relaxation exercise. Tell participants that this exercise releases the tension that built up while they created their artwork and encourages the members of the group to form bonds with one another. Explain what you are going to do and then lead the group in the following exercise:

Join hands, if you can. Close your eyes. Imagine that you are walking through a meadow full of flowers, just like the ones you just drew and painted. On the count of one, slowly take a deep breath through the nose. On the count of two, slowly exhale through the mouth and release all the tension in your body.

When everyone has completed the breathing/relaxation exercise, explain that Lesson 7 has concluded. Thank everyone for participating and tell the members of the group that you are pleased with their progress. (You may wish to thank yourself silently and tell yourself that you are doing a good job.) Remind the group that you will return for the eighth lesson on (day, date, and time). After the group leaves the room, hang the artwork in the gallery area.

Figure 85

Figure 86

Figure 87

Figure 88

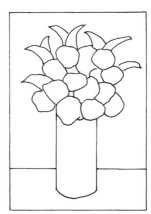
Figure 89

Lesson Plan B8

SUBJECT: Value and form

OBJECTIVES: Ensure that participants recognize and understand value and form in nature and in art.

Help participants to successfully draw a cone, a pyramid, and a cube using value to create form.

SUPPLIES: Heavyweight drawing paper (several sheets for each participant)

Pencils (no. 2) with erasers (one for each participant)

Vine charcoal (several sticks for each participant and for the facilitator)

Rulers (one for each participant and for the facilitator)

Easel with pad of oversize paper (large newsprint pad) (for the facilitator's use)

Black thick-line felt-tip marker (for the facilitator's use)

Charcoal drawings of a cone, a pyramid, and a cube (included in this lesson)

Reproductions of drawings that emphasize value and form (the work of Rembrandt, Michelangelo, and van Gogh are good examples)

PROCEDURE:

Arranging the Room

Arrange tables and chairs for the participants in a U or horseshoe shape. If a participant in a wheelchair wants to use a work board, attach the board to the wheelchair. Set the pad of oversize paper on the easel and place them in the opening of the U or horseshoe. Stand next to the easel to conduct the lesson.

Leading the Discussion

Begin the discussion by writing "Tools of the Trade: Value and Form" on the oversize pad or chalkboard (if available). Then write the words *value* and *form* below the title of the lesson. Ask group members to define the words, if they recall the definitions from Lesson A8. (*The correct response for value is that value is the darkness and lightness in a drawing, and that value also can be described as the shadows or shading in a drawing. The correct response for form is that form is three-dimensional mass created by using value.*) To illustrate value and form, display reproductions of drawings that primarily use black, white, and gray tones. The drawings of Rembrandt, Michelangelo, and van Gogh are good examples of art that incorporates value and form. As you display the reproductions and allow group members a few moments to study them, ask the participants questions such as the following:

- Where are the darkest and lightest values?
- How do you feel when you look at the drawings?
- What types (e.g., landscape, still life, seascape, portrait) of art are represented?
- Do the forms depicted in the drawings appear to be realistic and three-dimensional?
- What did the artist use to make the forms appear to be three-dimensional?

Display the charcoal drawings of a cone, a pyramid, and a cube. Ask the group members to indicate the values they see in the drawings and to show you the lightest area and the

---

Facilitators should note that this lesson may be too long for some groups, but that it can easily be broken into three sessions: 1) draw the cone, 2) draw the pyramid, and 3) draw the cube. A breaking point for the sessions is indicated in the text with three asterisks.

116

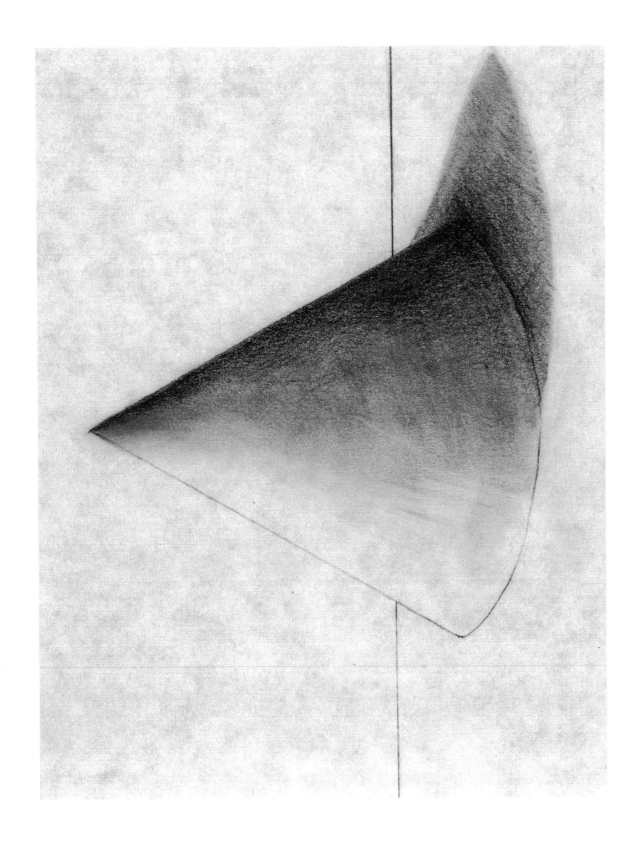

118

darkest area on the drawing. Explain to the participants that in the lesson they will draw a cone, a pyramid, and a cube by using value.

Leading the Drawing Demonstration

Distribute several sheets of heavyweight drawing paper, no. 2 pencils with erasers, and a stick of vine charcoal to each participant. Tape the corners of the heavyweight drawing paper to the tables or work boards of participants who have difficulty stabilizing their papers. Inform the participants that they will draw the cone first.

Begin the demonstration by asking the group members to turn their papers to the vertical position and to take their pencils and draw along with you. As you draw an upward-curving line near the bottom of the paper, ask the participants to draw along with you (Figure 90). Then draw a line that begins at the left side of the curve and moves up diagonally (right) (Figure 91). Ask the participants to do the same. Complete the line drawing of the cone by drawing a line from the top of the cone to the right side of the curve (Figure 92). Ask the participants to do the same. To give the cone the appearance that it is sitting on another object, draw two horizontal lines on either side of it (Figure 93).

Instruct group members to assess their drawing. If they are not happy with it, ask them to draw another. Provide step-by-step instructions if group members need them.

After everyone completes the line drawing of the cone, explain to participants that they will add value, or shading and shadows, to the drawing with which they are the most satisfied to create a three-dimensional form. To add value to the drawing, they will use vine charcoal. Ask everyone to pick up the stick of vine charcoal and examine it. Inform the group members that vine charcoal is made from actual vines that have been processed into the charcoal they are now holding. Explain that the stick of charcoal is very light and fragile. Reassure the participants that it is all right to break the charcoal into smaller, easier-to-handle pieces. To illustrate your point, break a stick of charcoal into smaller pieces.

Begin adding value to the drawing of the cone by asking participants to place the drawing they have chosen on the table or work board in front of them and to draw along with you. Set the scene by telling them that the light is hitting the cone on the left side, making a shadow on the right side. As you shade the right side of your cone drawing, ask the group to take the charcoal and draw along with you (Figure 94). Explain that because there would be a shadow on the surface on which the cone is sitting, this shadow should also be drawn. Ask the participants to use the charcoal to fill in the shadow. Instruct them to make the shadow gradually smaller as they move away from the cone (Figure 95).

After the group has finished shading the cone, ask the group members to review their drawings and to ask questions regarding the shading process. Allow sufficient time for participants' questions before proceeding with the lesson.

***

The next part of the lesson involves drawing and adding value to a pyramid. Begin by directing participants' attention to the displayed example of a pyramid. Ensure that everyone has a ruler, a clean sheet of heavyweight drawing paper, and a no. 2 pencil. Tape down the corners of the paper for participants who have difficulty stabilizing it. Explain to the participants that the pyramid is only slightly different from the cone. Illustrate your point by asking group members to study the displayed drawing of the pyramid. Ask the group to identify the differences. (*The correct response is that the curve at the bottom of the cone has been replaced with the two V-shaped lines of the pyramid. Also, there is a central line from the top of the pyramid to the bottom.*) Once the group has responded correctly, ask the group

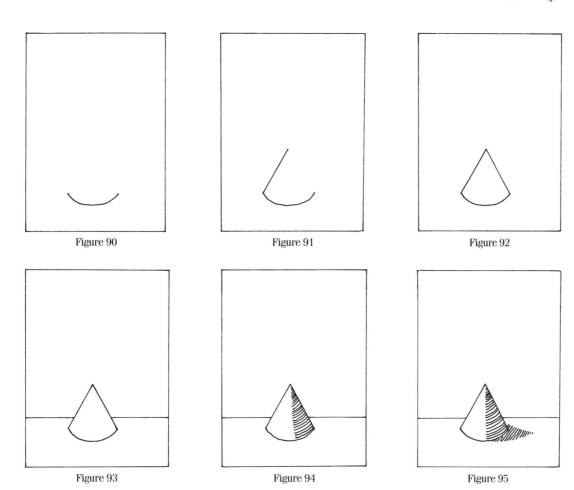

Figure 90 Figure 91 Figure 92

Figure 93 Figure 94 Figure 95

members to turn their papers to the vertical position and to draw along with you using their pencils. Offer assistance to participants who have difficulty with the drawing, and remember to build their self-esteem by encouraging them as they draw.

Begin the pyramid by taking the ruler and drawing a widely angled V toward the bottom of the page (Figure 96). Then draw a vertical line. Start at the bottom of the V and move up diagonally (Figure 97). Repeat this diagonal line on the opposite side of the pyramid (Figure 98). Then draw a line down the center of the pyramid (Figure 99). This center line completes the line drawing of the pyramid. To give the pyramid the appearance that it is placed on another object, draw two lines on either side of the pyramid (Figure 100).

Once the participants have completed their drawings, ask them to assess the drawings. If they are not satisfied, encourage them to draw another pyramid. Provide instructions for participants who need them.

Once all participants are satisfied with their line drawing, tell group members that they will use the vine charcoal to apply value, or shading, to the drawing of the pyramid with which they are the most satisfied, to create form. Ask them to draw along with you.

Begin adding value to the drawing of the pyramid by asking participants to place the drawing they have chosen on the table or work board in front of them and to draw along with you. Set the scene by telling them that the light is hitting the pyramid on the right side, making a shadow on the left side. As you shade the left side of your pyramid drawing, ask the group to take the charcoal and draw along with you (Figure 101). Explain that because there would be a shadow on the surface on which the pyramid is sitting, this shadow should also be drawn. Ask the participants to use the charcoal to fill in the shadow. Instruct them to make the shadow gradually smaller as they move away from the pyramid (Figure 102).

***

The participants have completed drawing and adding value and form to a cone and a pyramid. The next drawing, a cube, is more difficult to draw because there are more lines and angles in a cube. Review the instructions that follow before drawing the cube with the group.

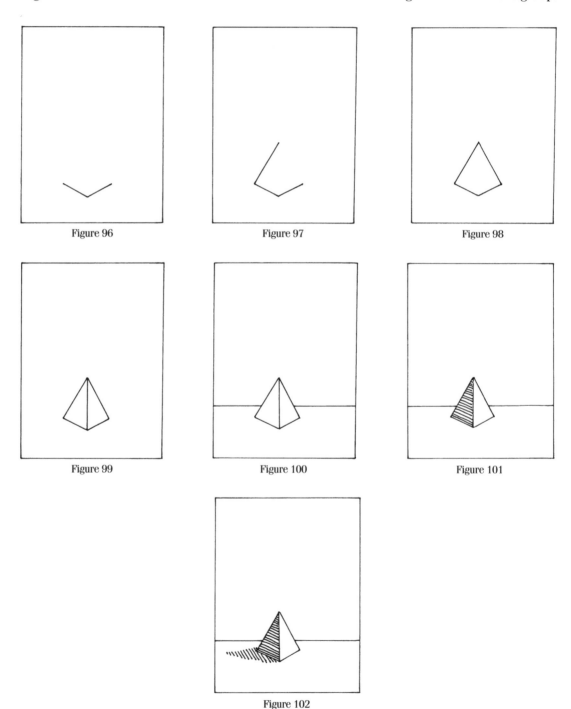

Figure 96

Figure 97

Figure 98

Figure 99

Figure 100

Figure 101

Figure 102

Ensure that participants have a ruler, a clean sheet of heavyweight drawing paper, and their pencils. Explain that because the cube has many lines, everyone will use a ruler to draw these lines. Tape down the corners of the paper for participants who have difficulty stabilizing it. Direct group members' attention to the drawing of a cube, which you put on display at the beginning of the lesson. Ask the group where the light is coming from and where the darkest and lightest values are in the drawing. After the group correctly answers the questions, ask participants to turn their papers to the horizontal position and to draw along with you.

Begin the cube by drawing a vertical line in the middle of the page near the bottom (Figure 103). Then draw a straight, diagonal line that leads to the right at the bottom of the vertical line (Figure 104). Next, draw a straight, diagonal line that leads to the left at the bottom of the vertical line (Figure 105). The next line to be drawn is a straight diagonal line that leads to the right at the top of the vertical line (Figure 106). This line is parallel to the line below it. Draw a straight, diagonal line that leads to the left at the top of the vertical line (Figure 107). This line is parallel to the line below it. Draw one vertical line to complete the right side of the cube and one vertical line to complete the left side of the cube (Figures 108 and 109). Then, at the top left, draw a straight, diagonal line (Figure 110). Ask the group to tell you which lines are parallel. Complete the cube by drawing a straight, diagonal line to close the top of the cube (Figure 111). Ask participants to tell you which lines are parallel. To give the cube the appearance that it is sitting on another object, draw two horizontal lines on either side of the cube (Figure 112).

The line drawing of the cube is now complete. Participants who are not satisfied with the results of their first drawing may want to try again. Provide step-by-step instructions for participants who need them.

Once all participants are satisfied with their drawings, explain that value needs to be added next in order to create form.

Refer to the drawing of the cube you displayed at the beginning of the session. Ask the participants to locate the darkest area on the cube. (*The correct response is the shadow.*)

Ask the participants to draw along with you as you draw and shade the dark area using the vine charcoal.

Begin adding value to the drawing of the cube by asking participants to place the drawing they have chosen on the table or work board in front of them. Set the scene by telling them that the light is hitting the cube on the left side, making a shadow on the right side (Figure 113). As you shade the right side of your cube drawing, remind the group to take the charcoal and draw along with you. Ask participants to identify the other areas of shadow on the cube. Shade those areas on your drawing. Explain that because there would be a shadow on the surface on which the cube is sitting, this shadow should also be drawn. Ask the participants to use the charcoal to fill in the shadow. Instruct them to make the shadow gradually smaller as they move away from the cube (Figure 114).

The cube drawing is now complete. Encourage participants to admire their work for a few moments. Congratulate them (and yourself) for accomplishing so much during the session.

Ending the Lesson

To conclude Lesson 8, ask the participants to sign their drawings and show them to the rest of the group. Ask whether anyone would like to display his or her drawings in the gallery area. Explain to the group members that you will hang all the drawings after they participate in a closing breathing/relaxation exercise. Tell participants that this exercise releases the tension that built up while they created their artwork and encourages the members of the

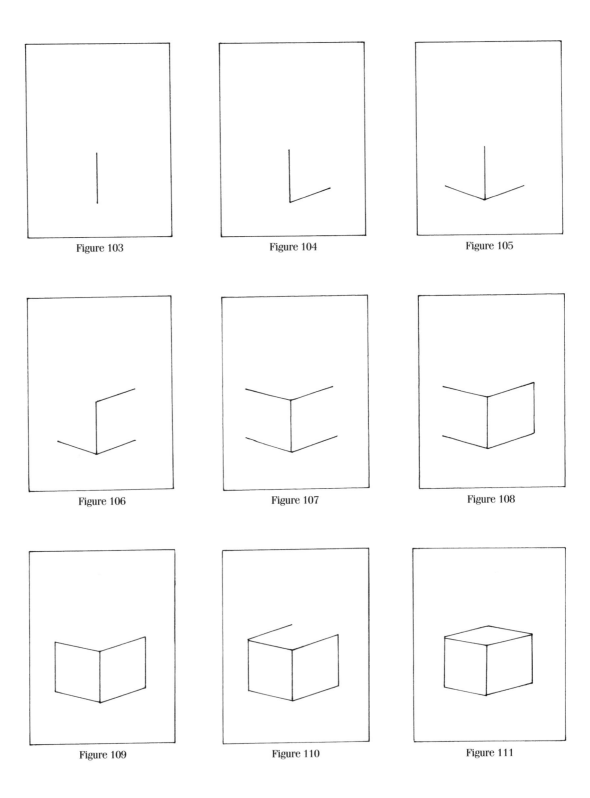

Figure 103

Figure 104

Figure 105

Figure 106

Figure 107

Figure 108

Figure 109

Figure 110

Figure 111

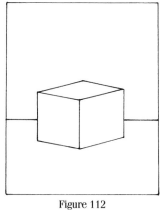
Figure 112

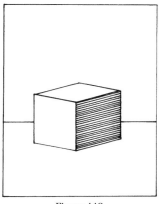
Figure 113

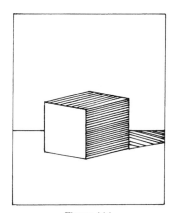
Figure 114

group to form bonds with one another. Explain what you are going to do and then lead the group in the following exercise:

Join hands, if you can. Close your eyes. On the count of one, slowly take a deep breath through the nose. On the count of two, slowly exhale through the mouth.

When everyone has completed the breathing/relaxation exercise, explain that Lesson 8 has concluded. Thank everyone for participating and tell the members of the group that you are pleased with their progress. Remind the group that you will return for the ninth lesson on (day, date, and time). After the group leaves the room, hang the artwork in the gallery area.

Lesson Plan B9

SUBJECT: Overlapping forms: Perspective and space

OBJECTIVES: Ensure that participants understand the concept of and are able to recognize overlapping forms in works of art.

Help participants to successfully draw a simple still life using their knowledge of overlapping forms to create perspective and space.

SUPPLIES: Heavyweight drawing paper (several sheets for each participant)

Construction paper (variety of colors)

Pencils (no. 2) with erasers (one for each participant and one for the facilitator)

Felt-tip markers (a full set of colors for each participant and for the facilitator)

Stapler

Cellophane tape

Apples and oranges (several of each fruit)

Easel with pad of oversize paper (large newsprint pad) (for the facilitator's use)

Black thick-line felt-tip marker (for the facilitator's use)

"Overlapping forms drawing example" (included in this lesson) (one for each participant)

Reproductions of drawings or paintings illustrating overlapping forms (e.g., the works of Cézanne and William Harnett)

PROCEDURE:

Arranging the Room

Arrange tables and chairs for the participants in a U or horseshoe shape. If a participant in a wheelchair wants to use a work board, attach the board to the wheelchair. Set the pad of oversize paper on the easel and place them in the opening of the U or horseshoe. Stand next to the easel to conduct the lesson.

Leading the Discussion

Begin the lesson by writing "Tools of the Trade: Overlapping Forms—Perspective and Space" on the oversize pad or on the chalkboard (if available). Explain to the members of the group that in this lesson they will learn how overlapping forms create perspective and space. Ask the participants to define perspective and space. If they cannot or they do not provide full explanations, you should define perspective for them as a method of drawing that is used to create space or depth in works of art and that space is the sense of depth (three dimensions) that is seen in a painting or drawing. Make the group aware that artists use perspective to create the illusion of three-dimensional space in the mind of the viewer. To illustrate your points, show the group the reproductions of drawings and paintings from various media that incorporate overlapping forms to create perspective and space. Explain that when an artist draws or paints objects that align along the same line of vision, the objects closer to the viewer will overlap the objects that are farther away from the viewer.

Illustrate this principle of overlapping forms in perspective by placing the apples and oranges together on a table top (Figure 115). Ask the participants to view the configuration in order to fully understand the concept of overlapping forms.

126

Figure 115

Distribute a copy of "overlapping forms drawing example" to each participant and explain that the group will copy this drawing in order to learn about overlapping forms. Also distribute a pencil with eraser, several sheets of heavyweight drawing paper, and a set of felt-tip markers to each member of the group. Using cellophane tape, secure the corners of the drawing paper to the table or work board for participants who have difficulty steadying the paper.

Leading the Drawing Demonstration

Begin the demonstration by asking participants to use a pencil with eraser for their drawings. (They will need the eraser to help create the overlapping forms.) Instruct group members to turn their papers to the horizontal position. Ask them with what object should they begin the drawing. (*The correct response is to begin by drawing the large cylinder, which is on the right side of the drawing example.*) Encourage everyone to draw along with you. First, draw a curved line at the lower right part of the paper (Figure 116). Second, draw two vertical lines, one on either side of the curved line, up from the curved line (Figure 117). Third, draw an ellipsis at the top of the two vertical lines (Figure 118). Fourth, draw a large circle over the lower left corner of the cylinder (Figure 119). Fifth, using the pencil eraser, erase the lower left corner of the cylinder (Figure 120). Sixth, draw a smaller circle that overlaps the first circle that you drew (Figure 121). Seventh, erase the lower left side of the large circle (Figure 122). Finally, draw two horizontal lines to represent a surface on which the circles and cylinder sit (Figure 123).

Inform the participants that they can add other objects to their drawing, such as other overlapping forms or designs found on the wall behind the circles and cylinder or on the table. Explain to group members that once they have completed their pencil drawing, they can darken the pencil lines by tracing over them using a felt-tip marker. The drawing should be completed by adding color to it. Demonstrate by adding color to your drawing using the multicolored markers. Ask participants to do the same.

Adding a construction paper backing enhances the appearance of the drawing. Ask each participant to choose a sheet of construction paper whose color coordinates with their artwork. Staple the construction paper to the drawing.

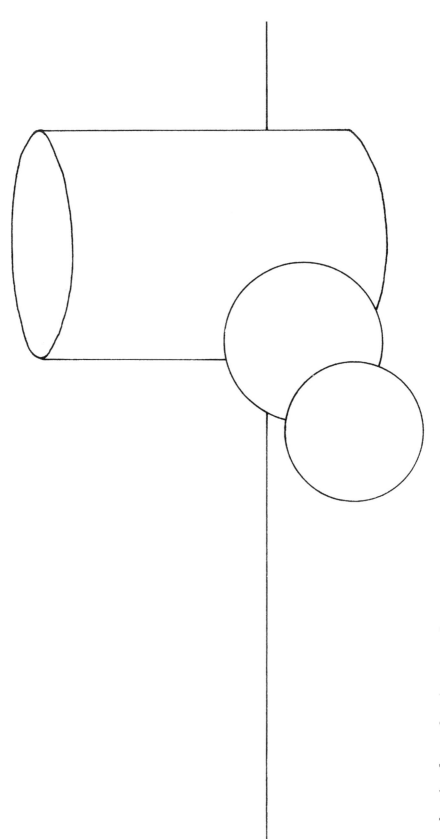

Overlapping forms drawing example

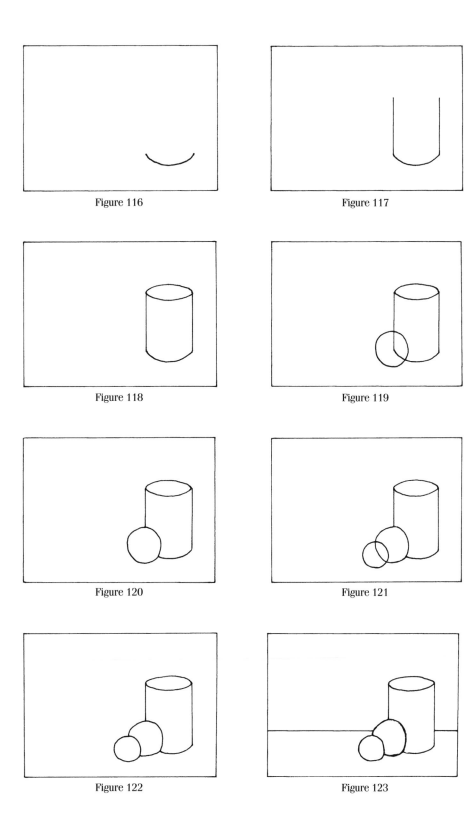

Figure 116

Figure 117

Figure 118

Figure 119

Figure 120

Figure 121

Figure 122

Figure 123

Ending the Lesson

To conclude Lesson 9, ask the participants to sign their work and show it to the rest of the group. Ask whether anyone would like to display his or her drawings in the gallery area. Explain to the group members that you will hang all the drawings after they participate in a closing breathing/relaxation exercise. Tell participants that this exercise releases the tension that built up while they created their artwork and encourages the members of the group to form bonds with one another. Explain what you are going to do and then lead the group in the following exercise:

Join hands, if you can. Close your eyes. On the count of one, slowly take a deep breath through the nose. On the count of two, slowly exhale through the mouth.

When everyone has completed the breathing/relaxation exercise, explain that Lesson 9 has concluded. Thank everyone for participating and tell the members of the group that you are pleased with their progress. Remind the group that you will return for the tenth and final lesson on (day, date, and time). After the group leaves the room, hang the artwork in the gallery area.

Lesson Plan B10

SUBJECT: Proportion in perspective and space

OBJECTIVES: Ensure that participants are able to recognize and understand the concept of proportion in works of art.

Help participants to successfully draw a simple landscape that demonstrates an understanding of proportion in perspective and space.

SUPPLIES: Heavyweight drawing paper (several sheets for each participant)

Construction paper (make available a variety of colors)

Oil pastels (a variety of colors for each participant and for the facilitator)

Pencils (no. 2) with erasers (one for each participant)

Cellophane tape

Easel with pad of oversize paper (large newsprint pad) (for the facilitator's use)

Black thick-line felt-tip marker (for the facilitator's use)

"Proportion in perspective and space drawing example" (included in this lesson) (one copy for each participant)

Reproductions of landscapes (drawings, paintings, or photographs) that illustrate proportion (good sources are magazines, greeting cards, and calendars; works of art by American artist Andrew Wyeth, French impressionist Alfred Sisley, and French artist Claude Lorrain are good examples)

PROCEDURE:

Arranging the Room

Arrange tables and chairs for the participants in a U or horseshoe shape. If a participant in a wheelchair wants to use a work board, attach the board to the wheelchair. Set the pad of oversize paper on the easel and place them in the opening of the U or horseshoe. Stand next to the easel to conduct the lesson.

Leading the Discussion

Begin the lesson by writing "Tools of the Trade: Proportion in Perspective and Space" on the oversize pad or on the chalkboard (if available). Inform the participants that in this final lesson they will learn about the use of proportion in works of art that contain perspective and space.

Explain to the group that proportion is the comparative size of one object in relationship to another object. Illustrate the concept by using the reproductions of landscapes that you have gathered. These landscapes should show objects becoming smaller as they are placed farther away from the viewer. An excellent example of the concept of proportion is an illustration or photograph that contains telephone poles that gradually get smaller as they recede into space. Landscapes with large trees in the foreground and small trees in the background are also good examples of proportion. These illustrations can readily be found in magazines, calendars, or greeting cards. An excellent fine art example of proportion is Andrew Wyeth's painting *Christina's World*.

Inform participants that they will draw a landscape using the principles of perspective, space, and proportion.

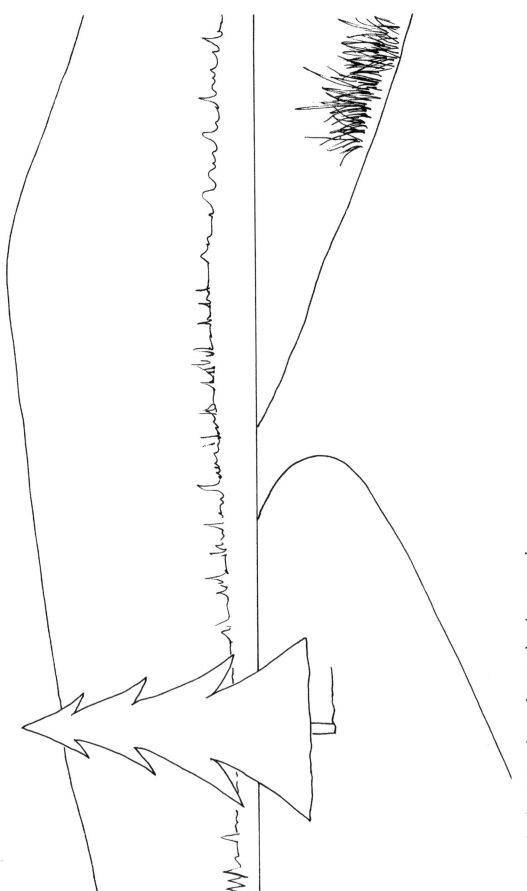

Proportion in perspective and space drawing example

Leading the Drawing Demonstration

Distribute one copy of "proportion in perspective and space drawing example" to each participant. Explain to the group that the artist who drew the example used proportion to create the illusion of space. Point to the tree on the left side of the drawing and explain that the tree is large because it is in closer proximity to the viewer. Add that the trees in the background near the mountains are smaller because they are farther away from the viewer, and that the grasses on the right side of the drawing are larger because they are in closer proximity to the viewer. Make the group aware that the artist also used the principles of perspective in this drawing. Draw participants' attention to the fact that the stream is wide in the foreground of the drawing and that, as it recedes into space, it gradually narrows.

Distribute several sheets of heavyweight drawing paper and a no. 2 pencil with an eraser to each participant. Using cellophane tape, secure the corners of the horizontally oriented drawing paper for participants who have difficulty stabilizing their paper.

Ask the other participants to turn their papers to the horizontal position and to draw along with you as you draw the horizontal line of the horizon. Start at about one third of the way up the page (Figure 124). Then draw a curved line to represent a mountain range and two lines to represent a stream (Figures 125 and 126). Next, draw one vertical line on the left side of the paper to represent a tree trunk and a large triangular shape over the vertical line (Figures 127 and 128). Then carefully erase the lines contained within the triangular shape (Figure 129). Once you have erased the lines, draw a jagged line just above the line of the horizon and near the foot of the mountains (Figure 130). The peaks of the jagged line should vary in height. The line represents the trees. Draw some lines in the foreground to represent grasses (Figure 131).

As you complete the drawing demonstration, invite the participants to refine the large tree shape on the left by erasing some lines and adding others. Another line can be added at the base of the tree to form a sturdy tree trunk (Figure 132). If group members wish to add other objects to their drawings, encourage them to do so.

When participants appear to be finished with their drawings, explain that color can be added to the drawing. Distribute one set of oil pastels to each participant. Demonstrate the use of the oil pastels by adding color to your drawing on the oversize pad. Ask group members to add color to their drawings along with you.

Ending the Lesson

When the participants have completed their landscapes, ask the participants to sign the piece and choose a coordinating color of construction paper to use as a mat for their artwork. Ask whether anyone would like to display his or her landscape in the gallery area. Explain to the group members that you will hang all the landscapes after they participate in a closing breathing/relaxation exercise. Tell participants that this exercise releases the tension that built up while they created their artwork and encourages the members of the group to form bonds with one another. Explain what you are going to do and then lead the group in the following exercise:

Join hands, if you can. Close your eyes. Visualize the landscape you just finished. On the count of one, take a deep breath through the nose. On the count of two, exhale through the mouth.

Do the exercise twice.

Explain to the members of the group that now that they have finished the drawing and painting lessons, class will continue to meet to develop the ability to critically think about

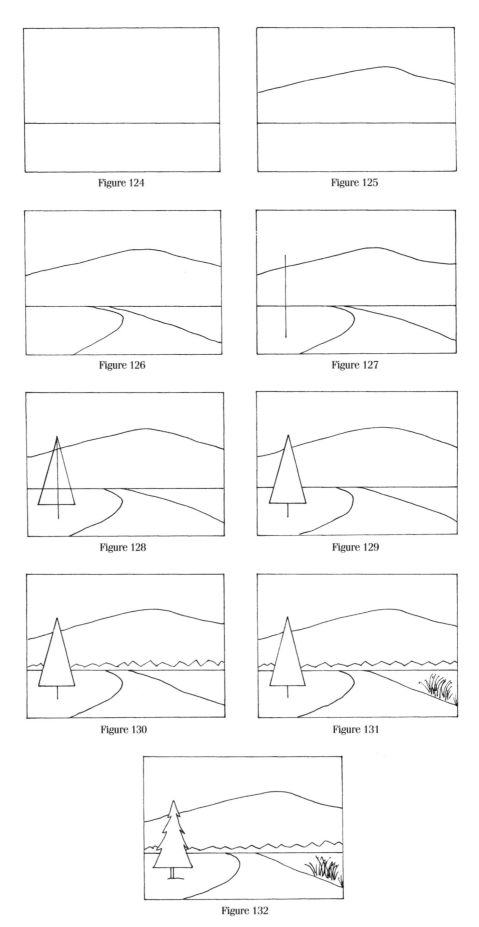

Figure 124

Figure 125

Figure 126

Figure 127

Figure 128

Figure 129

Figure 130

Figure 131

Figure 132

134

art. Inform the participants that they will use the six basic elements of art to review and evaluate their own artwork. Explain that after they review and evaluate their own artwork, they will view and learn about works of art drawn and painted by master artists throughout history. Tell the participants that they will also have the opportunity to create their own works of art using concepts in the masterworks.

Be sure to mention that an art exhibition can be organized at the end of the critical thinking section. Suggest to participants that an exhibition of their artwork or that of a guest artist can be organized.

Remember to thank all the participants and praise their work. (Give yourself a big pat on the back for a job well done!) After the group leaves the room, hang all the paintings in the gallery area for residents, staff, and visitors to admire as they pass.

Lesson Plan C1

SUBJECT:	Elements of art: Line
OBJECTIVES:	Help participants to recognize the element of art, line, in works of art.
	Help participants create a painting using the element of art, line.
SUPPLIES:	Sketchbook (8" × 10" pad)
	Black thick-line felt-tip marker (for the facilitator's use)
	Tempera nontoxic poster paints (nontoxic; red, green, blue, yellow, and white)
	Plastic squeeze bottles (two bottles for each color paint)
	Paintbrushes, 2" utility brushes (one for each participant and one for the facilitator)
	Small plastic bowls or cups for the white tempera poster paint (one for each participant and one for the facilitator)
	Cardboard dividers for boxed fruit or eggs
	Cellophane tape
	Newspapers (to protect work surfaces from paint or markers)
	Aprons (one for each participant)
	Paper towels
	Visual examples—reproductions of artwork that contain line from books, magazines, postcards, or other sources (line drawings done in pen and ink or pencil are good examples)
	Reproductions of the paintings of Jackson Pollack (Pollack's paintings provide excellent examples of a linear painting technique)

PROCEDURE:

Arranging the Room

Arrange tables and chairs so that you can reach all of the participants easily. Place participants in wheelchairs who use work boards near you so that you can easily assist them and so that they are not physically isolated from the group. Using a U- or circular-shaped table allows you to sit in the center of it, with several participants seated at each side of the table. Using a rectangular-shaped table allows you to sit on one side of it, with participants on each side and across from you. (You may also sit at the end of a rectangular-shaped table, with participants on either side of the table.) Cover the table with newspapers or other covering to protect the work surface from paint. Place the art supplies beside you for easy access while you conduct the lesson.

Leading the Discussion

After the participants are seated and comfortable, begin the lesson with a demonstration/discussion designed to enable the participants to recognize the element of art, line, in works of art and to verbally communicate with one another. Remember to make the discussion fun and nonthreatening to the group. Open the sketchbook and draw a straight line using the black thick-line felt-tip marker. Ask the participants to describe what you have drawn. Allow them sufficient time to respond. Draw additional lines that are jagged, scalloped, and wavy.

Facilitators should note that for group members with short attention spans or short-term memory losses, this lesson can be completed easily in two sessions: 1) painting the cardboard dividers with white paint and 2) creating the linear painting on the white cardboard surface.

Ask the group to describe what you have drawn. After they respond, inform group members that you will show them some pictures that contain the element of art, line. Show the reproductions of Jackson Pollack's paintings. Explain that Pollack painted the originals in the 1940s and 1950s and that his technique was to spread large canvases on the floor and to walk around on them as he dripped paint in order to form linear designs. Ask the participants to point to and describe the lines in the examples. If participants need assistance, point to the various lines in the work and describe the lines using whatever words best describe them.

Leading the Demonstration

To begin the demonstration, explain to the participants that you will create a painting using the element of art, line. Ask them to watch you carefully as you paint. Inform the group that the first step in creating this painting is covering a cardboard egg or fruit divider with white paint. Place a cardboard egg or fruit divider on the table in front of you. Dip a 2" paintbrush into a bowl of white poster paint and spread the paint over the convex (curving exterior) side of the cardboard divider.

After you have covered the cardboard divider with white paint, distribute a cardboard divider, a container filled with white paint, and a 2" paintbrush to each participant. Also, help participants to put on their aprons. Tack down the edges of the cardboard divider using cellophane tape for any participant who has difficulty stabilizing the divider.

Ask the participants to dip their paintbrushes into the white paint and to paint the convex side of their cardboard dividers. After group members cover the surface of the cardboard, ask them to apply a second coat of paint. The second coat of paint should completely cover the cardboard surface. Set the dividers to the side to dry. Be sure that the wet dividers are out of the reach of participants until the paint dries.

Ask the group to watch as you demonstrate the next step in creating the linear painting. Place your painted cardboard egg or fruit divider on the table in front of you. Take one of the plastic squeeze bottles of paint and squirt a small amount around in a linear fashion on the painted cardboard (Figure 133). Show the group what you have painted. Ask the members to identify the color you used. Then take a squeeze bottle of a different color of paint and squirt the color over the lines that you have already painted on the cardboard surface (Figure 134). Show the painting to the participants again and ask them to identify the other color you used. Repeat this procedure using as many colors as you wish.

When the group has commented on the painting and the painting is finished, put it to the side to dry, out of the reach of the art group participants. Ask the participants if they would like to try creating a linear painting. Enthusiastically assure the group that this type of painting is a lot of fun. Enthusiasm is infectious!

Creating the Linear Painting

Begin the painting project by passing to each participant his or her painted cardboard fruit or egg divider. Tape down the edges of the cardboard for any participant who cannot stabilize his or her cardboard. Explain to the group that everyone will create a linear painting just as you did in the demonstration painting. Participants' confidence is more apt to develop and grow if you supervise each person as he or she creates the linear painting. Supervision also will prevent accidents and provide individualized assistance. As each participant paints, the other members of the group should watch.

Begin painting with each participant just as you did in the demonstration. Allow the participant to select the colors and squeeze the paint onto the white cardboard surface.

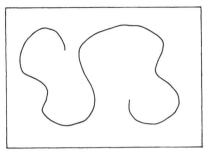

Figure 133

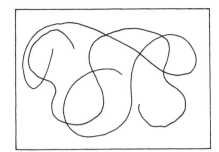

Figure 134

Remind everyone to watch as each person creates a linear painting. When each painting is completed, set it aside to dry, and ensure that the paintings are out of the reach of the group members. Continue to paint with the group members until they tire of the activity or until it is time for the session to end.

Ending the Lesson

To close the lesson, display all of the paintings. Ask each participant to sign his or her work using a felt-tip marker. If a group member is unable to sign his or her name, ask the person if you may sign the name for him or her. Remember to respect the participant's wishes if he or she prefers not to sign the piece. Once everyone who wishes to has signed his or her painting, explain that Lesson 1 has concluded. Thank everyone for participating, and tell the members of the group that you are pleased with their progress. Remind the group that you will return for the second lesson on (day, date, and time). After the group leaves the room, hang the artwork in the gallery area.

The participants' artwork should be removed periodically and saved in individual portfolios for a review and evaluation session (see Part 3 of this section) that is held after the completion of each section of lessons. The portfolios can be created by stapling two large sheets of heavyweight drawing paper together to form a large envelope. Participants may decorate their portfolios, which then also become works of art. You may wish to devote a part of Lesson C1 or C2 to this endeavor.

Lesson Plan C2

SUBJECT: Elements of art: Color (Wear colorful clothing or accessories to the class.)

OBJECTIVES: Ensure that participants are able to recognize the six basic colors of the rainbow: red, orange, yellow, green, blue, and purple.

Help participants to successfully create a rainbow using the six basic colors of the rainbow in watercolor.

SUPPLIES: White tissue paper (several sheets for each participant and for the facilitator)

Heavyweight watercolor paper (several sheets for each participant and for the facilitator)

Construction paper (a variety of colors)

Paper towels

Newspapers (to protect work surfaces from paint)

Cellophane tape

Watercolor paintbrush, 1" flat, soft bristle (one for each participant and one for the facilitator)

Watercolor paint sets (one for each participant and one for the facilitator)

Felt-tip marker (any color; for the facilitator's use)

Paper or plastic cups filled with water

Scissors

Stapler

Color samples (one sample [e.g., construction paper, fabric] of each of the six basic colors of the rainbow)

PROCEDURE:

Arranging the Room

Arrange the tables and chairs so that you can reach all of the participants easily. Place participants in wheelchairs who use work boards near you so that you can easily assist them and so that they are not physically isolated from the group. Using a U- or circular-shaped table allows you to sit in the center of it, with several participants seated at each side of the table. Using a rectangular-shaped table allows you to sit on one side of it, with participants on each side and across from you. (You may also sit at the end of a rectangular-shaped table, with participants on either side of the table.) Cover the table with newspapers or other covering to protect the work surface from paint. Place the art supplies beside you for easy access while you conduct the lesson.

Leading the Discussion

Begin the lesson by discussing the six basic colors of the rainbow. Display your color samples one by one. As you display each color, ask the participants to identify it, and ask the group to point out this color in the room. (Ensure that all six colors are represented in the room before the lesson.) Most of the members of the group should be able to participate in this discussion. However, for group members who find it difficult to join in, identify the color of the sample you are displaying, and indicate the color in the room. Repeat this procedure for the remaining color samples.

At the completion of this exercise, ask the participants where in nature can they find all six colors, especially after it rains. (*The correct response is in a rainbow.*) Ask group members to describe a rainbow that they have seen. Allow sufficient time for their responses. Conclude the discussion by reviewing the six basic colors in a rainbow.

Leading the Demonstration

Place a sheet of the heavy watercolor paper on the table in front of you and place a sheet of white tissue paper on top of the watercolor paper. Use the cellophane tape to tack down the corners of the watercolor and tissue papers to the table to prevent them from slipping. Place a small cup of water; the 1" flat, soft-bristle paintbrush; and a watercolor set near you. Inform the participants that you will create a rainbow using the six basic colors that you discussed a few minutes ago. Ask the group to watch as you paint.

First, dip your brush into the cup of water and then into the red watercolor paint. Be sure that the brush is fairly wet with paint. Quickly paint an arc of red across your sheet of tissue paper (Figure 135). The color will bleed through to the watercolor paper underneath, as will the other colors that you apply. (*Note:* Do not lift the tissue paper until you complete the rainbow and all six colors have dried.) Allow the red paint to dry. Remember to clean and dry paintbrushes before each new color is applied.

Second, paint an arc using orange paint above the red arc on the white tissue paper (Figure 136). Allow the orange arc to dry. Third, paint an arc of yellow just above the orange arc (Figure 137). Allow the yellow arc to dry. Fourth, paint an arc of green above the yellow arc (Figure 138). Fifth, when the green paint has dried, complete the rainbow by painting an arc of blue above the green arc and an arc of purple above the blue arc (Figure 139).

When the blue and purple paints have dried, lift the tissue paper rainbow from the surface of the table. As you lift the tissue paper, you will see that a second rainbow has formed on the watercolor paper beneath the tissue paper.

Show the rainbow on the tissue paper and the rainbow on the watercolor paper to the participants. Explain to them that they will have an opportunity to paint their own rainbows. Before you begin leading the painting project, however, place your freshly painted rainbow to one side, out of the reach of group members.

Leading the Painting Project

Place one sheet of heavyweight watercolor paper in front of each participant. Then place a sheet of white tissue paper on top of the watercolor paper. To prevent the papers from slipping, tape the corners of the watercolor and tissue papers to the table. Provide each participant with a cup of water; a 1" flat, soft-bristle paintbrush; and a set of watercolor paints. Inform group members that they will paint their own rainbow. Remember to compensate for participants' cognitive losses by providing instruction slowly enough so that everyone can execute each step. Assist participants who need guidance with the painting process.

Direct the participants to wet their paintbrushes in the cup of water and dip them in the red paint. Instruct the group to paint a red arc on their papers.

Once the red arc dries, instruct the group to paint an orange arc above the red arc. Continue the project by instructing them to paint the yellow, green, blue, and purple arcs.

When everyone has finished painting his or her rainbow, remove each tissue paper rainbow from the watercolor paper and place them away from the group to dry thoroughly. The watercolor paper remains on the work table. Ask participants to display their rainbows that are painted on the watercolor paper to other members of the group. Then discuss the colors that you used to create the rainbow.

The tissue paper rainbows can be displayed in a window. To prevent the rainbows from tearing, make construction paper frames for them. Ask participants to watch you as you

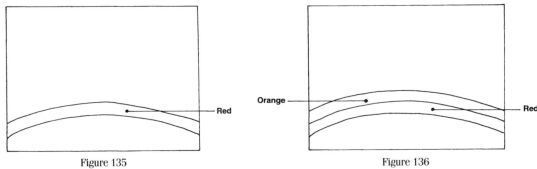

Figure 135

Figure 136

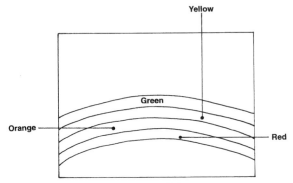

Figure 137

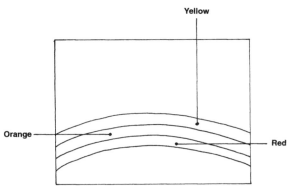

Figure 138

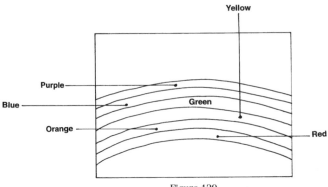

Figure 139

make the frames and attach the rainbows to them. Also ask each member to choose a color of construction paper for the frame.

To make the frame, select a sheet of construction paper, and fold the paper in half (Figure 140). Draw a dotted line using a felt-tip marker about 1" from the edges of the paper. (See the dotted line in Figure 141; *do not* draw the line along the folded edge. You may wish to have the dotted lines pre-drawn or the frames pre-cut before the session [to save time and to forestall any problem behavior from participants.]) Next, cut through both thicknesses of paper along the dotted line (Figure 142). After cutting around the dotted line on the construction paper, you will have a rectangular piece of construction paper and a paper frame (Figure 143). Discard the rectangular piece of construction paper and open the paper frame (Figure 144). Staple this paper frame around one of the tissue paper rainbows. Cut off any excess tissue paper from around the edges of the frame. Continue this process until you have created a construction paper frame for each rainbow. After stapling all of the tissue paper rainbows to the frames, hang the rainbows in a window so that the light shines through the paper and gives the appearance of an actual rainbow. (You may also wish to display the rainbows painted on the watercolor paper. To display these rainbows, staple a sheet of construction paper to the back of each painting.

Ending the Lesson

To close the lesson, display all of the paintings. Ask each participant to sign his or her work using a felt-tip marker. If a group member is unable to sign his or her name, ask the person if you may sign the name for him or her. Remember to respect the participant's wishes if he or she prefers not to sign the piece. Once everyone who wishes to has signed his or her painting, explain that Lesson 2 has concluded. Thank everyone for participating, and tell the members of the group that you are pleased with their progress. Remind the group that you will return for the third lesson on (day, date, and time). After the group leaves the room, hang the artwork in the gallery area.

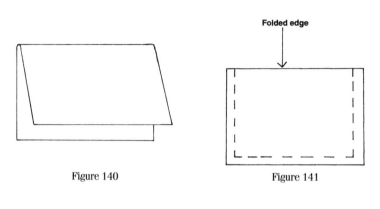

Figure 140

Folded edge

Figure 141

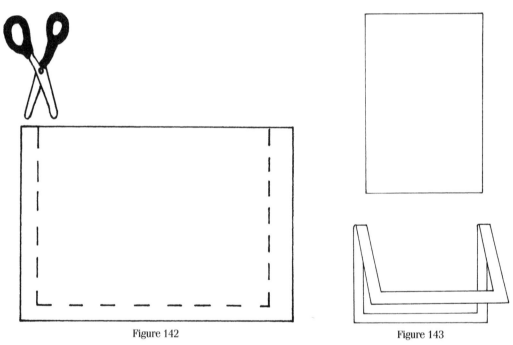

Figure 142

Figure 143

Figure 144

Lesson Plan C3

Subject: Elements of art: Shape and pattern

Objectives: Ensure that participants are able to recognize the elements of art, shape and pattern, in the U.S. flag.

Help participants to successfully create a large U.S. flag using torn paper shapes.

Supplies: Construction paper (red, white, and blue; many sheets of each color)

Kraft paper (white or brown; by the roll)

White glue in squeeze bottles (one bottle for each participant and for the facilitator)

Scissors

Black thick-line felt-tip marker (for the facilitator's use)

Adhesive stars (white)

Push pins or thumbtacks

Large reproduction of the U.S. flag

Procedure:

Arranging the Room

Arrange the tables and chairs so that you can reach all of the participants easily. Place participants in wheelchairs who use work boards near you so that you can easily assist them and so that they are not physically isolated from the group. Using a U- or circular-shaped table allows you to sit in the center of it, with several participants seated at each side of the table. Using a rectangular-shaped table allows you to sit on one side of it, with participants on each side and across from you. (You may also sit at the end of a rectangular-shaped table, with participants on either side of the table.) Cover the table with newspapers or other covering to protect the work surface from glue. Place the art supplies beside you for easy access while you conduct the lesson.

Leading the Discussion

After the participants are seated and comfortable, initiate a discussion designed to enable the participants to recognize the elements of art, shape and pattern, in the U.S. flag. Remember to make the discussion fun and nonthreatening to the group. Begin by displaying the reproduction of the U.S. flag. Ask the group to describe what you are displaying by telling you the colors they see, how many stripes they see, and how many stars they see in the flag.

Explain to the group that the blue area on the flag is a rectangle and that the stripes are long rectangles. In addition, explain that the stars create a pattern against the blue background and that the stripes also form a pattern. Ask the participants to recall any personal stories about the American flag. (Many participants will have memories of World War II and will be very willing to share them.) Remember to keep this discussion brief. If a participant begins to ramble, gently redirect the group's attention to creating the flag. Inform the group that in this lesson everyone will work together to create a large U.S. flag.

Facilitators should note that this lesson may be taught as a long-term project. If you wish to teach it in this way, divide the lesson into two sessions: 1) tearing the construction paper into square shapes and 2) assembling the flag by gluing the torn construction paper squares onto the flag outline (assembling the flag may require several sessions to complete).

Leading the Flag-Making Procedure

Begin the procedure by distributing one sheet of red construction paper to each participant and one to yourself. Explain that by tearing the paper into squares and gluing the squares onto an outline of the flag, the group will create a large U.S. flag. Hold the red construction paper upright (vertical) and tear a strip approximately 3" wide (Figure 145). The strip should have ragged edges, so reassure the group that the tear does not need to be straight. Ask the participants to tear their sheets of red construction paper in the same manner. You may need to help some participants begin the procedure by tearing a small section of their red construction paper.

After participants have torn strips from the sheet of construction paper, demonstrate to the group the way to tear each strip into several squares. Each square should be approximately 3" on all sides (Figure 146). Then ask the group to do the same. Assist participants who have difficulty tearing the paper. Instruct the group to tear two more sheets of red construction paper. After all of the red paper is torn, stack the squares in a pile away from the group's work area.

Next, distribute one sheet of blue construction paper to each participant and to yourself. Instruct participants to tear this sheet in the same manner as they did when they tore the red construction paper. Because the blue area of the flag is relatively small, one sheet of blue paper for each participant should be sufficient for the group flag. Complete the paper-tearing process by distributing one sheet of white construction paper to each participant and asking participants to tear this sheet of paper in the same manner as they did when they tore the red and blue paper. Each participant should tear two sheets of white construction paper. After the group tears the white construction paper, stack the 3" paper squares and place them out of the reach of the group.

Leading the Flag-Assembly Procedure

After the participants have torn the red, blue, and white sheets of construction paper and the 3" paper squares have been placed out of the group's reach, roll out a piece of kraft paper and cut it to a 3-foot length. Use a felt-tip marker to draw the outlines of the stripes and the blue rectangle in which the stars are located. (You may draw six or seven stripes if the area is too small for the 13 stripes that are contained in a regulation-size U.S. flag. If this is the case, explain to the group that their flag will not have all 13 stripes and the reason why.) The stripes can be drawn using either straight or wavy lines (Figure 147).

Distribute one container (squeeze bottle) of white glue to each participant and to yourself. Divide the 3" squares of red construction paper among you and the participants. Place the large drawing of the flag on the table in front of the participants, or tack it to a wall or other sturdy vertical surface at a level that each participant is able to reach easily. (Remember to compensate for participants using wheelchairs or other assistive devices.) If you place the drawing of the flag on the table in front of the group, place it in the middle of the table, with the participants seated around the table (Figure 148).

Start assembling the flag by marking each stripe with the word "red" or "white" (Figure 149). Next, apply white glue to the back of one of the red construction paper squares and attach the square to one of the stripes marked "red" on the flag (Figure 150). Ask participants to glue their red squares onto the drawing. Continue gluing squares to all of the red stripes until the stripe is a solid red color (Figure 151). Reassure participants that it is acceptable for the construction paper squares to overlap.

When the first "red" stripe is completely covered with red squares, distribute the white construction paper squares to the participants and to yourself. Glue the white squares onto a stripe on the drawing of the U.S. flag labeled "white" and ask participants to glue the pieces of white construction paper onto the drawing of the flag (Figure 152).

When the white stripe is completely covered, apply the red squares to the next stripe, which is labeled "red." Invite everyone to join in. Continue gluing the construction paper squares onto the areas of the flag labeled "red" and "white." All of the stripes must be covered with red or white construction paper squares.

When the red and white areas are completely covered with squares, begin gluing the blue construction paper squares to the upper left corner of the drawing of the flag and ask participants to complete the blue area (Figure 153).

Once all of the rectangular areas of the flag are covered with construction paper squares, apply the white adhesive stars to the blue area of the flag. Ask each participant to apply several stars to the blue area. Fill the area with stars. When all of the stars have been applied, the flag is complete.

Ending the Lesson

Ask the group members to view the finished flag and admire their work. To close the session, lead the group in singing a patriotic song, such as "My Country 'Tis of Thee" ("America"), "You're a Grand Old Flag," or "America, the Beautiful." Then explain that Lesson 3 has concluded. Thank everyone for participating, and tell the members of the group that you are pleased with their progress. Remind the group that you will return for the fourth lesson on (day, date, and time). After the group leaves the room, hang the flag in the gallery area.

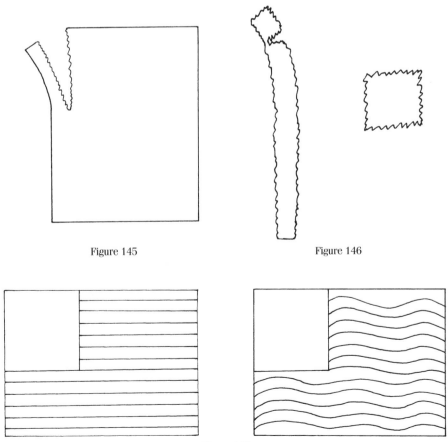

Figure 145

Figure 146

Figure 147

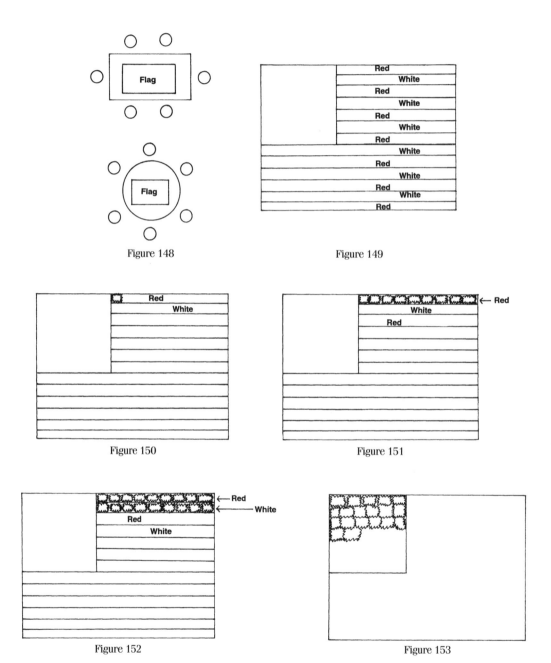

Figure 148

Figure 149

Figure 150

Figure 151

Figure 152

Figure 153

Lesson Plan C4

SUBJECT: Elements of art: Pattern and shape

OBJECTIVES: Ensure that participants are able to understand and recognize the elements of art, pattern and shape.

Help participants to successfully create a design that incorporates the elements of pattern and shape using paper squares.

SUPPLIES: Construction paper (several sheets in a variety of colors)

White 8½" × 11" paper (one sheet for each participant)

12" ruler (for the facilitator's use)

Scissors (two to three pairs)

Felt-tip marker (any color, one for the facilitator)

White glue in squeeze bottles (one bottle for each participant and for the facilitator)

"One-inch grid pattern" (included in this lesson)

Reproductions of the paintings of Piet Mondrian (can be obtained from books from the public or university library)

PROCEDURE:

Preparing the Art Supplies

Some preparation is required in order to teach this lesson. Valuable class time must not be consumed by creating the art supplies. Therefore, before class you should assemble the supplies used in this lesson: the construction paper squares and one copy of the "one-inch grid pattern" for each participant.

Prepare the construction paper squares by selecting a sheet of red construction paper. Use the felt-tip marker and the ruler to mark off 1" increments along the width of this sheet of construction paper (Figure 154). Place a sheet of yellow and a sheet of blue construction paper against the sheet on which you have marked the 1" increments. Hold the three sheets together and cut the paper into strips along each 1" line (Figure 155).

Then take one 1" strip of paper and mark off 1" increments along its length (Figure 156). Place the marked 1" strip of paper on top of two additional strips of paper. Cut through all three strips of paper along each 1" mark that you have drawn. When you have finished cutting, you will have many 1" squares of red, yellow, and blue construction paper.

After dividing several sheets of construction paper into 1" squares, photocopy the "one-inch grid pattern" onto one sheet of white 8½" × 11" paper for each participant and for yourself (to conduct the demonstration).

Arranging the Room

Arrange the tables and chairs so that you can reach all of the participants easily. Place participants in wheelchairs who use work boards near you so that you can easily assist them and so that they are not physically isolated from the group. Using a U- or circular-shaped table allows you to sit in the center of it, with several participants seated at each side of the table. Using a rectangular-shaped table allows you to sit on one side of it, with participants seated on each side and across from you. (You may also sit at the end of a rectangular-shaped table, with participants on either side of the table.) Cover the table with newspapers or other covering to protect the work surface from glue. Place the art supplies beside you for easy access while you conduct the lesson.

149

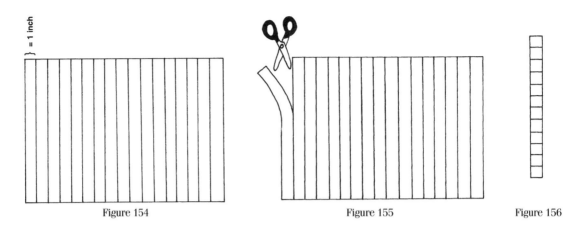

Figure 154   Figure 155   Figure 156

Leading the Discussion

When the participants are seated and comfortable, show them the reproductions of the paintings of Piet Mondrian. Explain to the group that Mondrian painted squares in the primary colors, red, blue, and yellow. His paintings have rhythm and pattern because of the way he arranged the shapes and colors. Ask the group to study Mondrian's paintings and point to and identify the shapes and colors in them. Once everyone has done so, inform the participants that in this lesson they will have an opportunity to create a similar design using 1" squares of colored construction paper.

Leading the Demonstration

Ask the group to watch as you demonstrate how to create the design. Remember to work slowly enough for all participants to see and understand what you are doing, and to explain each step as you execute it. Also remember to encourage participants as they work. First, place a copy of the "one-inch grid pattern," a bottle of white glue, and several 1" paper squares on the table in front of you. Second, select a paper square, apply glue to it, and place it anywhere on the "one-inch grid pattern" (Figure 157). (*Note*: The 1" construction paper squares can be placed either in a random or an organized arrangement. For example, the paper squares can be glued next to one another or they can be spaced apart. Remember that some participants may be capable of organizing a pattern, however, others may not. Also, remember that the squares do not have to fit exactly inside the grid. Some participants may be capable of covering the entire surface of their "one-inch grid pattern" with colored construction squares and may wish to do so, whereas other participants may not. The objective of the lesson is that each participant uses whatever organizational and manual dexterity skills he or she possesses in order to create a colorful design. Keep in mind that it is the process of creating the design that is important, not the product that is created.) Third, select another paper square, apply glue to it, and place it anywhere on the "one-inch grid pattern" (Figure 158).

After you have glued several paper squares to the copy of the "one-inch grid pattern," show the grid pattern to the group. Explain to the group that everyone will now create a design of his or her own.

Distribute one copy of the "one-inch grid pattern," a bottle of glue, and a few 1" squares of construction paper to each participant. Direct the participants to apply glue to the paper squares and to glue them onto their own "one-inch grid pattern." Some participants may need assistance. Remember to be patient with the participants and to proceed at a pace that is comfortable for them.

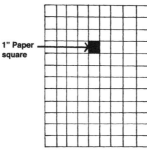

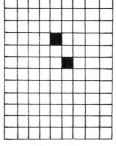

Figure 157 Figure 158

Ending the Lesson

After everyone finishes his or her design, ask each participant to select a coordinating color of construction paper. Assist any participant who has difficulty choosing. Complete the design project by asking the group members to glue their designs onto the coordinating sheet of construction paper.

Once everyone has completed these steps, ask the participants to sign their designs, if they are able to do so. Show each design to the entire group. Explain that Lesson 4 has concluded. Thank everyone for participating, and tell the members of the group that you are pleased with their progress. Remind the group that you will return for the fifth lesson on (day, date, and time). After the group leaves the room, hang the artwork in the gallery area.

Lesson Plan C5

Subject: Elements of art: Value and form

Objectives: Ensure that participants are able to understand and recognize the elements of art, value and form.

Help participants to successfully create a three-dimensional ornament.

Supplies: Heavyweight watercolor paper (one sheet for each participant and for the facilitator)

Lightweight cardboard or tag board

Newspapers

Paper towels

Construction paper or other colored paper (a variety of colors whose values range from light [pink or lavender] to dark [black])

Tempera nontoxic poster paints (two colors of the facilitator's choice)

Small plastic bowls or cups for poster paint (two for each participant and two for the facilitator)

Small plastic bowls or cups for water (one for each participant and one for the facilitator)

Paintbrushes, 1" size (one for each participant and one for the facilitator)

Scissors (one pair for each participant and one pair for the facilitator)

Single-hole punch

Felt-tip markers (any color; one for each participant and one for the facilitator)

Aprons (one for each participant and one for the facilitator)

Cellophane tape

Small toy ball

Hole punch

Curl-type ribbon (any color; 1 foot long for each participant and for the facilitator)

Procedure:

Preparing the Art Supplies

Some preparation is required in order to teach this lesson. Valuable class time must not be consumed by creating the art supplies. Therefore, before class you should assemble the supplies used in this lesson and make the the 3" cardboard circle patterns. Create these cardboard patterns by placing an inverted drinking glass or other object that is round and approximately 3" in diameter onto a piece of lightweight cardboard or tag board and drawing around the rim using a felt-tip marker. Take scissors and cut out the circle you have drawn. Draw and cut one circle pattern for each participant in your group.

Arranging the Room

Arrange the tables and chairs so that you can reach all the participants easily. Place participants in wheelchairs who use work boards near you so that you can easily assist them and so that they are not physically isolated from the group. Using a U- or circular-shaped table

---

Facilitators should note that if they find this lesson too lengthy for one session, they may conduct it in two sessions: 1) drawing and painting the 3" circles and 2) cutting the circles and assembling them to create a hanging ornament.

allows you to sit in the center of it, with several participants seated at each side of the table. Using a rectangular-shaped table allows you to sit on one side of it, with participants seated on each side and across from you. (You may also sit at the end of a rectangular-shaped table, with participants on either side of the table.) Cover the table with newspapers or other covering to protect the work surface from paint. Place the art supplies beside you or on a supply cart for easy access while you conduct the lesson.

Leading the Discussion

Initiate a discussion about the elements of art, value and form. Begin by displaying a piece of lightly colored (e.g., pink, lavender) construction paper. Ask the participants to identify the color of this piece of paper. Then ask whether the color is light or dark. If none of the group members answers correctly, tell the group that this color is light, which means that it is light in value. Next, show the learners a piece of black construction paper and tell them that this color is dark, which means that it is dark in value. Test the comprehension capabilities of group members by showing them other colors of paper and asking the group to identify the colors and their value. If some participants do not seem to fully understand, continue to review value until you feel certain all of the learners understand.

After discussing the concept of value, introduce the concept of form by showing the participants a small toy ball. Ask the group to describe this toy. Guide the discussion by asking questions such as the following:

- What is this?
- What color is it?
- Is the color light in value or dark in value?
- What shape is this?

Even if a group member should answer the questions correctly, reinforce the idea that the ball is round and that it is a three-dimensional form. Point to other three-dimensional forms found in the room, such as desks, tables, chairs, and books. Explain to the participants that everyone will create a three-dimensional round ornament to hang in their rooms or in the classroom.

Creating the Art Project

Distribute a sheet of heavyweight watercolor paper, three small bowls or cups (one for water, two for paint), two colors of your choice of tempera nontoxic poster paint, a 1" paintbrush, a 3" cardboard circle pattern, a felt-tip marker, a pair of scissors, and an apron to each participant and to yourself. Pour each color of paint into a separate bowl or cup. Pour water into one cup or bowl of each group member. Help the participants put on their aprons and become organized for the lesson. Tape down the corners of the watercolor paper for participants who have difficulty stabilizing the paper. You may wish to tape the circle patterns to the watercolor paper. To do so, roll a piece of cellophane tape onto the back of the circle pattern and gently stick the pattern on the watercolor paper.

Initiate the creative process by placing a 3" cardboard circle pattern onto a piece of heavyweight watercolor paper. Ask the participants to draw along with you as you take a felt-tip marker and trace the outline of this pattern. Move the pattern to another area on the paper and trace it again. You now have two circle outlines. Assist all participants who need help. Make sure each participant has drawn two outlines. Use a pair of scissors to cut out two cardboard circles. Ask the participants to cut out their circles. Assist all participants who need help.

Once everyone has cut out two circles, take a 1" paintbrush, dip it into the color of your choice, and paint one side of one circle. Repeat these steps on one side of the second circle. Instruct group members to paint one side of their circles in the same manner. As the paint dries, instruct the participants to rinse their paintbrushes in the bowl or cup of water and dry them with a paper towel.

When the paint has dried, turn the circles over and paint the other sides using the second color. Ask the group to paint along with you. As the paint dries, direct the participants to rinse their brushes in the bowl or cup of water and dry them with a paper towel. Then remove the paints and brushes from the work area.

When the paint has dried completely, take the scissors and cut a slit halfway across the diameter of each cardboard circle (Figure 159). If you feel confident that participants can cut slits in their own circles, draw a line along which they can cut on each circle. Be sure to emphasize to participants that they must stop at the end of the line. However, if you feel that participants are not able to complete this step, cut the slits for each circle yourself.

After slits are cut into each circle, you can assemble the circles into the three-dimensional round ornament. First, turn one circle so that the slit is at the bottom of the circle and turn the second circle so that the slit is at the top. Second, open each slit by pulling one edge of each piece of cardboard up slightly and then slide the circles together (Figure 160). Assist participants who need help completing this step. The three-dimensional round ornament should resemble Figure 161.

Next, fold the two circles together. Use the single-hole punch to punch a hole approximately ¼" from the top of the fold through all thicknesses of the cardboard (Figure 162). Complete the three-dimensional round ornament by inserting a 1 foot long ribbon through the punched holes and tying the ends together (Figure 163). The three-dimensional round ornament is ready to hang.

Ending the Lesson

When participants have completed their ornaments, ask each member of the group to show his or her ornament to the rest of the group. Inquire as to whether each artist would like to hang the ornament in his or her room or in the classroom. Make sure to honor each participant's preference.

Your art group may comprise participants who have knowledge of or an interest in art history and would enjoy viewing masterworks. For these group members, you can continue the curriculum by referring to Part 3 of this section. This material will help you to plan lessons that introduce the group to historical artworks.

If your art group comprises participants with significant cognitive impairments, explain to the group that this is the end of this set of lessons. You may wish to award each participant a certificate of course completion. Before going to the program evaluation section (Section III), you may wish to organize an art exhibition of the participants' work, which you have saved in portfolios like those discussed at the end of Lesson Plan C1. Thank all the participants and praise their work. (Give yourself a big pat on the back for a job well done!) After the group leaves the room, hang all the ornaments the participants have not taken with them in the gallery area for residents, staff, and visitors to admire as they pass.

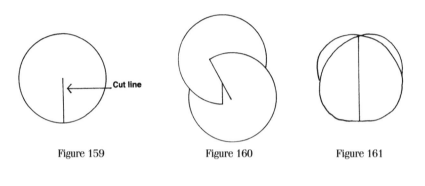

Figure 159   Figure 160   Figure 161

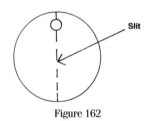

Figure 162

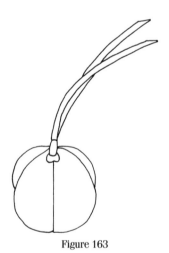

Figure 163

Part 3

Critical Thinking: Broadening the Base of "What Is Art?"

Evaluating Works of Art

Maintain a positive atmosphere and an atmosphere conducive to sharing thoughts and feelings at all times during the evaluation discussion. Be generous with praise and support for the participants' efforts.

Select at least one piece from each participant's portfolio for review and evaluation.

Broaden the evaluation process by showing and evaluating your own or a local artist's artwork.

Exposing Older Adults to Art History

Make the presentation of art history interesting and enjoyable by using slides, videos, films, and various types of reproductions (e.g., posters, postcards, books).

Foster self-confidence in participants by leading art activities designed to introduce masterworks to the participants.

Explore the world of art exhibitions by inviting a local artist to exhibit his or her work in your facility or by organizing an art exhibition of the participants' work.

The concept of critical thinking is often overlooked by facilitators of art classes that are offered to older adults in formal settings, such as adult day centers and nursing facilities. One reason is that facilitators tend to get caught up in the hands-on experience of creating art. They may forget or may not be aware that helping participants in the art group to evaluate their own artwork and exposing them to masterworks can enhance the participants' experience of art. Another reason is that facilitators can "buy into" many of the myths associated with aging, one of which is that older people with and without disabilities have no opinions or feelings about what they see and experience. Either they are not asked what they think or feel or sometimes they are ridiculed or ignored if they volunteer the information. Consequently, older people feel removed from the rest of humanity. I mentioned earlier in the book that your task as facilitator is to help reanimate participants' lives and to help them reconnect with others by teaching them how to create and learn to evaluate works of art in a group setting.

When participants are given an opportunity to create, think about, and react to artwork, their intellect and emotions are engaged. As you ask questions about the artwork, the participants are able to connect or reconnect with their thoughts and feelings. When the participants answer and ask questions about works of art, their critical sensibility grows.

Part 3 of the curriculum is divided into two steps, "Evaluating Works of Art" and "Exposing Older Adults to Art History." "Evaluating Works of Art" contains guidelines, sample questions, and activities that will help you lead discussions about works of art. Discussing works of art is an excellent way to learn to evaluate art.

The discussions should begin with a review of the participants' own artwork. The review and evaluation process can be conducted in one class session. The six basic elements of art that are taught in Lesson Plans A and B and the five elements taught in Lesson Plans C are used as the foundation for the review discussion questions. Once the participants feel comfortable using these elements of art to evaluate their own art, they are able to evaluate masterworks.

The section "Exposing Older Adults to Art History" takes the art evaluation process one step farther. By participating in activities designed to stimulate discussion, the members of the art group get an opportunity to view and evaluate masterworks. This section also contains activities that are designed to guide the participants as they incorporate the ideas used by the masters into their own art.

Appendix A, "Art History Time Line," is helpful in planning art history lessons. The time line contains a short summary of each period in art history and lists some of the artists of the period and their works.

EVALUATING WORKS OF ART

Learning how to evaluate art is the first step in thinking critically about art. Evaluating art involves a careful study and appraisal of the work. To properly evaluate art, a foundation must be established. The foundation for evaluation is the six basic elements of art (line, color, shape, pattern, value and form, and perspective and space) presented in the lesson plans section. Participants used these elements during the lessons to create their artworks, and they can use them here to evaluate the work of other artists. The elements of art are also used by art critics and art historians to evaluate works of art. Using these elements to evaluate masterworks is especially important when viewing abstract art, or what is casually referred to as "modern art." These works of art may look strange to participants. Without a logical method, such as that of the six basic elements, for evaluating or viewing the art, participants often reject these pieces. Using the six basic elements of art to evaluate modern art, the participants have a point of reference from which to evaluate what they see. Group members may not always like what they see, but this method of evaluation helps them gain an appreciation for modern art.

One of the most effective ways to facilitate an art evaluation session is to conduct a discussion that allows everyone to state opinions and facts about the work(s) of art. Whether or not you have little or no art training and/or are unaccustomed to leading a discussion, the following guidelines, sample questions, and activities will help you to organize and lead discussions in which works of art are evaluated.

Selecting the Artwork

Before beginning the evaluation process, ask group members whether they would enjoy reviewing and discussing a few pieces of their artwork. Explain to participants that evaluating their art provides an excellent way to review what they have learned about art. Members of the group who like the idea should be asked for their permission to review their artwork. Some members may not like the idea. Do not force anyone to participate if he or she does not wish to do so. After receiving permission from the interested participants, begin selecting pieces.

First, gather together the participants' portfolios, which contain the works of art created during the class sessions. Second, select three or four of the best pieces from each portfolio. As you review each participant's work, keep the following factors in mind: 1) Select artwork that fulfills the objectives of the particular lesson, 2) request the same quantity of pieces from each participant, and 3) take into consideration each participant's physical and mental abilities as you select. In conjunction with considering all three factors, rely on your judgment to select good pieces of art for discussion.

Arranging the Room

The environment in which the discussion of the participants' art takes place is important. The following guidelines will help you to select and arrange this environment:

- Ensure that the room is quiet and free of pedestrian traffic.
- Place the chairs in a U or horseshoe shape.
- Arrange the artwork on an easel (try to display only one participant's art at a time to minimize confusion and to focus the viewers' attention on the artwork) or on another vertical surface in the opening of the U or horseshoe shape so that all participants can see it easily.
- Place an easel and oversize pad of paper (large newsprint pad) with a black felt-tip marker in the opening of the U or horseshoe shape.
- Close any draperies or blinds to eliminate glare, and/or move participants who have sensitive eyes away from any source of glare.
- Ensure that all of the participants can see you, the artwork, and the easel pad.

Part 1 of Section II, "Social Exchange: Building a Community," explains how to create an atmosphere that is conducive to sharing thoughts and feelings. You may want to refresh your memory by reviewing the text. Once this atmosphere has been established and the artwork is in place, the discussion can begin.

Leading the Discussion

Because participants are familiar with their own artwork and it is less complex than are masterworks, it is best for participants to learn how to evaluate art by reviewing their own artwork. In order to conduct positive review and evaluation sessions, guidelines are necessary.

It is important to maintain a positive atmosphere during the discussion. Because participants may be sensitive to comments made about their artwork, emphasize the positive qualities in all the works and provide a great deal of positive feedback to the participants. Phrase all suggestions for improvement in a positive way, such as, "I really like your landscape drawing, Mr. Jones, but I think you could make your next drawing even better by making it larger. You might consider using the entire page for your next drawing. What do you think?" Positive, encouraging comments from you and the group members enable participants to see the progress they have made in the class.

As I stated earlier in the book, the foundation for evaluating art is the six basic elements of art that were introduced in the lesson plans section. Begin the discussion by asking group members if they can recall the six basic elements. If all of the elements have not been introduced at the time of the evaluation session, inquire about the elements that have been introduced. As participants name the elements, list them on the oversize pad on the easel. After you have listed the elements of art on the oversize pad, ask the group specific questions about each element using the key words "what," "when," "where," "how," and "why" as a guide. The following questions, which incorporate these key words, can be used to help you in leading an art evaluation discussion.

1. Do you see the use of line in this artwork? If so, where?
2. What do the lines used in the artwork express?
3. Can you describe the lines you see (e.g., are they short, long, curved, straight, some other type of line)?
4. What shapes do you see in the artwork? Can you describe these shapes?
5. Are the shapes you see in the artwork geometric? If so, are the shapes squares, rectangles, triangles, or some other geometric shape?
6. Do you see patterns in the artwork? If so, can you describe the patterns (e.g., are the patterns floral, striped, checked, some other pattern)?
7. What colors do you see in the artwork?
8. Why do you think the artist used red (or any other color) in the artwork?
9. Do you see complementary colors in the artwork? If so, what are the colors?
10. What is the overall tonal value of the artwork? Is the artwork mostly light, dark, or gray?
11. Are light and dark values used to create the forms? If so, where are these seen in the artwork?
12. Has the entire page been used for the image?
13. Has the space on the page been used effectively? Can you describe the use of space in this piece (e.g., does the use of space in the work seem large, small, somewhere in between)?
14. Did the artist use perspective to draw or paint objects in the artwork? If so, can you describe the use of perspective in the artwork?
15. Could you use some of this artist's ideas in your own work? If so, how? If not, why?

To conclude the discussion of each participant's artwork on a positive note, ask group members what they like best about each piece and tell the group what you like best about each piece.

Broadening the Scope

As the group becomes familiar with and more comfortable in evaluating works of art, you can broaden the scope of the evaluation process and provide an easy transition to evaluating masterworks. One way to accomplish this is to show a few pieces of your work to the group, if you are an artist and feel the group would understand and enjoy viewing and reviewing your work. Ask the group to evaluate your artwork using the six basic elements of art and the 15-question guide. Another way to broaden the scope and provide an easy transition to evaluating masterworks is by inviting a local artist to show his or her work. Choose an artist whose work you feel would be interesting to the group. The best choice of artist would probably be a portraitist, a landscapist, and/or a still life artist because these forms are the most familiar and because two of these forms are taught in the lessons. Once you have selected the artist, explain to him or her that your group is learning how to evaluate works of art using the six (or five, if you taught the C lessons) basic elements of art, and ask him or her for permission to discuss the work using these elements. Inform the artist that you will be asking him or her to explain how and why the works on display were created. Invite the artist to share with the group how he or she begins each work of art and where he or she finds ideas for each piece. In order to ensure that the artist is familiar and comfortable with the questions to be used during the discussion, send him or her a copy of the list of questions well in advance of the presentation.

Promote the event and build anticipation for it by publicizing the artist's visit for several weeks before the event. If you feel that all residents of the facility or clients at the center would enjoy this type of presentation, invite everyone to attend. Ask staff for help.

Select a room for the artist's presentation that is free from distractions. If you or the guest artist plan to show slides, ensure that the lights in the room can be dimmed and that a slide projector and a projection screen are available. If you are working with a small group, arrange the room in the same manner as you did for the participants' artwork evaluation discussions. (The arrangements would, of course, be different if the entire facility, older adults and staff, were in attendance.) Arrange the participants' chairs in a U or horseshoe shape, with the artist's work placed in the opening of the U or horseshoe. If slides of the work are to be shown, place the projection screen in the open space of the U. Before beginning the presentation, ensure that no one's view is obstructed and that everyone is comfortable. Make the event a festive occasion by serving light refreshments after the presentation.

EXPOSING OLDER ADULTS TO ART HISTORY

In its entirety, the history of art can be overwhelming, but when broken down into sections that are manageable and of interest to the participants, art history becomes an important adjunct to the experience of creating art. The following guidelines and activities will help you expose your art group participants to art history.

The method I have used to introduce art history to older adults has four steps: 1) selecting the artwork to be studied, 2) presenting and evaluating the artwork, 3) doing art activities, and 4) attending art exhibitions.

Access to the following equipment and resources is necessary in order to present masterworks to the art group participants:

- Easel with pad of oversize paper
- Black thick-line felt-tip marker
- Slide projector (ensure that all electrical equipment is working properly before participants arrive for the presentation)
- Projection screen or wall painted white
- Extension cords
- Duct tape (to secure cords to the floor in order to prevent accidents)

- Audiocassette player (some art history slide programs, such as those produced by the National Gallery of Art in Washington, D.C., are accompanied by narration recorded on audiocassette)
- Television monitor
- VCR
- Books containing color reproductions of works of art
- Color reproductions of works of art (postcards and posters can be purchased from stores, art museums [see Appendix B], and libraries)
- Color slide reproductions of works of art (colleges and university and some public libraries make available slides to lend; companies that market slides and many art museum gift shops and gift catalogs make available slides to purchase or borrow; see Appendix B)
- Videos about artists (available for purchase or loan from stores, libraries, and audiovisual companies [see Appendix B]; many programs air on public television, local access, local college and community college television stations, and cable television channels and can be videotaped)

After locating sources for the equipment and supplies, begin selecting artwork for the participants to view and evaluate.

Selecting the Artwork

To begin the study of art history, select works of art that contain images that are easily identifiable. If you know everyone in the group well, you may wish to select a few works that relate in some way to the various life experiences of which you are aware. For example, if a member of the group is a retired horticulturalist, you might select a painting that depicts plants.

This section ("Exposing Older Adults to Art History") of the curriculum is very flexible. For example, you may wish to present an art history component that runs for six sessions and includes all five categories of art listed below, or you may wish to present only one or two sessions. You may wish to refer to Appendix A and design your own art history categories and lessons. As the facilitator, you must decide what is best for you and for the members of the group.

Five categories of art that groups generally enjoy are the following: landscapes, portraits and figures, still lifes, impressionist and post-impressionist painting, and American painting. A sixth category, modern art, can be introduced when participants become familiar with the history of art and the process of evaluating art. The easiest way to begin a study of art history is by selecting one of the categories that is of interest to the art group participants and selecting reproductions.

Should you wish to present a more comprehensive study of a particular category of art, I have provided a list of artists and one well-known work he or she produced for each category, which is followed by a brief description of the category. Refer to Appendix A for a more complete list of the periods of art and their representative artists.

Landscapes

Artists
John Constable (*Stoke-by-Nayland*)
Joseph Turner (*The Slave Ship*)
Camille Corot (*Papigno*)
Francois Millet (*The Sower*)

Gustave Courbet (*The Stone Breakers*)
Camille Pissarro (*The Artist's Garden at Fragny*)
Berthe Morisot (*Seascape, Isle of Wight*)
Claude Monet (*Water Lilies, Giverny*)
Vincent van Gogh (*The Starry Night*)
Paul Cézanne (*Mont Sainte-Victoire Seen from Bibemus Quarry*)
Marguerite Thompson Zorach (*Man Among the Redwoods*)

Landscapes are fairly self-explanatory. The artist, regardless of the historical period, attempted to re-create nature on canvas as he or she or the society of the time perceived it.

French painters Courbet, Corot, and Millet and English landscapists Turner and Constable painted scenes in the style of realism, popular during the 19th century. Morisot, Pissarro, and Monet worked in the style of impressionism late in the 19th century, and the work of Cézanne and van Gogh broke ground for the styles of painting that followed them. Marguerite Thompson Zorach introduced the style of French modernism to the United States.

Portraits and Figures

Artists
Leonardo da Vinci (*Mona Lisa*)
Michelangelo (the Sistine Chapel ceiling)
Peter Paul Rubens (*The Raising of the Cross*)
Rembrandt van Rijn (*The Night Watch*)
Elisabeth Vigée-Le Brun (*Self-Portrait*; the cover of Germaine Greer's book *The Obstacle Race* includes this portrait)
Edgar Degas (*Prima Ballerina*)
Henri de Toulouse-Lautrec (*At the Moulin Rouge*)
Mary Cassatt (*The Bath*)
John Singer Sargent (*Madame X*)
Andrew Wyeth (*Christina's World*)

Portraits and figures have been drawn or painted throughout history, but until the Renaissance (14th–17th centuries) images were two-dimensional (e.g., Russian religious icons, prehistoric cave paintings). Leonardo da Vinci and Michelangelo were leading artists of the Renaissance. Prominent portrait and figure painters of the 17th century baroque period were Rubens and Rembrandt. Vigée-Le Brun, a principal artist of the 18th century, was the first person to paint portraits of Marie Antoinette. Degas, Toulouse-Lautrec, and Cassatt painted in the impressionistic styles of the late 19th century. Andrew Wyeth is a popular American artist of the 20th century.

Still Lifes

Artists
Jean-Baptiste Chardin (*Back from the Market*)
Edouard Manet (*Flowers in a Crystal Vase*)
Claude Monet (*Vase of Chrysanthemums*)
Paul Cézanne (*Fruit Bowl, Glass, and Apples*)
Vincent van Gogh (*Sunflowers*)
Georgia O'Keeffe (*Yellow Cactus Flowers*)
Janet Fish (*Tanqueray Bottles*)
Margaretta Angelica Peale (*Still Life with Watermelon and Peaches*)

Still lifes can often be seen within paintings of figures and interiors, but some artists painted still lifes as a form of painting. Chardin, Monet, Cézanne, Manet, and van Gogh painted many everyday items, such as fruit, flowers, and vases. The 19th century American artist Margaretta Angelica Peale excelled in still lifes. The American artist Georgia O'Keeffe rendered sections of flowers in gigantic proportions. Janet Fish, another American, paints modern objects such as gin bottles and crystal goblets in the style of photorealism.

Impressionist and Post-Impressionist Painting

Artists

Camille Pissarro (*Peasant Girl with a Straw Hat*)
Claude Monet (*Water Lilies, Giverny*)
Auguste Renoir (*Le Moulin de la Galette*)
Lilla Cabot Perry (*Haystacks, Giverny*)
Helen M. Turner (*Morning News*)

Impressionists wanted to depict the natural appearances of objects with dabs and strokes of paint in order to simulate actual reflected light. As a result, these artists were the first to paint entire works of art outdoors. (Before impressionism, artists sketched their ideas in nature but painted in their studios.) Some characteristic features of impressionist painting are the use of dabs of color to represent fleeting images, several layers of paint to create thick textures on the canvas, lack of detail, technique of blurred edges to the subjects depicted, and ordinary objects and common people as subject matter.

American Painting

Artists

Winslow Homer (*Northeaster*)
Thomas Eakins (*The Gross Clinic*)
Albert Pinkham Ryder (*The Race Track* [*Death on a Pale Horse*])
John Singer Sargent (*Madame X*)
Grant Wood (*American Gothic*)
Thomas Hart Benton (*City Activities with Subway*)
Cecilia Beaux (*Dorothea in the Woods*)
Edward Hopper (*Early Sunday Morning*)
Georgia O'Keeffe (*Dark Abstraction; Music: Pink and Blue*)
Jacob Lawrence (*The Migration of the Negro*)

Until the late 19th century many American artists, such as Mary Cassatt and John Singer Sargent, studied and lived in Europe and painted European scenes. Toward the end of the Victorian era, more American painters began working in the United States, painting images specific to America. Some painters, such as portraitist Cecilia Beaux, worked first in Europe, and then returned to the United States. Beaux herself returned to work and teach at the Pennsylvania Academy of Fine Arts in Philadelphia.

Winslow Homer and Thomas Eakins worked in the United States and painted scenes and people that depicted American culture and the underlying psychological nuances that made American life different from European life.

Early in the 20th century, Edward Hopper painted starkly realistic scenes of contemporary life, often imbued with a sense of isolation and loneliness. Regional artists Thomas Hart Benton and Grant Wood portrayed people and scenes of the midwestern United States in the 1930s. Georgia O'Keeffe painted a wide variety of subjects, including the skyscrapers of New

York City and close-ups of flowers. African American history comes alive in the paintings of Jacob Lawrence.

Modern Art

Artists
Henri Matisse (*Harmony in Red*)
George Braque (*Le Courrier*)
Pablo Picasso (*Les Demoiselles d'Avignon*)
Vasily Kandinsky (*Improvisation*)
Paul Klee (*Ad Parnassum*)
Mark Rothko (*Earth and Green*)
Marc Chagall (*I and the Village*)
Jackson Pollack (*Autumn Rhythm*)
Lee Krasner (*Cornucopia*)
Helen Frankenthaler (*Before the Caves*)

As group members become familiar with creating art and examining art history, you can introduce a sixth category of art that many participants will call "modern art." Modern art can be used as a general term for art that contains unrecognizable subject matter or unrealistic-looking images. More descriptive terms used for this style of art are nonobjective, abstract, or nonrepresentational art. Many artistic styles of the 20th century can be defined as modern art. This style is difficult for some participants to appreciate because it is nonrepresentational, but by using the six basic elements of art as a foundation for evaluating art and incorporating an open mind and careful observation, modern art can be understood and appreciated by participants.

The beginnings of modern art can be seen in the early 20th century works of artists such as Matisse, Braque, Picasso, and Kandinsky. The use of bright colors; flat, angular shapes; and distorted images were introduced by these artists. Images that have no bearing on material reality depicted in their work became even more abstract after World War II. This development is reflected in the artwork of Pollock, Rothko, Krasner, and Frankenthaler.

Presenting and Evaluating the Artwork

After selecting the works of art for an art history lesson, you should prepare the presentation of the artwork.

Arranging the Room

You will want to refer to "Arranging the Room" in the section on evaluating works of art (p. 160) and to the list of supplies on pages 162–163 to help you prepare for the presentation.

Leading the Discussion

Once the room is set up and the participants are seated, begin the presentation. As you show each work of art to the participants, talk about the artist who created it. Mention a few facts about the period of time in which the artist worked and some biographical data about him or her. When leading the discussion, remember to ask questions that use the words "what," "when," "where," "how," and "why," and, as you discuss the artist, use the word "who." Try to ask follow-up questions by asking for examples or for the group member to explain more fully. The following questions can be used as a guide for the discussion.

1. Who is the artist?
2. Where and when did the artist live? What type of artwork did the artist create?
3. What world events occurred during the artist's life?
4. Are these events reflected in his or her work? How?
5. What is the artist trying to show us in this work?
6. Do you think the artist was successful with this work?

Some personal feelings may be expressed by group members while viewing the artwork. Freely discuss these feelings and your own feelings as you view the art, but remember to moderate the discussion effectively. If you see a group member becoming overly agitated, change the subject or ask facility staff for assistance. Remember always to respond to participants in a positive way. The following questions can be used as a guide for the discussion.

1. Do you like this work of art? Why or why not?
2. How do you feel when looking at this artwork?
3. What did the artist do in the piece to cause you to feel this way?
4. How do the colors make you feel?
5. Could you change the piece to make viewers feel differently? If so, how?
6. How do you think the artist was feeling when he or she created this work? What causes you to think this way?

After discussing the artist and any personal feelings the artwork evoked in the participants, ask questions about the six basic elements of art. (These questions are found on p. 161.) It is important to ask these questions because the six basic elements are the foundation of all works of art and reviewing them will help participants to recall the information better.

When presenting and evaluating the six categories of art (see p. 161) ask specific questions about each category, as in the following.

Landscapes are pictures of outdoor scenes. As you show the landscape, ask the group participant to be aware of the colors, light, setting, and activity or activities in the drawing or painting. Use the following questions as a guide for the discussion:

1. What type of scene is this?
2. What do you see in this scene?
3. What kind of light do you see in the scene?
4. What time of day is it? How can you tell?
5. What season is it? How can you tell?
6. What colors did the artist use?
7. What is the mood of the scene?
8. What is happening in the scene?
9. How did the artist use texture?
10. How are perspective and space used?
11. Where is this scene? What country is depicted?
12. Have you ever been in a place like this? If so, where?

Portraits and figures have been drawn and painted throughout history. As group members view these works of art, ask them to carefully study the subjects in the artwork. Ask them to note the expressions on the face(s), the age(s), and the clothing of the subject(s), as well as the colors and the light seen in the artwork. The following questions can be used as a guide for the discussion.

1. How old is the subject of the drawing or painting? What causes you to think this way?
2. Is the subject a woman, man, or child?
3. What is he or she feeling? What causes you to think this way?
4. What is he or she thinking? What causes you to think this way?
5. What colors did the artist use?
6. How did the artist use light?
7. How did the artist use texture?
8. Is the subject indoors or outdoors?
9. What is the subject wearing?
10. What period in history is depicted? How can you tell?
11. What is the time of day?
12. What is the financial status of the subject? How can you tell?

Still lifes depict objects seen in everyday life. As group members view the artwork, ask them to be aware of the objects that are depicted and the way(s) in which the artist used the six basic elements of art. The following questions can be used as a guide for the discussion.

1. What objects are depicted in the drawing or painting?
2. What colors did the artist use?
3. How did the artist use texture?
4. How did the artist use light?
5. How did the artist use pattern?
6. How did the artist use value to create form?
7. How did the artist create depth? Did the artist use perspective, overlapping forms, or both?
8. Where is this scene?
9. What time in history is depicted? How can you tell?
10. What is the time of day?
11. Are the objects depicted expensive? How can you tell?
12. Who might own objects like those depicted?

Impressionists changed art by drawing or painting much of their work outdoors and capturing their impressions of light falling on an object or a person. As participants study these works of art, ask them to note the use of light, color, and texture; the subject of the artwork; and the way(s) in which details are rendered. The following questions can be used as a guide for the discussion.

1. Do you like this painting? Why or why not?
2. How does the artwork make you feel? Why?
3. What do you see in this piece?
4. Where was this work of art created?
5. How did the artist use color?
6. How did the artist apply the paint—in thick dabs or with smooth strokes?
7. Do you see the use of line in the artwork, and how is it used?
8. What shapes do you see in the artwork and are they geometric or organic (see Part 1 for an explanation of "organic")?
9. Are the shapes very clear or are they blurred? What causes you to think this way?
10. Is there texture or pattern in this artwork, and if so, what kind?
11. Did the artist use perspective to create space, and if so, can you describe what the artist did?

12. Did the artist use a wide range of values (darks and lights) in this artwork, and if so, can you describe the values?

Many, although not all, **American painters** depict the American landscape, the American people, and the American way of life. Ask the participants to view these artworks with these facts in mind. The following questions can be used as a guide for the discussion.

1. Do you like this work of art? Why or why not?
2. What or who is the subject of this artwork?
3. Did the artist use line in the work, and if so, can you describe the use of line?
4. What shapes do you see in this artwork?
5. What textures and patterns do you see in this piece?
6. What colors do you see in the painting?
7. How is light used in this artwork?
8. Did the artist use a wide range of values (darks and lights) in this artwork, and if so, can you describe what the artist did?
9. Did the artist use perspective in this work?
10. Does anything about the painting suggest that the artist was American, and if so, can you describe why?
11. Does the work depict an American scene, and if so, can you describe why it is an "American" scene?
12. Does anything in the artwork suggest the time in history it was created, and if so, can you describe why?

Although **modern art** may look strange to an untrained eye, these works can be better appreciated when approaching them with an open mind and by observing them carefully. The following questions can be used as a guide for discussion.

1. Do you like this painting? Why or why not?
2. How does this artwork make you feel? Why?
3. What do you see in the artwork?
4. What colors do you see?
5. What shapes do you see?
6. How is line used?
7. How are perspective and space used?
8. How are texture and pattern used?
9. How is light used? What tells you this?
10. If there is a subject depicted in the artwork, where is the subject?
11. When was this artwork done? How can you tell?
12. Why did the artist create this artwork? What is the artist trying to tell the viewer?

Brainstorming

After the group has viewed the artwork, you may wish to review and assess what the participants remember from your presentation. Brainstorming is a good technique to use for this review and assessment process. Brainstorming is a nonjudgmental problem-solving technique that allows everyone in the group to contribute ideas, thoughts, and feelings. It allows the participants to talk about the artwork they have just seen. All contributions are spontaneous.

To begin the brainstorming process, ask the participants to recall anything (no matter how small or insignificant it may seem, and remember to respond positively to each contribution) they remember from the artwork they have just seen. As the group recalls what they remember, list these items on the oversize pad. If no one responds to your first inquiry, call on specific individuals or, to prompt responses, list what you recall about the works of art.

Once you have compiled a lengthy list, use it to ask the participants specific questions about the works of art. Remember to use the words "who," "what," "where," "when," "how," and "why." Ask many questions. The more questions you ask, the clearer and more interesting the discussion. The following general guidelines will help you to conduct this discussion.

1. *Ask a survey question*: What can you tell me about the artwork we have just seen?
2. *Call on participants individually to respond to a question*: Mary, how did the artist use blue in the painting of the boat?
3. *Ask follow-up questions*: Why? Do you all agree? Can you give me an example? Can you tell us more?
4. *Respond to the participants' answers in a positive way*: "That's an excellent observation, John."
5. *Give the participants time to think after asking a question.*
6. *Invite the participants to ask their own questions*: Do you have any questions about the paintings or artists?

At the conclusion of brainstorming, you will know what the participants remembered most about the presentation. You will also realize what they liked and disliked about the artwork. Use this information as a guide in planning other art history presentations.

ART ACTIVITIES

After presenting and evaluating masterworks, your next step in exposing older adults to art history is conducting art activities that help to acquaint group members with masterworks while they create works of art of their own. To conduct these activities, you will need access to good-quality reproductions and the basic art supplies listed in Table 1 (see p. 9). Books with high-quality color reproductions of masterworks can be obtained from a university or public library. Posters and smaller-size reproductions can be purchased from the companies listed in Appendix B. Art museums also make reproductions available for sale. Check the museum gift shops or request a mail-order catalog. After gathering the supplies, arrange the room in the same manner as you did in the lessons section and begin the activities. Three activities are included here to assist you.

Activity 1
Copy a Masterwork (Line Drawing)

SUPPLIES: Easel with oversize pad of paper and a black thick-line felt-tip marker (for the facilitator's use)

Artist's drawing pencils (4B or 6B; one for each participant)

Heavyweight drawing paper (several sheets for each participant)

Kneaded art erasers (one for each participant)

Reproduction of a simple line drawing done by a master (van Gogh's landscapes or still lifes work well)

PREPARATION: Photocopy one copy of the line drawing for each participant.[1] If you use a poster-size reproduction, display it so all participants can see it. Ensure that everyone has the supplies and a copy of the line drawing needed for this activity and that they are within easy reach before beginning the activity.

PROCEDURE:

Once everyone is seated and comfortable, begin to discuss the drawing using the six basic elements of art as a foundation. Then instruct the participants to copy the line drawing. If you perceive that the group needs help to begin drawing, draw a small section of the artwork on the oversize pad. Because this activity is designed to be an independent activity, minimize the amount of drawing you do. Instruct the group to begin just as you did and to draw the lines lightly. Encourage the participants' efforts. Remind them that if they are not satisfied with their drawing at any time, they may begin again on a fresh sheet of paper or use their eraser to correct small sections with which they are dissatisfied.

After participants have completed their line drawings, ask each group member to show his or her artwork to the rest of the group. Explain to group members that because their work is a copy of another artist's work, they cannot sign their own names to the copy. Inform them that they can state that the drawing is a copy of a line drawing by the original artist.

Display the completed line drawings in the gallery area. Thank everyone who participated.

---

[1]Certain restrictions on this type of photocopying were approved by Congress in 1980. The restrictions are as follows: Instructors may make multiple copies (cannot exceed one copy per learner in a course) for classroom use or for purposes of discussion, provided that only one drawing or painting per book or periodical is used; the instructor decides to use the artwork so close in time to its actual use that it would not be reasonable to expect a timely response to a request for permission; the copying is done for only one course; and there are no more than nine occurrences of multiple copying during one term.

Activity 2
Copy a Masterwork (Painting)

SUPPLIES: Easel with oversize pad of paper and a black thick-line felt-tip marker (for the facilitator's use)

Artist's drawing pencils (4B or 6B; one for each participant)

Tempera nontoxic poster paints (red, yellow, blue, white, green, and any other colors you desire)

Heavyweight drawing paper (several sheets for each participant)

Plastic or paper cups (to hold water and paint; participants may share paints, but have an adequate supply on hand so that group members can easily reach them)

Paintbrushes (two or three brushes for each participant)

Paper towels

Newspapers or other covering (to protect work surfaces from paint)

Aprons (one for each participant)

Color reproduction of a masterwork (e.g., van Gogh's *Still Life: Vase with Fourteen Sunflowers* or another of his sunflower paintings; Cézanne's *Apples and Oranges* or another of his still lifes; Manet's *Flowers in a Crystal Vase*, *Lilacs and Roses*, or another of his floral still lifes)

PREPARATION: Display a large (poster size, if possible) reproduction for all to see and distribute smaller reproductions for the participants to use at their tables. If you use individual copies of different works, ask each participant to select a reproduction to copy. Distribute the supplies to the group before you begin the activity.

PROCEDURE:

Once everyone is seated and comfortable, ask participants to look at the copy of the masterwork. Discuss the painting using the six basic elements of art as a foundation. Then instruct the participants to copy the painting. If you perceive that the group members need help to begin painting, instruct them to draw the image on the paper before they apply the paints. As an example, draw a small section of the painting on the oversize pad and ask the group to observe and draw along with you. Mix a few colors to refresh the participants' memories of the color mixing process and apply the paints to your drawing. Because this activity is designed to be an independent activity, minimize the amount of drawing or painting you do. Positively encourage everyone to proceed on his or her own. Remind the participants that if they are not satisfied with their painting at any time, they may begin again on a fresh sheet of paper.

After group members complete their paintings, ask each person to show his or her artwork to the rest of the group. Explain to group members that because their work is a copy of another artist's work, they cannot sign their own names to the copy. Inform them that they can state that the painting is a copy of a painting by the original artist.

Display the completed paintings in the gallery area. Thank everyone who participated.

Activity 3
Create a Work of Art in the Style of a Masterwork

SUPPLIES: The supplies will vary depending on the artwork you select for this activity, but the following are the basic necessary supplies:

Easel with oversize pad of paper and a black thick-line felt-tip marker

Tempera nontoxic poster paints (red, yellow, blue, white, black, green, and any other colors you desire)

Paintbrushes (two or three brushes for each participant)

Artists' drawing pencils (4B or 6B; one for each participant)

Black permanent felt-tip markers (one for each participant)

Heavyweight drawing paper (several sheets for each participant)

Construction paper (in a variety of colors)

Plastic or paper cups (to hold water and paint; participants may share paints, but have an adequate supply on hand so that group members can easily reach them)

Scissors (one pair for each participant)

Glue (one container for every two participants)

Rulers (one for each participant)

Paper towels

Newspapers or other covering (to protect work surfaces from paint)

Aprons (one for each participant)

Color reproductions of a masterwork (e.g., Mondrian's *Composition with Red, Blue, and Yellow*, van Gogh's *The Starry Night*, Matisse's *Beasts of the Sea* or another of his paper cutout works, still life paintings of any artist)

PREPARATION: Display a large (poster size, if available) reproduction for all to see and distribute smaller reproductions of the same painting to the participants. Also distribute the art supplies to group members before you begin the activity.

PROCEDURE:

After everyone is seated and comfortable, ask participants to look at the copy of the masterwork. Explain to them that this reproduction is to be used only as a guide to creating their own artwork in the style used by the original artist (i.e., they should not copy the masterwork but implement the ideas used to create it). Initiate a discussion of the reproduction using the six basic elements of art as a foundation. Ask group members to explain how they can incorporate the ideas used in the masterwork in their artwork. If the participants are hesitant to answer these questions, provide them with the following examples:

• If Matisse's paper cutouts are used as the foundation for a participant's creation, cut out shapes of different colors and sizes from the construction paper and arrange them in an interesting composition on a sheet of heavyweight drawing paper.

• If van Gogh's *The Starry Night* is used as the foundation for a participant's creation, paint a brilliant sunny day using bright, swirling colors, as van Gogh did in his painting.

• If Mondrian's *Composition with Red, Blue, and Yellow* is used as the foundation for a participant's creation, draw large squares on your oversize pad, and outline them in black felt-tip marker. Paint the squares using the secondary colors orange, green, and purple.

Because this art activity is designed to be an independent activity, minimize the amount of drawing or painting you do. Positively encourage everyone to proceed on his or her own. Remind the participants that if they are not satisfied with their work, they may begin again on a fresh sheet of paper.

After group members complete their artworks, ask each person to show his or her piece to the rest of the group. Display the completed artwork in the gallery area. Thank everyone who participated.

Before dismissing the group, explain to participants that they have completed Set A (or Set B) of the materials and technical skills and the critical thinking components of the art curriculum. Review the following pages about organizing an art exhibition and tell the group that an exhibition of members' artwork or the work of a local artist can be organized.

Explain that over the next few days you will be evaluating the program and asking them for suggestions about how to improve it. Emphasize that all suggestions, positive or negative, are welcome. If circumstances allow you to continue the program, explain that after the evaluation the group can continue to meet, if this is what everyone desires.

ART EXHIBITIONS

As group members learn about art and create works of art of their own, begin to introduce the concept of the art exhibition, a necessary component of the art world. Exhibitions provide artists with opportunities to display their work and to communicate their ideas to the community. If your facility or center is equipped to host an exhibition, invite a local artist, a group of local artists, or the art group participants to exhibit their work. The exhibit can be as simple or as elaborate as you wish. The exhibit may be mounted exclusively for the residents or clients of and visitors to the facility, or it can be mounted for the community, perhaps as part of a larger celebration (e.g., National Nursing Home Week, Mental Illness Awareness Week, Alzheimer's Disease Awareness Month) at your facility or health care agency. If your facility or center is not equipped to host an exhibition, you can arrange for it to be held in a public forum, such as a mall, bank, library, or town square. Before proceeding with the idea, however, ask the artist or artists whether they would like to display their artwork and to help plan the exhibit. If they respond enthusiastically, begin planning the event.

In planning the exhibit, you should remember that the artwork selected must be matted and/or framed properly in order to present it in the best possible manner. Often, frame shops donate mats, frames, and labor to organizations, senior centers, and nursing facilities. The next steps are to secure the venue and to publicize the event, particularly if the venue is a public place, such as a shopping mall. Some ways to publicize the exhibition are to list the exhibit in the cultural events section of a local newspaper and to send announcements of the exhibition to the family and friends of the artists as well as to community leaders well in advance of the event. Local newspapers often welcome an opportunity to visit your facility and write a short article about the exhibition and the artists. Call the paper's news or lifestyle editor and ask if the paper would be interested in reporting on your art exhibit.

If the exhibition is being held in the facility or center, you should organize a reception for the artist and the residents of the facility. As a part of this reception, ask the artist or artists to talk about their artwork and the process of creating it. At the conclusion of the talk, residents or clients can ask questions about the artwork.

An art exhibition is a rewarding and positive learning experience for everyone. Consider the ideas in this section, inform the art group members about them, and ask them for their contributions. Then begin planning your art exhibit.

Section III

Evaluation

At the end of each set of lessons and "Critical Thinking," you should evaluate your art program. Evaluation comprises seven levels: 1) evaluating your goals, 2) evaluating yourself, 3) evaluating the participants, 4) evaluating the physical space, 5) evaluating the art supplies, 6) evaluating the lesson plans, and 7) facilitating the participants' evaluation. Levels 1–6 each contain a set of questions to be answered by the group facilitator; Level 7 contains a set of questions to be answered by the group participants.

To begin the program evaluation, take a few minutes to reflect on what you have accomplished with the group and jot down a few notes. Then review the goal statements that you wrote as you planned the art course.

1. Did you reach your expectations? Why or why not? In what ways would you change your expectations?
2. Was the length of the course satisfactory? What would you change?
3. Was the length of each class session adequate?
4. Was the number of sessions presented before evaluation satisfactory?

After answering questions about your goals, reflect on your feelings about leading the group.

1. Did you enjoy leading the group? Why or why not?
2. Did you enjoy teaching the course? Why or why not?
3. Did the participants respond well to you? Why or why not?
4. Were you prepared for each group session? Why or why not?
5. Were you enthusiastic about the content of the lessons? Why or why not?
6. Did you use class time well?

Take a moment to review the participants and their reactions to the sessions.

1. Did the participants seem interested in the art group? Why or why not?
2. Were the participants physically able to accomplish the artwork?
3. Were the participants capable of understanding what they were asked to do?
4. Did the group contain an appropriate number of participants?
5. Did the participants work well together? Why or why not? What would you change for the next art group?

The space in which the art group was held had an impact on the success or failure of the group. Take time to evaluate the physical space.

1. Was the location acceptable? Why or why not?
2. Was the size of the space adequate? Why or why not?
3. Was the ambient noise level acceptable? Why or why not?
4. Was the lighting adequate or inadequate? Why or why not?
5. Was the equipment (e.g., tables, chairs, sink, audiovisual equipment) satisfactory? Why or why not?
6. Were the gallery and storage areas adequate? Why or why not?

The supplies used for the art lessons must be appropriate for the group. Answering the following questions will help you to evaluate the art supplies.

1. Were the supplies appropriate for the artwork the participants were asked to do? Would other supplies be more appropriate? If so, what are these supplies?
2. What supplies do you need to add to the list?
3. What supplies should you omit from the list?
4. What supplies do you need to replace?

The lesson plan is the foundation upon which each group session is built. It is important to review these plans.

1. Was the concept/subject of the lesson clear? If not, why?
2. Were the objectives clear? If not, why?

3. Were the participants able to achieve the objectives? If not, why?
4. Were all the supplies needed for the lesson listed on the lesson plan?
5. Was the procedure for conducting the lesson clear? If not, why?

The final level of program evaluation is the evaluation of the group by its participants. Most of the participants will have thoughts and feelings about what they have learned, and some may have suggestions for improvement. Conduct this evaluation using a written or oral questionnaire or using a combined written and oral questionnaire. Questions to be used for this evaluation are as follows:

Interest and Expectations

1. Were you interested in the course? Why or why not?
2. Were you able to understand what was expected of you?
3. Were you physically able to accomplish what was expected of you?
4. Did the course meet your expectations? Why or why not?
5. Did you feel comfortable in the group? Why or why not?

Group Facilitator

1. Did the facilitator adequately explain what was expected of you?
2. Were you provided with opportunities to express your views?
3. Was the facilitator prepared for each lesson?
4. Was the use of examples and visual materials adequate and interesting?
5. Were you supported in your efforts? Were you complimented for good work?

Physical Space and Supplies

1. Was the physical space or classroom adequate for the group? What about the size of the space, noise level, lighting, and access to rest rooms?
2. Were the tables and chairs comfortable for you to work at?
3. Did you enjoy displaying your artwork? Why or why not?
4. Were the supplies satisfactory? Were they easy to use?
5. Was the temperature of the classroom comfortable for you? If not, why?

The Future

1. Do you want the group to continue? Why?
2. What would you change about the group to make it better?

Once you and the participants have answered the evaluation questions, take some time to reflect on the answers. After doing so, ask yourself the following questions:

1. Do you want to continue facilitating the group?
2. Do the participants want the group to continue?

Your answers to these two questions will determine the direction the art group will take. Several possibilities exist that you may want to consider, as follows:

• If you do not want to continue leading the group but the participants want the group to continue, perhaps there is someone else who would be willing to lead the group.
• If you want the group to continue but the participants do not, consider a break of a month or two or a restructuring of the course.

- If you and the participants find that creating artwork is not appropriate or satisfactory, discontinue the group and move on to activities that everyone will enjoy.
- If you and the participants want the group to continue, forge ahead with renewed energy and creativity.

If you decide to continue the group, make any changes necessary in your teaching methods, the course materials, and the physical space, or write new goal statements. An art program that is well planned, organized, and led by an enthusiastic facilitator reaps many rewards for all, such as renewed enthusiasm and interest in life and the joy of creating and sharing artwork with others. After all your hard work, give yourself a well-deserved pat on the back and enjoy all the artwork that has been created.

Select Bibliography

Albers, J. (1963). *Interaction of color*. New Haven: Yale University Press.

Andresen, G. (1995). *Caring for people with Alzheimer's disease: A training manual for direct care providers*. Baltimore: Health Professions Press.

Balkema, J.B. (1986). *The creative spirit: An annotated bibliography on the arts, humanities, and aging*. Washington, DC: National Council on the Aging.

Beaubien, J. (1976). *Artists and the aging: A project handbook*. St. Paul, MN: Community Programs in the Arts and Sciences–St. Paul–Ramsey Arts Council.

Berger, J. (1972). *Ways of seeing*. London: British Broadcasting Corporation/Penguin Books.

Brommer, G.F., & Horn, G.F. (1985). *Art in your world*. Worcester, MA: Davis Publications.

Burnside, I.M. (1978). *Working with the elderly: Group processes and techniques*. North Scituate, MA: Duxbury Press.

Butler, R. (1975). *Why survive? Being old in America*. New York: Harper & Row.

Campbell, M.S., Driskell, D., Levering Lewis, D., & Ryan, D.W. (1987). *Harlem Renaissance art of black America*. New York: Harry N. Abrams.

Canaday, J. (1981). *Mainstreams of modern art*. New York: Holt, Rinehart & Winston.

Cane, F. (1983). *The artist in each of us*. Craftsbury Common, VT: Art Therapy Publications.

Chilvers, I. (Ed.) (1990). *The concise Oxford dictionary of art and artists*. Oxford, England: Oxford University Press.

Clair, A.A. (1996). *Therapeutic uses of music with older adults*. Baltimore: Health Professions Press.

Craig, J. (1980). *Human development*. Englewood Cliffs, NJ: Prentice Hall.

Crosson, C. (1976, January). Art therapy with geriatric patients: Problems of spontaneity. *American Journal of Art Therapy*, pp. 51–56.

Dalley, T. (Ed.) (1984). *Art as therapy: An introduction to the use of art as a therapeutic technique*. London: Tavistock Publications.

Daval, J. (1989). *History of abstract painting*. Paris: Fernand Hazan.

de la Croix, H., & Tansey, R.G. (1975). *Gardner's art through the ages*. New York: Harcourt Brace Jovanovich.

Edwards, B. (1979). *Drawing on the right side of the brain.* Los Angeles: J.P. Tarcher.

Erikson, J.M. (1988). *Wisdom and the senses. The way of creativity.* New York: Norton.

Fingesten, P. (1963). *Basic facts of art history for examination review.* New York: Crowell-Collier Publishing.

Flack, A. (1986). *Art and soul. Notes on creating.* New York: E.P. Dutton.

Fowler, M., & McCutcheon, P. (1991). *Songs of experience.* New York: Ballantine Books.

Franck, F. (1973). *The zen of seeing-seeing/Drawing as meditation.* New York: Vintage Books.

Freeman, S. (1987). *Activities and approaches for Alzheimer's.* Knoxville, TN: The Whitfield Agency.

Gerdts, W.H. (1981). *Painters of the humble truth: Masterpieces of American still life 1801–1939.* Columbia: University of Missouri Press.

Gombrich, E.H. (1995). *The story of art* (16th ed.). London: Phaidon.

Gordon, R., & Forge, A. (1986). *The last flowers of Manet.* New York: Harry N. Abrams.

Graubarth-Szyller, B.R., & Padgett, J.D. (1989). *Longevity therapy.* Philadelphia: Charles Press.

Greenberg, P. (1987, July). Introduction. *Art Education*, pp. 6–7.

Greenberg, P. (1987). *Visual arts and older people. Developing quality programs.* Springfield, IL: Charles C Thomas.

Greer, G. (1979). *The obstacle race: The fortunes of women painters and their work.* New York: Farrar, Straus, & Giroux.

Hale, G. (1979). *The source book for the disabled.* New York: Paddington Press/Grossett & Dunlap.

Hartt, F. (1979). *History of Italian Renaissance art.* Englewood Cliffs, NJ: Prentice Hall and New York: Harry N. Abrams.

Heller, N.G. (1987). *Women artists: An illustrated history.* New York: Cross River Press.

Hoffman, D.H., Greenberg, P., & Fitzner, D.H. (1980). *Lifelong learning and the visual arts: A book of readings.* Reston, VA: National Art Education Association.

Hoffman, D.H., & Masem, E. (1977, April). The relationships of the arts and leisure to elderly persons: An annotated bibliography. *Art Education*, pp. 16–19.

Hughes, R. (1980). *The shock of the new.* New York: Alfred A. Knopf.

Jackson, J.E., Katzman, R., & Lessin, P.J. (1992). *Alzheimer's disease: Long term care.* San Diego, CA: San Diego State University.

Janson, H.W. (1995). *History of art* (5th ed.). New York: Harry N. Abrams.

Jones, J.E. (1980). *Teaching art to older adults: Guidelines and lessons.* Atlanta: Georgia State University.

Koch, K. (1977). *I never told anybody: Teaching poetry writing in a nursing home.* New York: Random House.

Levi, J. (1961). *Modern art: An introduction.* New York: Pitman Publishing.

Lewis, H.P. (1987, July). Art and older adults: An overview. *Art Education*, pp. 4–5.

London, P. (1989). *No more secondhand art: Awakening the artist within.* Boston: Shambhala Publications.

Mace, N.L., & Rabins, P.V. (1991). *The 36-hour day. A family guide to caring for persons with Alzheimer's disease, related dementing illness and memory loss in later life.* (Rev. ed.). Baltimore: The Johns Hopkins University Press.

Maclay, E. (1977). *Green winter—Celebrations of old age.* New York: Reader's Digest Press.

Mendelowitz, D.M. (1976). *A guide to drawing.* New York: Holt, Rinehart & Winston.

Miller, S. (1982, April). Attitudes of arts instructors and students. *Educational Gerontology*, pp. 176–181.

Mittler, G.A. (1989). *Art in focus.* Mission Hills, CA: Glencoe Publishing.

National Gallery of Art. (1980). *Post-impressionism: Cross-currents in European and American painting 1880–1906.* Washington, DC: Author.

Nesbitt, J.A. (Ed.) (1986). *The international directory of recreation-oriented assistive device sources.* Marina Del Rey, CA: Lifeboat Press.

Nouwen, H.J.-M., & Gaffney, W.J. (1974). *Aging.* Garden City, NY: Doubleday.

Roger, J., & McWilliams, P. (1989). *You can't afford the luxury of a negative thought.* Los Angeles: Prelude Press.

Sandel, S.L., & Johnson, D.R. (1987). *Waiting at the gate: Hope and creativity in the nursing home.* New York: Haworth Press.

Shives, J.S., & Fait, H.F. (1990). *Recreational service for the aging.* Philadelphia: Lea & Febiger.

Simmons, S., III, & Winer, M.S.A. (1977). *Drawing: The creative process.* Englewood Cliffs, NJ: Prentice Hall.

Spies, W. (undated). *Albers.* New York: Harry N. Abrams.

Zeiger, B.L. (1976, January). Life review in art therapy with the aged. *American Journal of Art Therapy*, pp. 47–50.

Appendix A
Art History Time Line

The art history time line provided here introduces participants to art history. It enumerates the periods of art history, types of art executed during each period, and artists who worked during each period. Use this appendix to help you select periods of art and artists of interest for your group. After making your selections, you can begin to do research into the periods and artists for your presentation. University and public libraries are excellent sources of information.

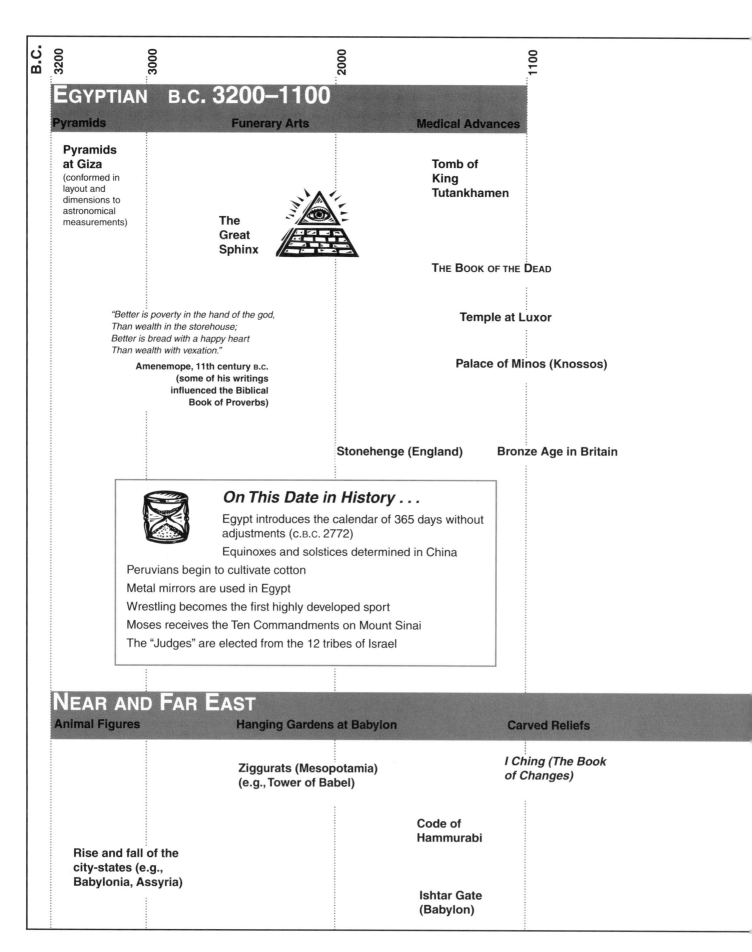

B.C.

B.C.	3200	3000	2000	1100

EGYPTIAN   B.C. 3200–1100

Pyramids · **Funerary Arts** · **Medical Advances**

Pyramids at Giza
(conformed in layout and dimensions to astronomical measurements)

The Great Sphinx

Tomb of King Tutankhamen

THE BOOK OF THE DEAD

"Better is poverty in the hand of the god,
Than wealth in the storehouse;
Better is bread with a happy heart
Than wealth with vexation."

Amenemope, 11th century B.C.
(some of his writings influenced the Biblical Book of Proverbs)

Temple at Luxor

Palace of Minos (Knossos)

Stonehenge (England)   **Bronze Age in Britain**

On This Date in History . . .

Egypt introduces the calendar of 365 days without adjustments (C.B.C. 2772)

Equinoxes and solstices determined in China

Peruvians begin to cultivate cotton

Metal mirrors are used in Egypt

Wrestling becomes the first highly developed sport

Moses receives the Ten Commandments on Mount Sinai

The "Judges" are elected from the 12 tribes of Israel

NEAR AND FAR EAST

Animal Figures · **Hanging Gardens at Babylon** · **Carved Reliefs**

Ziggurats (Mesopotamia)
(e.g., Tower of Babel)

I Ching (The Book of Changes)

Code of Hammurabi

Rise and fall of the city-states (e.g., Babylonia, Assyria)

Ishtar Gate (Babylon)

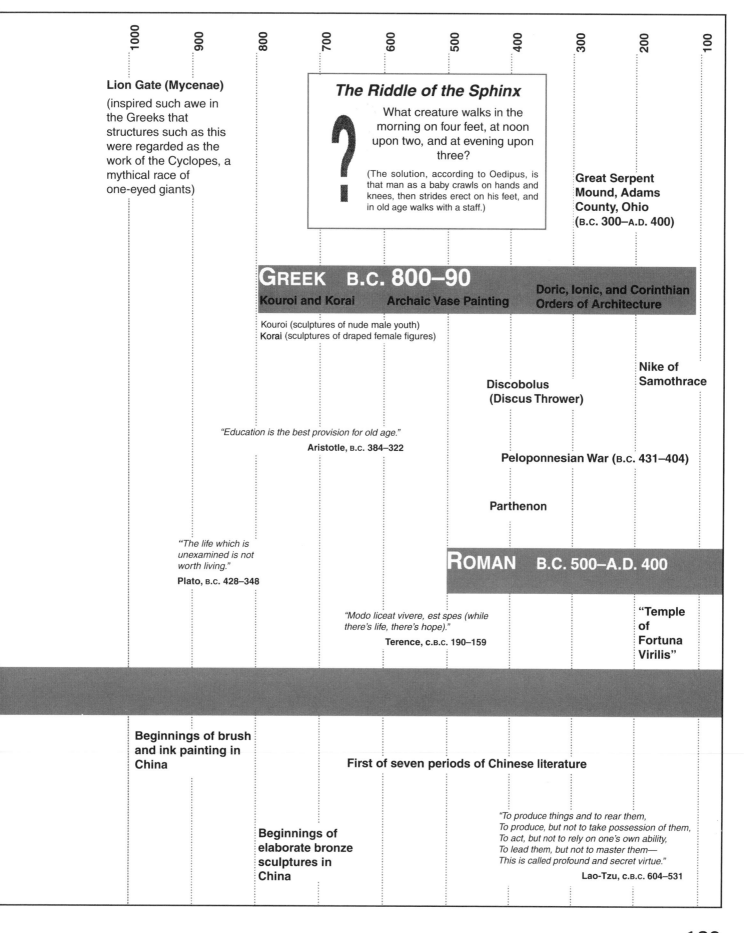

1000 900 800 700 600 500 400 300 200 100

Lion Gate (Mycenae)

(inspired such awe in the Greeks that structures such as this were regarded as the work of the Cyclopes, a mythical race of one-eyed giants)

The Riddle of the Sphinx

?

What creature walks in the morning on four feet, at noon upon two, and at evening upon three?

(The solution, according to Oedipus, is that man as a baby crawls on hands and knees, then strides erect on his feet, and in old age walks with a staff.)

Great Serpent Mound, Adams County, Ohio (B.C. 300–A.D. 400)

GREEK   B.C. 800–90

Kouroi and Korai   Archaic Vase Painting   Doric, Ionic, and Corinthian Orders of Architecture

Kouroi (sculptures of nude male youth)
Korai (sculptures of draped female figures)

Nike of Samothrace

Discobolus (Discus Thrower)

"Education is the best provision for old age."
Aristotle, B.C. 384–322

Peloponnesian War (B.C. 431–404)

Parthenon

"The life which is unexamined is not worth living."
Plato, B.C. 428–348

ROMAN   B.C. 500–A.D. 400

"Modo liceat vivere, est spes (while there's life, there's hope)."
Terence, C.B.C. 190–159

"Temple of Fortuna Virilis"

Beginnings of brush and ink painting in China

First of seven periods of Chinese literature

"To produce things and to rear them, To produce, but not to take possession of them, To act, but not to rely on one's own ability, To lead them, but not to master them— This is called profound and secret virtue."
Lao-Tzu, C.B.C. 604–531

Beginnings of elaborate bronze sculptures in China

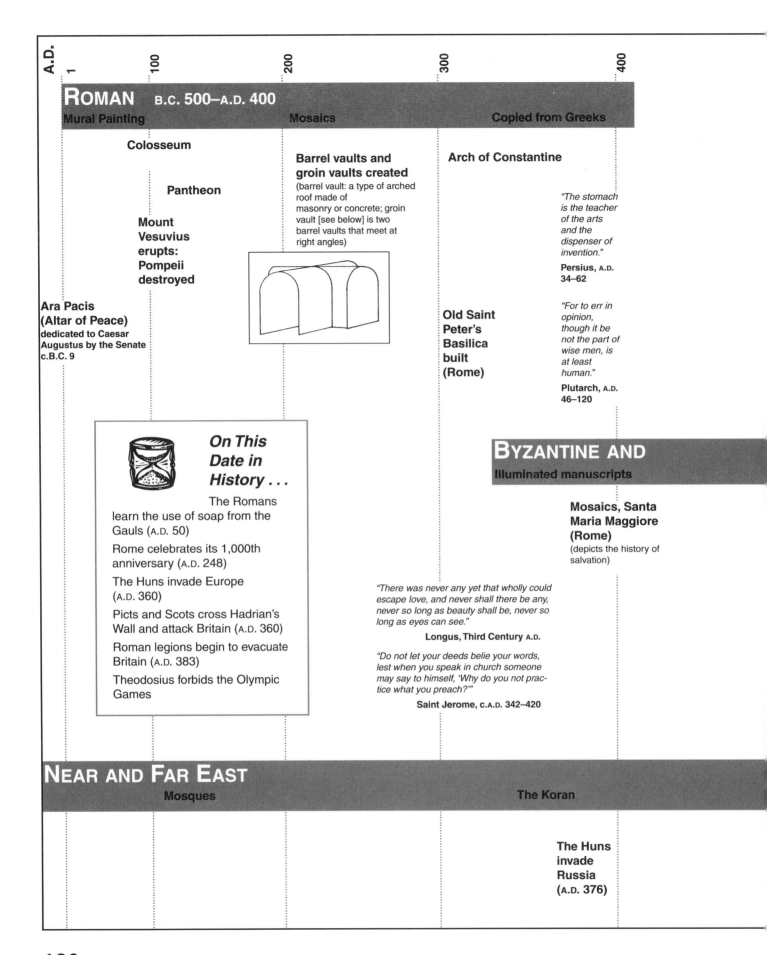

ROMAN   B.C. 500–A.D. 400

Mural Painting   **Mosaics**   **Copied from Greeks**

Colosseum

Barrel vaults and groin vaults created
(barrel vault: a type of arched roof made of masonry or concrete; groin vault [see below] is two barrel vaults that meet at right angles)

Arch of Constantine

Pantheon

Mount Vesuvius erupts: Pompeii destroyed

Ara Pacis (Altar of Peace)
dedicated to Caesar Augustus by the Senate c.B.C. 9

Old Saint Peter's Basilica built (Rome)

"The stomach is the teacher of the arts and the dispenser of invention."
Persius, A.D. 34–62

"For to err in opinion, though it be not the part of wise men, is at least human."
Plutarch, A.D. 46–120

On This Date in History . . .

The Romans learn the use of soap from the Gauls (A.D. 50)

Rome celebrates its 1,000th anniversary (A.D. 248)

The Huns invade Europe (A.D. 360)

Picts and Scots cross Hadrian's Wall and attack Britain (A.D. 360)

Roman legions begin to evacuate Britain (A.D. 383)

Theodosius forbids the Olympic Games

BYZANTINE AND

Illuminated manuscripts

Mosaics, Santa Maria Maggiore (Rome)
(depicts the history of salvation)

"There was never any yet that wholly could escape love, and never shall there be any, never so long as beauty shall be, never so long as eyes can see."
Longus, Third Century A.D.

"Do not let your deeds belie your words, lest when you speak in church someone may say to himself, 'Why do you not practice what you preach?'"
Saint Jerome, C.A.D. 342–420

NEAR AND FAR EAST

Mosques   **The Koran**

The Huns invade Russia (A.D. 376)

500 | 600 | 700 | 800 | 900

ROMANESQUE
The Middle Ages

Utrecht Psalter
(important illuminated manuscript produced during the rule of the successors to Charlemagne)

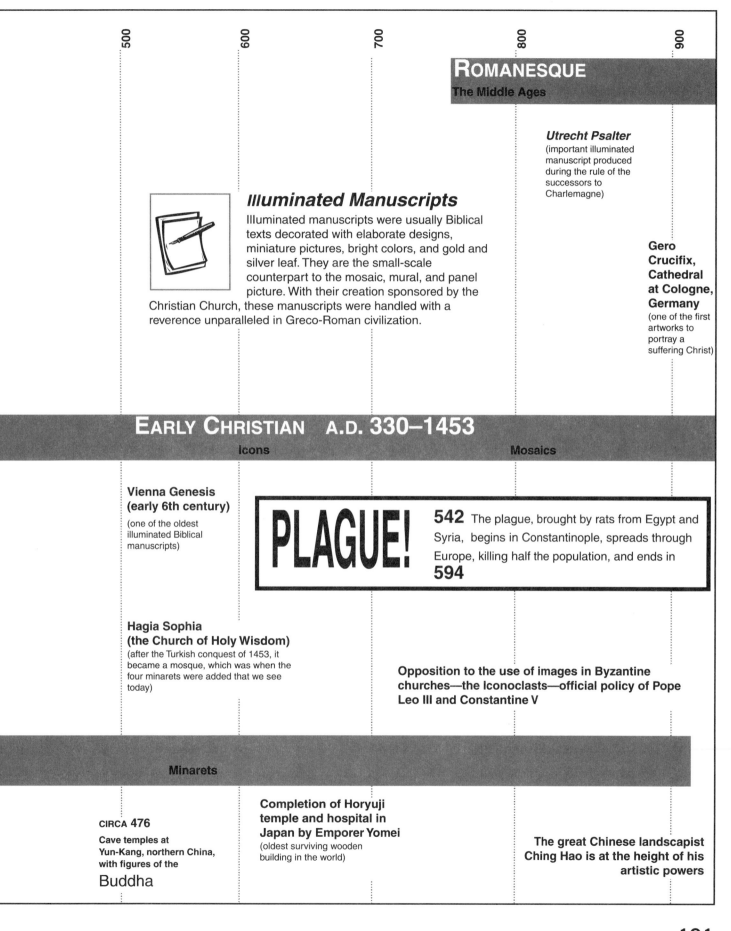

Illuminated Manuscripts

Illuminated manuscripts were usually Biblical texts decorated with elaborate designs, miniature pictures, bright colors, and gold and silver leaf. They are the small-scale counterpart to the mosaic, mural, and panel picture. With their creation sponsored by the Christian Church, these manuscripts were handled with a reverence unparalleled in Greco-Roman civilization.

Gero Crucifix, Cathedral at Cologne, Germany
(one of the first artworks to portray a suffering Christ)

EARLY CHRISTIAN   A.D. 330–1453
Icons   Mosaics

**Vienna Genesis
(early 6th century)**
(one of the oldest illuminated Biblical manuscripts)

PLAGUE!
542 The plague, brought by rats from Egypt and Syria, begins in Constantinople, spreads through Europe, killing half the population, and ends in **594**

**Hagia Sophia
(the Church of Holy Wisdom)**
(after the Turkish conquest of 1453, it became a mosque, which was when the four minarets were added that we see today)

Opposition to the use of images in Byzantine churches—the Iconoclasts—official policy of Pope Leo III and Constantine V

Minarets

CIRCA **476**

Cave temples at Yun-Kang, northern China, with figures of the
Buddha

Completion of Horyuji temple and hospital in Japan by Emporer Yomei
(oldest surviving wooden building in the world)

The great Chinese landscapist Ching Hao is at the height of his artistic powers

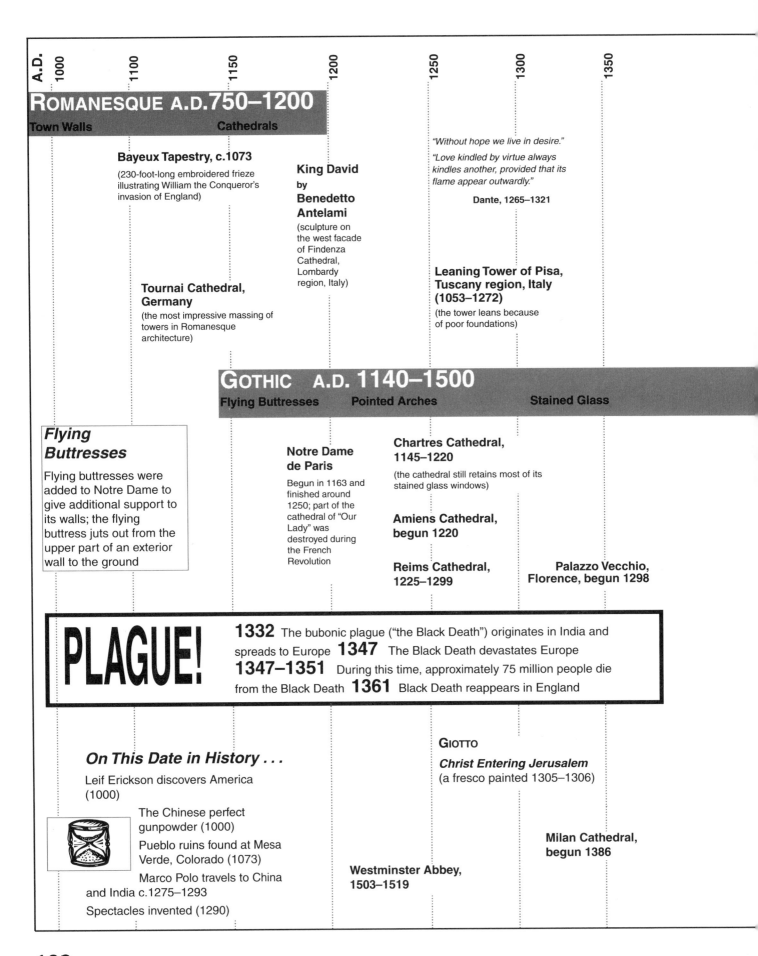

A.D.

1000 | 1100 | 1150 | 1200 | 1250 | 1300 | 1350

ROMANESQUE A.D. 750–1200

Town Walls   Cathedrals

Bayeux Tapestry, c.1073
(230-foot-long embroidered frieze illustrating William the Conqueror's invasion of England)

King David
by
Benedetto
Antelami
(sculpture on the west facade of Findenza Cathedral, Lombardy region, Italy)

"Without hope we live in desire."
"Love kindled by virtue always kindles another, provided that its flame appear outwardly."
Dante, 1265–1321

Tournai Cathedral, Germany
(the most impressive massing of towers in Romanesque architecture)

Leaning Tower of Pisa, Tuscany region, Italy (1053–1272)
(the tower leans because of poor foundations)

GOTHIC A.D. 1140–1500

Flying Buttresses   Pointed Arches   Stained Glass

Flying Buttresses

Flying buttresses were added to Notre Dame to give additional support to its walls; the flying buttress juts out from the upper part of an exterior wall to the ground

Notre Dame de Paris
Begun in 1163 and finished around 1250; part of the cathedral of "Our Lady" was destroyed during the French Revolution

Chartres Cathedral, 1145–1220
(the cathedral still retains most of its stained glass windows)

Amiens Cathedral, begun 1220

Reims Cathedral, 1225–1299

Palazzo Vecchio, Florence, begun 1298

PLAGUE! **1332** The bubonic plague ("the Black Death") originates in India and spreads to Europe **1347** The Black Death devastates Europe **1347–1351** During this time, approximately 75 million people die from the Black Death **1361** Black Death reappears in England

On This Date in History . . .

Leif Erickson discovers America (1000)

The Chinese perfect gunpowder (1000)

Pueblo ruins found at Mesa Verde, Colorado (1073)

Marco Polo travels to China and India c.1275–1293

Spectacles invented (1290)

GIOTTO
Christ Entering Jerusalem
(a fresco painted 1305–1306)

Milan Cathedral, begun 1386

Westminster Abbey, 1503–1519

192

RENAISSANCE C.1400–1600

Beginning of Oil Painting   **Self-Expression**   **Revival of the Classics**

R enaissance literally means "rebirth." The movement began in Italy and spread to northern Europe. The Renaissance marked a return to the values of the Greek and Roman worlds. Architectural design was based on mathematical ratios and painting conveyed a fidelity to nature.

In Italy and Southern Europe

Painting and sculpture as personal expression of the artist

Onorata Rodiana (Rodiani) (died 1452)
Because (it is believed that) she painted strictly in tempera, none of her work has survived, and if any has, it is disputed that she painted it; she was tried for murder in the early 15th century and pardoned, and lived out her life in military service

Leonardo da Vinci (1452–1519)
Painter, sculptor, architect, scientist
Mona Lisa (c.1503–1505), *The Last Supper* (c.1495–1498)

Donatello (1386–1466)
Greatest sculptor of the 15th century
David (c.1425–1430)

Sandro Botticelli (1444/5–1510)
The Birth of Venus

Michelangelo (Buonarroti) (1475–1564)
Sculptor, painter, architect; greatest sculptor of the 16th century
David (1501–1504), *Moses* (c.1513–1515), ceiling of the Sistine Chapel (1508–1512), Saint Peter's Cathedral (as architect, 1546–1564)

Raphael (Sanzio) (1483–1520)
Painter of figures
Galatea (1513), *Madonna del Granduca* (c. 1505)

Titian (1488/90–1576)
After Raphael's death, the most sought-after portraitist of the age
Bacchanal (c.1518), *Christ Crowned with Thorns* (c.1570)

Tintoretto (1518–1594)
Christ Before Pilate (1566–1567)

"El Greco" (Domenikos Theotocopoulos) (1541–1614)
Greatest of the Mannerists of the Venetian School; perhaps the first Expressionist (see 20th century) painter
The Burial of Count Orgaz (1586)

In Northern Europe

Franco-Flemish painting

Diptychs and triptychs
(diptych: a painting or altarpiece consisting of two parts usually hinged together; triptych: a painting or altarpiece consisting of one central panel and two hinged panels on either side of the central panel)

Jan van Eyck (Holland, 1384–1441)
Painter of Flemish figures
With his brother Hubert, *The Ghent Altarpiece* (triptych, completed 1432)

Albrecht Dürer (Germany, 1471–1528)
Painter of figures and landscapes; engraver
Adam and Eve (1504), *The Four Apostles* (1523–1526)

Hans Holbein (Germany, 1497–1543)
Life-like portraits
Henry VIII (1540)

Hieronymus Bosch (Flanders, 1450–1516)
Humorous paintings of dream imagery, good and evil
The Garden of Delights (triptych, c.1500)

Mechteld toe Boecop (Holland)
One of the most accomplished female painters of her day
The Last Supper (1547)
Adoration of the Shepherds (1574)

The Reformation

A religious movement started in Germany in 1517 by Martin Luther, the Reformation sought to correct real or imagined abuses in the Roman Catholic Church. It rejected the supremacy of the Pope, modified much of the doctrine of the Church, and established Protestantism.

"If music be the food of love, play on; Give me excess of it, that, surfeiting, The appetite may sicken, and so die."
Shakespeare, *Twelfth Night*, 1601

BAROQUE 1600s

Ornate, Complex Forms   **Bold Ornamentation**   **Sensual Figures**

> Art of the baroque period is a response to the Reformation. Works were created to coax people back to the Roman Catholic Church. The use of light was important, but not all artists used light in the same way (e.g., compare Vermeer with Rembrandt). Rembrandt was the leading artist of the baroque period.

Caravaggio (1573–1610)
Strong use of light in figure painting
Huge canvases at Saint Luigi dei Francesi

Artemisia Gentileschi (1593–c.1653)
Judith Beheading Holofernes
One of her favorite subjects was the biblical heroine Judith, who saved her people by beheading the Assyrian general Holofernes; Caravaggio was a great influence on her work

Rembrandt van Rijn (Holland, 1606–1669)
Painter of religious portraits (especially Old Testament subjects) and of aristocrats
The Night Watch (1642)

Franz Hals (Holland, 1580–1666)
Painter of common people and subjects
The Jolly Toper (1627) (a toper is a drunkard)

Judith Leyster (Holland, 1609–1660)
Portratist, landscapist, painter of still lifes
Boy with Flute (1630–1635)

Galileo
constructs astronomical telescope (1608)

Great Fire of London, 1666

Jan Vermeer (Holland, 1632–1675)
Painter of small, interior scenes
The Letter (1666)
"he translates reality into a mosaic as he puts it on canvas" (Janson, 1986, p. 534)

French Landscapists

Claude Lorrain (1600–1682)
A Pastoral (c.1650)

Nicolas Poussin (1594–1665)
The Rape of the Sabine Women (c.1636)

Peter Paul Rubens (Flanders, 1577–1640)
("Rubensesque" women)
The Garden of Love

Diego Velazquez (Spain, 1599–1660)
Painter of court of King Philip IV of Spain; portraitist
The Maids of Honor (1656)

Santa Fe, New Mexico founded (1605)
(later home to artists such as Georgia O'Keeffe and D.H. Lawrence)

"Youth is the time of getting, middle age of improving, and old age of spending."
Anne Bradstreet (c.1612–1672)

V E R S A I L L E S
Begun 1669, completed 1685; built for King Louis XIV of France to glorify him.
The gardens, which extend for several miles, were designed to be a continuation of the palace space.

NEAR AND FAR EAST

1644
Ming Dynasty ends

Taj Majal, a mausoleum built between 1630 and 1648 to honor a man's wife

ROCOCO 1700s
Fanciful Curved Asymmetrical Forms   **Elaborate Ornamentation**

"To wake the soul by tender strokes of art,
To raise the genius, and to mend the heart;
To make mankind, in conscious virtue bold,
Live o'er each scene, and be what they behold:
For this the Tragic Muse first trod the stage."
Alexander Pope (1688–1744)

William Hogarth (England, 1697–1764)
Figure painter; satirical social critic
The Rake's Progress (1735)

Elisabeth Vigee-Le Brun (France, 1755–1842)
Portraitist to Queen Marie Antoinette
Self-Portrait

Antoine Watteau (France, 1684–1721)
Painted erotic garden scenes
Embarkation for the Isle of Cythera (1717)

Jean-Baptiste Chardin (France, 1699–1779)
Still life painter
Back from the Market (1739)

RIVALRY!

Sir Joshua Reynolds (England, 1723–1792)
Portraits of English aristocrats
Mrs. Siddons as the Tragic Muse (1784)

Thomas Gainsborough (England, 1696–1764)
Portraits of English aristocrats
Mrs. Siddons (1785)

On This Date in History . . .

Mayan civilization destroyed by Spanish (by c.1700)

"Captain" Kidd hanged for piracy (1701)

Bach's "St. Matthew Passion" (1729)

Casanova escapes from Piombi in Venice (1751)

American Revolution (1776–1783)

Louis XVI executed (1793)

Perfectly preserved wooly mammoth found in Siberia (1799)

Rosetta Stone found (1799)

Beethoven composes Symphonies 5 and 6 (1808)

Mary Wollstonecraft Shelley writes *Frankenstein* (1818)

Florence Nightingale born (1820)

Abner Doubleday conducts first baseball game, in Cooperstown, New York (1839)

P.T. Barnum opens the "American Museum," an exhibition devoted to freaks, curios, and the like (1841)

First painted Christmas card designed (1846)

NEOCLASSICISM 1750–1850

Francisco Goya (Spain, 1746–1828)
Painter of war scenes
The Third of May, 1808 (1814–1815)

"Art is long, life short; judgment difficult, opportunity transient."
Goethe (1749–1832)

ROMANTICISM 1750–1850

For the first time the middle classes could afford to patronize the arts; paintings depicted nature as wild and picturesque

Eugene Delacroix (France, 1798–1863)
Liberty Guiding the People (1830)

1800	1810	1820	1830	1840	1850

NEOCLASSICISM ("NEW CLASSICISM") 1750–1850
Academic, Moralistic, Rational   **Revival of Styles of Classic Antiquity**

Jacques Louis David (France, 1748–1825)
Painted academic, political scenes
The Death of Marat (1793)

Monticello was designed and built by **Thomas Jefferson** between 1770 and 1806

Benjamin Latrobe, Architect
Baltimore Cathedral
Parts of the Capitol building
Portico of the White House

"Enlighten the people generally, and tyranny and oppressions of body and mind will vanish like evil spirits at the dawn of day."
Thomas Jefferson (1816)

Karl Langhans
The Brandenburg Gate, Berlin

Jean-Auguste Ingres (France, 1780–1867)
Painted academic, political scenes; student of Jacques Louis David
Odalisque (1814)

ROMANTICISM 1750–1850
Exotic Scenes   **Rich Palette of Color**

"Now Art, used collectively for painting, sculpture, architecture and music, is the mediatress between, and reconciler of, nature and man."
Coleridge (1818)

John Constable (England, 1776–1837)
Stoke-by-Nayland (1836)

1846 "Potato Famine" in Ireland; between 1850 and 1860, **914,000** Irish emigrate to America

Honore Daumier (France, 1808–1879)
Don Quixote Attacking the Windmills (c.1866)

John Henry Fuseli (Switzerland, 1741–1825)
The Nightmare (1785–1790)

Theodore Gericault (France, 1791–1824)
Mounted Officer of the Imperial Guard (1812)
The Raft of the "Medusa" (1818–1819)

Jean-Francois Millet (France, 1814–1875)
Landscapes that included peasants
The Sower (c.1850)

REALISM 1830–1850

William Blake (England, 1757–1827)
Poet, painter of dream-like scenes

John Singleton Copley (United States, 1738–1815)
Portrait of Paul Revere

Realism—Fidelity in Art to **Nature** or to Real Life and To Accurate Representation Without **Idealization**

Gustave Courbet (France, 1819–1877)
The Stone Breakers (1849) (destroyed in 1945)

Joseph Turner (England, 1775–1851)
The Slave Ship (1839)

Thomas Eakins (1844–1916)
The Gross Clinic (1875)

Camille Corot (France, 1796–1875)
Cartres Cathedral (1830)
La Danse des Nymphes (1851)

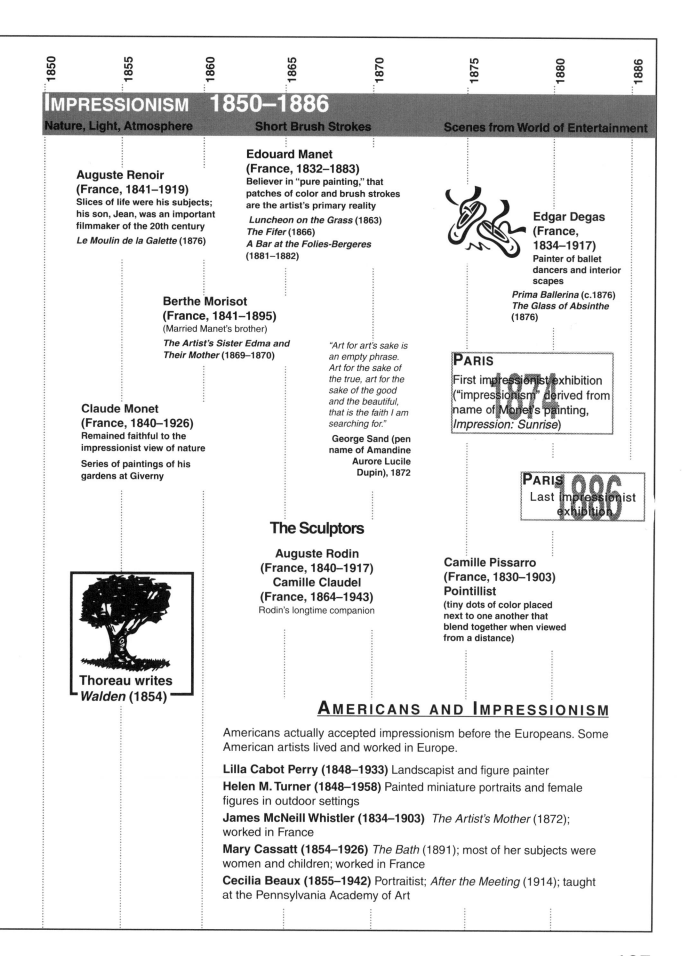

1850	1855	1860	1865	1870	1875	1880	1886

IMPRESSIONISM 1850–1886

Nature, Light, Atmosphere **Short Brush Strokes** **Scenes from World of Entertainment**

**Auguste Renoir
(France, 1841–1919)**
Slices of life were his subjects; his son, Jean, was an important filmmaker of the 20th century
Le Moulin de la Galette (1876)

**Edouard Manet
(France, 1832–1883)**
Believer in "pure painting," that patches of color and brush strokes are the artist's primary reality
Luncheon on the Grass (1863)
The Fifer (1866)
A Bar at the Folies-Bergeres
(1881–1882)

**Edgar Degas
(France,
1834–1917)**
Painter of ballet dancers and interior scapes
Prima Ballerina (c.1876)
The Glass of Absinthe
(1876)

**Berthe Morisot
(France, 1841–1895)**
(Married Manet's brother)
The Artist's Sister Edma and Their Mother (1869–1870)

"Art for art's sake is an empty phrase. Art for the sake of the true, art for the sake of the good and the beautiful, that is the faith I am searching for."

George Sand (pen name of Amandine Aurore Lucile Dupin), 1872

**Claude Monet
(France, 1840–1926)**
Remained faithful to the impressionist view of nature

Series of paintings of his gardens at Giverny

PARIS
First impressionist exhibition ("impressionism" derived from name of Monet's painting, *Impression: Sunrise*)
1874

PARIS
Last impressionist exhibition
1886

The Sculptors

**Auguste Rodin
(France, 1840–1917)
Camille Claudel
(France, 1864–1943)**
Rodin's longtime companion

**Camille Pissarro
(France, 1830–1903)
Pointillist**
(tiny dots of color placed next to one another that blend together when viewed from a distance)

**Thoreau writes
Walden (1854)**

AMERICANS AND IMPRESSIONISM

Americans actually accepted impressionism before the Europeans. Some American artists lived and worked in Europe.

Lilla Cabot Perry (1848–1933) Landscapist and figure painter

Helen M. Turner (1848–1958) Painted miniature portraits and female figures in outdoor settings

James McNeill Whistler (1834–1903) *The Artist's Mother* (1872); worked in France

Mary Cassatt (1854–1926) *The Bath* (1891); most of her subjects were women and children; worked in France

Cecilia Beaux (1855–1942) Portraitist; *After the Meeting* (1914); taught at the Pennsylvania Academy of Art

POSTIMPRESSIONISM　1886–1906

Artists who worked through the impressionist period but rebelled against and went beyond the limitations of the style

1876

Invention of the telephone

**Georges Seurat
(France, 1859–1891)**
Huge canvases, spent a year or
more on each
Bathers (1883–1884)
*Sunday Afternoon on the
Grande Jatte* (1886)
Side Show (1887–1888)

Paul Cézanne (France, 1839–1906)
Admirer of Delacroix's work
Fruit Bowl, Glass, and Apples (1879–1882)
*Mont Sainte-Victoire Seen from Bibemus
Quarry* (c.1898–1900)

**Buffalo Bill Cody
organizes his
"Wild West"
show**

*"He is the greatest artist who has
embodied, in the sum of his works,
the greatest number of the greatest
ideas."*

John Ruskin, 1843

**Henri Rousseau
(France, 1844–1910)**
Considered by Picasso and
contemporaries to be the
godfather of 20th century
painting

The Dream (1910)

Vincent van Gogh (Holland, 1853–1890)
Color was all-important to van Gogh; his greatest paintings
were created at Arles, in the south of France, in the last 2
years of his life; van Gogh committed suicide in 1890

*The Starry Night
Landscape with Cypress
Trees* (1889)

*Sunflowers series
Self-Portrait* (1889)

**Albert Pinkham Ryder
(United States,
1847–1917)**
Used biblical and literary
themes; thick layers of paint
Moonlit Cove (1880/1890)

1880 **Edison invents
the light bulb**

**Henri
de Toulouse-Lautrec
(France, 1864–1901)**
Pessimistic view;
insights beyond the
surface; influenced by
Gaugin
At the Moulin Rouge
(1892)

INVENTED **1880**
B I N G O

**Winslow Homer
(United States,
1836–1910)**
Seascapes
The Morning Bell (c.1866)

**Queen Victoria
dies; ruled British
Empire for more
than 50 years**

**John Singer Sargent
(United States, 1856–1925)**
Portraitist and landscapist
The Daughters of Edward Boit (1882)

**Paul Gaugin
(France,
1843–1903)**
Left his job and family
to live and work in
Tahiti
When Will You Marry?
(1892)

Picasso
"Blue Period"

Refers to the dominant color of his work
during this time as well as his mood.
Works such as *The Old Guitarist*, painted in 1903, were done in a distinctly
postimpressionist style. He had not yet
invented cubism.

A Life of Picasso, a series of books by
art expert and friend, John Richardson,
provides an excellent overview of
Picasso's early years, particularly this
period.

*We're made so that we love
First when we see them painted, things we have passed
Perhaps a hundred times nor cared to see;
And so they are better, painted—better to us,
Which is the same thing. Art was given for that.*

Robert Browning, 1855

FAUVISM 1900–1918
Unrealistic, Brilliant Color　Flat Patterns

CUBISM 1906–1914
Objects Seen from Several Sides At Once

Fauve is a French word meaning "the wild beasts." The work of Gaugin was a great influence on the fauves. The colors used were more brilliant than those used by the postimpressionists, and the objects that the fauves painted were boldly distorted. Fauvism's leading artist was Henri Matisse.

Using Cézanne's idea of employing cubes to show form and volume, cubists painted objects as seen from several sides at once. Cubism is an intellectual rather than an emotional approach to painting.

(Spain, 1881–1973)
The most important artist of the 20th century; invented cubism along with Georges Braque
Les Demoiselles d'Avignon (1906–1907), the first cubist painting
Three Musicians (1921)
Guernica (1937; one of Picasso's most important works; inspired by the terrorist bombing of Guernica, the ancient capital of the Basques of northern Spain, during the Spanish Civil War)

Marguerite Thompson Zorach (United States, 1887–1968)
Introduced fauvism to the United States

Henri Matisse (France, 1869–1954)
The Joy of Life (1905–1906)
Harmony in Red (1908–1909)
Jazz series

Georges Braque (France, 1881–1963)
Co-founder of cubism
Le Courrier (1913)

Maurice de Vlaminck (France, 1876–1958)
Landscapist

ABSTRACTION 1910–TODAY
(Nonobjective Art)　　　　　　　　　　　　　　　　Unrecognizable Subjects

Color, line, shape, and texture were used to evoke certain emotions in viewers

Piet Mondrian (Holland, 1872–1944)
Greatly influenced pop art
Composition with Red, Blue, and Yellow (1930)

Vasily Kandinsky (Russia, 1876–1944)
Wrote the book *Concerning the Spiritual in Art*
Also worked in expressionist style and had a great deal of influence on expressionists
Sketch I for "Composition VII" (1913)

EXPRESSIONISM 1905–1930
Rebellion Against Naturalism　　Dark Colors　　Distorted Images

Edvard Munch (Norway, 1863–1944)
Influenced by Gaugin, van Gogh, and Toulouse-Lautrec
The Scream (1893)

James Ensor (Belgium, 1860–1949)
Painter, printmaker, maker of masks
Intrigue (1890)

Ernst Ludwig Kirchner (Germany, 1880–1938)
Street, Dresden (1908)

On This Date in History . . .

1900	Freud writes *The Interpretation of Dreams*
1905	Einstein formulates the theory of relativity
1906	"Typhoid Mary" caught and confined
1909	First permanent waves are given by London hairdressers
1913	Charlie Chaplin's first movies debut (by 1917, he is earning $1 million a year)
1918	Worldwide influenza epidemic (by 1920, nearly 22 million dead)

1920
Debut of the first Expressionist film, *The Cabinet of Dr. Caligari*

ASHCAN SCHOOL 1908–1914
Scenes from the Modern, Urban World

School of art founded by Robert Henri (1865–1929), who was Edward Hopper's teacher

John Sloan (United States, 1871–1951)
Painted scenes of New York City

George Bellows (United States, 1882–1925)
Painted city and boxing scenes
Stag at Sharkey's (1909)

DADA 1915–1922
Celebration of the Absurd and Illogical

Founded by a group of artists, writers, photographers, and filmmakers as a reaction to the horrors of World War I. The artists worked in various styles (e.g., montage, collage), but used extremes in personal behavior and artistic style to exaggerate and emphasize the illogical and the absurd.
Several of the dadaists went on to found surrealism.

Marcel Duchamp (France, 1887–1968)
Used everyday objects ("ready-mades") to create works such as a bicycle wheel mounted onto a kitchen stool
Nude Descending a Staircase (1922)

Francis Picabia (France, 1879–1953)
Painter; founded the dadaist periodical *391*

FANTASY 1900s
Rich Colors   Child-Like Interpretation of World

Artists expressed their fantasies and dreams on canvas.

Marc Chagall (Russia, 1887–1985)
Memories of Russia
I and the Village (1911)

Paul Klee (Switzerland, 1879–1940)
More child-like images than Chagall
Park Near L(ucerne) (1938)

Man Ray (United States, 1890–1977)
Painter, sculptor, photographer, filmmaker
Work spanned both dada and surrealism
Chess-set (photograph, 1926)
Emak Bakia (film, 1927)
Shakespearian Equation: "Twelfth Night" (painting, 1948)

SURREALISM 1920s–1930s

Surrealism depicts the dream world, the subconsious and the unconscious mind, and the bizarre. The work produced resembles dada, but is positive in orientation. The surrealists sought to smash the conventions of the day.

Andre Bréton (France, 1896–1966)
Leader of surrealist movement
Author of the "Surrealist Manifesto"

Dorothea Tanning (United States, 1913–)
Palaestra (1947)
Two Words (1963)

Meret Oppenheim (Switzerland, 1913–1985)
"Object maker"
With Tanning, one of the first women to join the surrealist movement
Breakfast in Fur (1938)
(cup, saucer, and spoon covered in fur)

Salvador Dali (Spain, 1904–1989)
Painter, raconteur
Un Chien Andalou (1929, film with Luis Buñuel)
The Persistence of Memory (1931)
The Last Supper (1955)
Aphrodisiac Jacket (1936)
Dali Museum is located in St. Petersburg, Florida

Joan Miro (France, 1893–1983)
Painter
The Harlequin's Carnival (1924–1925)

Réne Magritte (France, 1898–1967)
The Treason of Images (1928–1929)
The Threshold of Liberty
The Great War (1964)

Luis Buñuel (Spain, 1900–1983)
The surrealist filmmaker
Un Chien Andalou (1929, with Salvador Dali)
L'Age d'Or (1930)
Land Without Bread (1932)
Los Olividados (1950)
Belle du Jour (1968)

"Subjectivity and objectivity commit a series of assaults on each other during a human life out of which the first one suffers the worse beating."

Andre Bréton, 1928

REGIONALISM   1930s–1940s
American Scene Painting

**Thomas Hart Benton
(Missouri, 1889–1975)**

The Arts of Life in America
(mural on permanent display
at the Whitney Museum of
American Art, New York City)

**Grant Wood
(Iowa, 1892–1942)**

American Gothic

**John Steuart Curry
(Kansas, 1897–1946)**

Tornado
Murals painted for the U.S.
Departments of Justice
and the Interior buildings,
Washington, DC

HARLEM RENAISSANCE
1920s–1930s

Art depicting the daily life experiences and cultural history of African Americans

Aaron Douglas (1899–1967) Painter
William H. Johnson (1901–1970) Painter, printmaker
Jacob Lawrence (1917–) Painter
Romare Bearden (1914–) Painter

**"Harlem had needed
something to smash. To
smash something is the
ghetto's chronic need."**

James Baldwin,
Native Son, **1955**

ABSTRACT EXPRESSIONISM   1940s–1960s
"Action Painting"   Rejection of Realistic Subject Matter   Dribbled, Spilled, Slashed Paint on Vast Canvases

**Lee Krasner
(United States,
1911–1984)**
Wife of Jackson Pollock
Celebration (1959–1960)

**Jackson Pollock
(United States,
1912–1956)**
Creator of the drip technique;
brilliant career cut short by
his suicide in 1956
One (1950)

**Helen
Frankenthaler
(United States,
1928–)**
Creator of the
stained canvas tech-
nique
Blue Causeway
(1963)

**Mark Rothko
(1903–1973)**
Creator of color field
painting
Earth and Green (1955)

Willem de Kooning (1904–)
Artist has Alzheimer's disease; his wife, Elaine, is also a
well-known abstract expressionist painter
Woman II (1952)

POP ART   1950s–1970s

Popular Culture as Basis: Comic Books, Advertisements, Cult of Celebrity

"In the future everyone will be world-famous for 15 minutes."
Andy Warhol, 1968

**Stuart Davis
(United States,
1894–1964)**
Combining elements
of cubism and
abstraction, Davis is a
godfather of pop art;
jazz was a primary
influence on his work
The Mellow Pad
(1945–1951)

**Andy Warhol
(United States, 1928–1987)**
Painter, photographer, filmmaker
pop icon
200 Campbell's Soup Cans (1962)
Marilyn Monroe Diptych (1962)
Sleep (1963) (6-hour-long film
   about a man sleeping)
The Chelsea Girls (film, 1966)

**Roy Lichtenstein
(United States, 1923–)**
Painter inspired by comic strips
Drowning Girl (1963)
As I Opened Fire (1964)

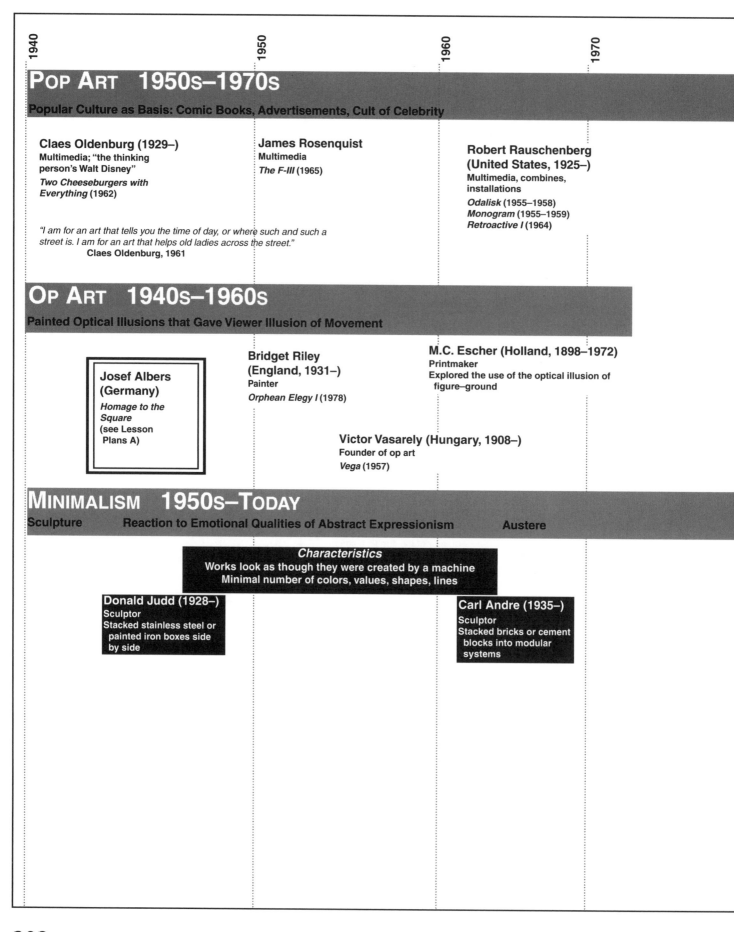

POP ART 1950s–1970s

Popular Culture as Basis: Comic Books, Advertisements, Cult of Celebrity

Claes Oldenburg (1929–)
Multimedia; "the thinking person's Walt Disney"
Two Cheeseburgers with Everything (1962)

James Rosenquist
Multimedia
The F-III (1965)

Robert Rauschenberg (United States, 1925–)
Multimedia, combines, installations
Odalisk (1955–1958)
Monogram (1955–1959)
Retroactive I (1964)

"I am for an art that tells you the time of day, or where such and such a street is. I am for an art that helps old ladies across the street."
Claes Oldenburg, 1961

OP ART 1940s–1960s

Painted Optical Illusions that Gave Viewer Illusion of Movement

Josef Albers (Germany)
Homage to the Square
(see Lesson Plans A)

Bridget Riley (England, 1931–)
Painter
Orphean Elegy I (1978)

M.C. Escher (Holland, 1898–1972)
Printmaker
Explored the use of the optical illusion of figure–ground

Victor Vasarely (Hungary, 1908–)
Founder of op art
Vega (1957)

MINIMALISM 1950s–TODAY

Sculpture   **Reaction to Emotional Qualities of Abstract Expressionism**   Austere

Characteristics
**Works look as though they were created by a machine
Minimal number of colors, values, shapes, lines**

Donald Judd (1928–)
Sculptor
Stacked stainless steel or painted iron boxes side by side

Carl Andre (1935–)
Sculptor
Stacked bricks or cement blocks into modular systems

George Segal (United States, 1924–)
Environments
Cinema (1963)

Robert Indiana (United States, 1928–)
Painter, sculptor
The Demuth Five (1963)
LOVE (1966)

Duane Hanson (United States, 1925–)
Sculptor of realistic figures
Tourists (1970)

PHOTOREALISM   LATE 1960s–TODAY
Paintings that Look Like Photographs

Janet Fish (United States, 1938–)
Tanqueray Bottles (1978)

Audrey Flack (United States, 1931–)
Painter
Queen (1975–1976)

John Baeder (United States, 1938–)
Majestic Diner (1977)
Modern Diner (1974)

Richard Estes (United States, 1936–)
Drugstore (1970)
Double Self-Portrait (1976)

Chuck Close (United States, 1940–)
Portraits

HARD-EDGE PAINTING   LATE 1950s–TODAY
Crisp, Precise Edges   Pure, Flat Colors

Ellsworth Kelly (United States, 1923–)
Painter, sculptor
Two Panels, Yellow and Black (1968)

Kenneth Noland (United States, 1924–)
Painter
Song (1958)

Appendix B

Sources for Prints and Audiovisual Materials

Many resources are available that can help you select works of art to show to participants. Begin by selecting one of the six categories of art history mentioned in Section II, Part 3. Then go to the university or public library and research books and magazine and newspaper articles about the category selected. The library may also loan other material, such as slides, reproductions, and video- and audiocassettes.

Check out whatever materials are suitable for your group. Remember that the art history lesson can be as simple as selecting a book with good color reproductions, showing these pictures of the artwork, and telling the group about the artist.

Another resource for art history materials is the reproductions of artwork on postcards or greeting cards or posters that can be purchased from art reproduction companies, art museums, and art museum catalogs. Individual slides or packets of slides of masterworks can be purchased from art slide companies or museum gift shops. Videos and other materials can be purchased from audiovisual companies.

Local art museums may conduct outreach programs for people with disabilities, in which an art historian travels to the facility to make a presentation about a category of art history that you have selected, or the group travels to the museum to hear a presentation by a docent, or trained tour guide. If the participants are able to travel, organize a trip to a local art museum, art gallery, or art center. Many museums will allow you to select the subject matter to be discussed during the tour.

A and F Video
Post Office Box 264
Genesco, New York   14454
Phone (716) 243-3122
Fax (716) 243-3438
Art history videos and laser discs; prints,
   slides, CD-ROM

Alarion Press
Post Office Box 1882
Boulder, Colorado   80306-1882
Phone (800) 523-9177
Fax (303) 443-9098
Art history videotapes, posters, workbooks

Art Extension Press
Post Office Box 389
Westport, Connecticut   06881
Phone (203) 256-9920
Color reproductions of works of art

Art Image Publications, Inc.
Post Office Box 568
Champlain, New York   12919
Phone (800) 361-2598
Fax (518) 298-5433
Prints, teaching kits

Art Video Library
Post Office Box 68
Ukiah, Oregon   97880
Phone (503) 427-3024
Rents art instruction videotapes; free
   brochure available

Artco Arts and Crafts
Post Office Box 33712
Las Vegas, Nevada   89133
Phone (702) 259-4485
Art instruction videotapes, free brochure
   available

Arts America, Inc.
9 Benedict Place
Greenwich, Connecticut   06830
Phone (800) 553-5278
Fax (203) 869-3075
Art history videotapes

Blockbuster Video
Locations nationwide
Documentaries of artists and their lives
   and motion pictures such as *Lust for Life*
   (Kirk Douglas as Vincent van Gogh), *The
   Agony and the Ecstacy* (Charlton Heston
   as Michelangelo), *Camille Claudel* (Isa-
   belle Adjani as Claudel), and *Vincent and
   Theo* (Tim Roth as van Gogh).

Catalyst Productions
Post Office Box 225
Albany, Oregon   97321
Phone (800) 228-5978
"How to paint" videotapes

Crystal Productions
Post Office Box 2159
Glenview, Illinois   60025
Phone (800) 255-8629
Fax (800) 657-8149
Books, CD-ROM, prints, posters, slides,
   videos

Dover Publications, Inc.
31 East 2nd Street
Mineola, New York   11501
No phone orders
Catalog of fine art and art instruction
   books

Elders Share the Arts
57 Willoughby Street
Brooklyn, New York   11201
Phone (718) 488-8565
Educational materials for art group
   facilitators

Films for the Humanities and Sciences
Post Office Box 2053
Princeton, New Jersey   08543-2053
Phone (800) 257-5126
Fax (609) 275-3767
Videos, CD-ROM

Getty Center for Education in the Arts
401 Wilshire Boulevard, Suite 950
Santa Monica, California   90401-1455
Phone (800) 223-3431
Videotapes, art education, professional
   development seminars and materials

The Museum Company
Locations in shopping malls nationwide
Posters, postcards, prints, and reproductions of fine art

Museum One, Inc.
35 Dover Chester Road
Randolph, New Jersey   07869
Phone (800) 524-1780
Slide and video programs about art history specially geared toward older adults

National Gallery of Art
Washington, DC   20565
Educational Resources: The National Gallery of Art lends color slide programs, films, and videos at no cost to the borrower except for return postage on the items borrowed. To receive a free catalog, write or call Department of Education Resources, Education Division (202) 842-6273.
Publications Sales: A large selection of color reproductions, slide sets, books, and videos about the Gallery's collection can be found in a free mail-order catalog. To receive the catalog, write or call Publications Sales (202) 842-6466.
Slide Library: Programs in their slide collection of over 50,000 works of art are loaned to the public free of charge. Some slide programs are accompanied by narration on audiocassette. For more information, write or call the Slide Library (202) 842-6100.

North Light Books
1507 Dana Avenue
Cincinnati, Ohio   45207
Phone (800) 289-0963
(513) 531-2222
Catalog of books about art and art instruction; also, art instruction book club

Parent Child Press
Post Office Box 675
Hollidaysburg, Pennsylvania   16648-0675
Phone (814) 696-7512
Fax (814) 696-7510
Books, videos, prints

Quinten Gregory Studios, Inc.
6800 South Cloverdale Road
Boise, Idaho   83709
Phone (800) 759-0859
"How to paint" videotapes

Reading and O'Reilly, Inc.
Wilton Programs
Post Office Box 302
2 Kensett Avenue
Wilton, Connecticut   06897
Phone (800) 458-4274
Fax (203) 762-8295
    (203) 762-2854
Videos, filmstrips, prints

Sandak
180 Harvard Avenue
Stamford, Connecticut   06902
Phone (800) 343-2806
Fax (203) 967-2745
Color slides

Shorewood Fine Art Reproductions, Inc.
27 Glen Road
Sandy Hook, Connecticut   06482
Phone (203) 426-8100
Catalog of reproductions of works of art

Starry Night Distributors, Inc.
19 North Street
Rutland, Vermont   05701
Phone and Fax (800) 255-0818
Books, prints, posters at discounted prices

Universal Color Slide Co.
8450 South Tamiami Trail
Sarasota, Florida   34238
Phone (800) 326-1367
Fax (800) 487-0250
Books, filmstrips, reproductions, color slides, videos

The University Prints
21 East Street
Post Office Box 485
Winchester, Massachusetts   01890
Phone (617) 729-8006
Fax (617) 729-8024
Print reproductions

Appendix C
Sources for Art Supplies

Art Supply Warehouse Express
5325 Departure Drive
Raleigh, North Carolina   27604
Phone (800) 995-6778

Catalog of art supplies; locations
  nationwide

Chaselle, Inc.
9645 Gerwig Lane
Columbia, Maryland   21046
Phone (800) 242-7355

Catalog of art supplies (retail store located
  in Columbia, Maryland)

Cheap Joe's Art Stuff
347 Industrial Park Drive
Boone, North Carolina   28607
Phone (800) 227-2788

Catalog of art supplies

Chroma Acrylics, Inc.
205 Bucky Drive
Lititz, Pennsylvania   17543
Phone (800) 257-8278

Catalog of artists' paints

Co-Op Artists' Materials
Post Office Box 53097
Atlanta, Georgia   30355
Phone (800) 877-3242
Fax (404) 872-0294

Catalog of reasonably priced fine art
  materials

Crescent Cardboard Co.
100 West Willow Road
Post Office Box X-D
Wheeling, Illinois   60090
Phone (800) 323-1055
        (708) 537-3400
Fax (708) 537-7153

Catalog and samples of art papers, poster
  board, mat board

209

Dick Blick
Department A, Post Office Box 1267
Galesburg, Illinois   61402
Phone (800) 447-8192
        (309) 343-6181
Catalog of art supplies; retail locations
    nationwide

Frame Fit Co.
Department AM
Post Office Box 8926
Philadelphia, Pennsylvania   19135
Phone (215) 332-0683
Catalog of frames and framing supplies

Fredrix Artist Canvas
111 Fredrix Alley
Lawrenceville, Georgia   30246
Phone (770) 963-5256
Canvas and other painting supports and
    supplies

Graphik Dimension Ltd.
2103 Brentwood Street
High Point, North Carolina   27263
Phone (800) 221-0262
        (919) 887-3700
Fax (910) 887-3773
Catalog of frames and framing supplies

H K Holbein, Inc.
Post Office Box 555
Williston, Vermont   05495
Phone (800) 682-6686
Paints

Jerry's Artarama, Inc.
Post Office Box 1105 AM
New Hyde Park, New York   11040
Phone (800) U-ARTIST
Catalog of art supplies; locations
    nationwide

The Napa Valley Art Store
1041 Lincoln Avenue
Napa, California   94558
Phone (800) 648-6696
Catalog of art supplies

Pearl Art & Craft
308 Canal Street
New York, New York   10013
Phone (800) 221-6845
Catalog of art supplies; also, retail
    locations nationwide

S & S Arts and Crafts
Post Office Box 513
Colchester, Connecticut   06415-0513
Phone (800) 243-9232
Catalog of art supplies

Sax Arts and Crafts
Post Office Box 51710
New Berlin, Wisconsin   53151
Phone (800) 323-0388
Catalog of art supplies

Testrite Instrument Co., Inc.
135AA Monroe Street
Newark, New Jersey   07105
Phone (201) 589-6767
All types and sizes of artists' easels

Utrecht
33 35th Street
Brooklyn, New York   11232
Phone (718) 768-2525
Catalog of reasonably priced art supplies;
    retail locations nationwide

Winsor and Newton
Post Office Box 1396
Piscataway, New Jersey   08855-1396
Phone (908) 562-0770
Paints

Yarka
65 Eastern Avenue
Essex, Massachusetts   01929
Phone (800) 582-ARTS
Art supplies

Appendix D

Sources for Adaptive Equipment and Activity Therapy

adaptAbility
Post Office Box 515
Colchester, Connecticut   06415-0515
Phone (800) 266-8856
Fax (800) 566-6678

Briggs Activity and Recreation Products
Post Office Box 1698
Des Moines, Iowa   50306-1698
Phone (800) 247-2343
Fax (800) 222-1996

Independent Living Aids, Inc.
27 East Mall
Plainview, New York   11803
Phone (800) 537-2118

Maddak, Inc.
Ableware, Inc.
Pequannock, New Jersey   07440-1993
Phone (201) 628-7600
Fax (201) 305-0841

Maxi Aids
42 Executive Boulevard
Farmingdale, New York   11735
Phone (800) 522-6294
Fax (516) 752-0689
    (516) 752-0521 (New York residents)

Nasco Activity Therapy
901 Janesville Avenue
Post Office Box 901
Fort Atkinson, Wisconsin   53538-0901
Phone (800) 558-9595
Fax (414) 563-8296

Pickett Enterprises
Post Office Box 11000
Prescott, Arizona   86304
Phone (602) 778-1896
Fax (602) 778-2112

Sportime Abilitations
One Sportime Way
Atlanta, Georgia   30340-1402
Phone (800) 850-8602
Fax (800) 845-1535

Appendix E
Professional Organizations

Alzheimer's Association
National and state chapters
919 North Michigan Avenue, Suite 1000
Chicago, Illinois   60611-1676
Phone (800) 272-3900
        (312) 335-8700 (in Illinois)

**Alzheimer's Disease Education and
    Referral (ADEAR) Center**
Post Office Box 8250
Silver Spring, Maryland   20907-8250
Phone (800) 438-4380
Fax (301) 495-3334 (after May 1, 1997,
    use area code 240)

**American Association of Retired
    Persons (AARP)**
National and local chapters
601 E Street, N.W.
Washington, DC   20049
Phone (800) 434-3401
        (202) 434-2277 (in Washington
            metro area)

American Art Therapy Association, Inc.
Chapters nationwide
1202 Allanson Road
Mundelein, Illinois   60060
Phone (708) 949-6064

**American Association for Adult and
    Continuing Education**
1200 19th Street, N.W., Suite 30
Washington, DC   20036
Phone (202) 429-5131

**American Occupational Therapy
    Association, Inc.**
4720 Montgomery Lane
Post Office Box 31220
Bethesda, Maryland   20824-1220
Phone (301) 652-2682 (after May 1, 1997,
    use area code 240)

American Society on Aging (ASA)
833 Market Street, Suite 512
San Francisco, California   94193
Phone (415) 974-9600

Center on Arts and the Aging
National Council on the Aging
West Wing 100
Washington, DC   20024
Phone (202) 479-1200

Center for the Study of Aging
706 Madison Avenue
Albany, New York   12208
Phone (518) 465-6927

**Gerontological Society of America
    (GSA)**
1275 K Street, N.W., Suite 350
Washington, DC   20005-4006
Phone (202) 842-1275
Fax (202) 842-1150

**National Art Education Association
    (NAEA)**
National and state chapters
1916 Association Drive
Reston, Virginia   22091
Phone (703) 860-8000

**National Association of Activity
    Professionals (NAAP)**
National and state chapters
1225 I Street, N.W., Suite 300
Washington, DC   20005
Phone (202) 289-0722

National Council on the Aging (NCOA)
600 Maryland Avenue, S.W.
West Wing 100
Washington, DC   20024
Phone (202) 479-1200

National Institute on Aging
National Institutes of Health
Health and Human Services Department
9000 Rockville Pike
Building 31, Room 5C35
Bethesda, Maryland   20892
Phone (301) 496-1752
Fax (301) 496-2525 (after May 1, 1997,
    use area code 240)

**National Recreation and Parks
    Association**
2775 South Quincy Street, Suite 300
Arlington, Virginia   22206-2204
Phone (703) 820-4940

**National Therapeutic Recreation
    Society**
2775 South Quincy Street, Suite 300
Arlington, Virginia   22206-2204
Phone (703) 578-5548

Appendix F
Periodicals

Activities, Adaptations and Aging
The Haworth Press, Inc.
6549 South Lincoln Street
Littleton, Colorado   80121
Phone (800) 532-4033
(303) 794-7676 (in Colorado)
Fax (803) 254-9379

American Artist
BPI Communications
1515 Broadway, Eleventh Floor
New York, New York   10036
Phone (800) 274-4100
(212) 536-5167 (in New York)
Fax (212) 536-5351

American Journal of Art Therapy
Vermont College of Norwich University
Montpelier, Vermont   05602
Phone (802) 828-8540
Fax (802) 828-8855

The American Journal of Occupational Therapy
American Occupational Therapy Association,
   Inc.
616 Tanner Mauk Road
Guilford, Connecticut   06437
Phone (800) 877-1383
(203) 652-2682 (in Connecticut)
Fax (203) 652-7711

Art in America
Brant Publications, Inc.
575 Broadway
New York, New York   10012
Phone (800) 925-8055
(212) 941-2800 (in New York)
Fax (212) 941-2937

Art Education
National Art Education Association
1916 Association Drive
Reston, Virginia   22091-1590
Phone (703) 860-8000
Fax (703) 860-2960

The Artist's Magazine
F & W Publications
1507 Dana Avenue
Cincinnati, Ohio   45207
Phone (513) 531-2222
Fax (513) 531-2902

ARTnews Magazine
Art News Associates
48 West 38th Street
New York, New York   10018
Phone (212) 398-1690
Fax (212) 768-4002

Arts and Activities
Publishers' Development Corporation
Suite 200
591 Camino de la Reina
San Diego, California   92108
Phone and Fax (619) 297-5352

Connections
Alzheimer's Disease Education and Referral
   Center (ADEAR Center)
Post Office Box 8250
Silver Spring, Maryland   20907-8250
Phone (800) 438-4380
Fax (301) 495-3334 (after May 1, 1997, use
   area code 240)

*Educational Gerontology: An International
   Journal*
Taylor & Francis
1101 Vermont Avenue, N.W.
Suite 200
Washington, DC   20005
Phone (202) 289-2174
Fax (202) 289-3665

Generations
American Society on Aging
833 Market Street
Suite 511
San Francisco, California   94103-1824
Phone (415) 974-9600
Fax (415) 974-0300

Modern Maturity
American Association of Retired Persons
3200 East Carson Street
Lakewood, California   90712
Phone (310) 496-2277
Fax (310) 496-4124

NAAP News
National Association of Activity Professionals
1225 I Street, N.W.
Suite 300
Washington, DC   20005
Phone (202) 289-0722

The Older Learner
Older Adult Education Network
American Society on Aging
833 Market Street
Suite 511
San Francisco, California   94103-1824
Phone (415) 974-9600
Fax (415) 974-0300

School Arts
50 Portland Street
Worcester, Massachusetts   01608
Phone (508) 754-7201
Fax (508) 753-3834

Therapeutic Recreation Journal
National Recreation and Parks Association
2775 South Quincy Street
Suite 300
Arlington, Virginia   22206-2204
Phone (703) 820-4940
Fax (703) 671-6772

Consult your local library, bookstore, and newsstand for arts and aging periodicals that may be published locally for your area.

Index

Page numbers follwed by "f" indicate figures; page numbers followed by "t" indicate tables.